D0147997

"This is not just another book on theology and evolution, but a serious attempt by well-established and emerging scholars to grapple with the most pressing theological issues that result from that engagement. By confining the discussion to key debates on the image of God, original sin, and the problem of evil from a range of different perspectives, the editors have achieved that rare combination of theological depth with philosophical sophistication in engagement with historical and contemporary perspectives on evolutionary theory. This is not only a book for serious scholars in this field, but—given that it encourages open and honest debate—it is also one that will be extremely useful for teaching and deserves to be fully embedded in theology courses as well as those in theology and science."

—**Celia Deane-Drummond**, professor of theology and director of the Center
for Theology, Science, and Human Flourishing, University of Notre Dame

"Too often reading books on science and religion by multiple authors feels like walking into a cramped room where everyone is shouting. This book feels more like entering a big open hall where there is room to breathe and room to think. It is not that anything goes—Christian theology has boundaries, what the contributors to this volume call "doctrines." Doctrines such as the image of God, the universality of sin among humans, and the goodness of God have not been overturned by the science of evolution. But evolution has called into question certain ways of explaining those doctrines. The contributors to the book show that the Christian tradition has the resources to explore different ways of explaining these doctrines without leaving the building. They are to be commended for drawing us further into that space."

—**Jim Stump**, senior editor, BioLogos

FINDING OURSELVES AFTER DARWIN

Conversations on the
Image of God, Original Sin, and the Problem of Evil

STANLEY P. ROSENBERG,
GENERAL EDITOR

MICHAEL BURDETT,
MICHAEL LLOYD,
AND BENNO VAN DEN TOREN,
ASSOCIATE EDITORS

Baker Academic
a division of Baker Publishing Group
Grand Rapids, Michigan

© 2018 by Stanley P. Rosenberg

Published by Baker Academic
a division of Baker Publishing Group
PO Box 6287, Grand Rapids, MI 49516-6287
www.bakeracademic.com

Printed in the United States of America

All rights reserved. No part of this publication may be reproduced, stored in a retrieval system, or transmitted in any form or by any means—for example, electronic, photocopy, recording—without the prior written permission of the publisher. The only exception is brief quotations in printed reviews.

Library of Congress Cataloging-in-Publication Data
Names: Rosenberg, Stanley P., 1961– editor.
Title: Finding ourselves after Darwin : conversations on the image of God, original sin, and the problem of evil / Stanley P. Rosenberg, general editor ; Michael Burdett, Benno van den Toren, and Michael Lloyd, associate editors.
Description: Grand Rapids : Baker Publishing Group, 2018. | Includes bibliographical references and index.
Identifiers: LCCN 2017052477 | ISBN 9780801098246 (pbk. : alk. paper)
Subjects: LCSH: Evolution (Biology)—Religious aspects—Christianity. | Religion and science. | Image of God. | Sin, Original. | Good and evil—Religious aspects—Christianity.
Classification: LCC BL263 .F39 2018 | DDC 233—dc23
LC record available at https://lccn.loc.gov/2017052477

Unless otherwise indicated, Scripture quotations are from the New Revised Standard Version of the Bible, copyright © 1989, by the Division of Christian Education of the National Council of the Churches of Christ in the United States of America. Used by permission. All rights reserved.

Scripture quotations labeled NIV are from the Holy Bible, New International Version®. NIV®. Copyright © 1973, 1978, 1984, 2011 by Biblica, Inc.™ Used by permission of Zondervan. All rights reserved worldwide. www.zondervan.com

Scripture quotations labeled ESV are from The Holy Bible, English Standard Version® (ESV®), copyright © 2001 by Crossway, a publishing ministry of Good News Publishers. Used by permission. All rights reserved. ESV Text Edition: 2011

Scripture quotations labeled NASB are from the New American Standard Bible®, copyright © 1960, 1962, 1963, 1968, 1971, 1972, 1973, 1975, 1977, 1995 by The Lockman Foundation. Used by permission.

18 19 20 21 22 23 24   7 6 5 4 3 2 1

In keeping with biblical principles of creation stewardship, Baker Publishing Group advocates the responsible use of our natural resources. As a member of the Green Press Initiative, our company uses recycled paper when possible. The text paper of this book is composed in part of post-consumer waste.

CONTENTS

INTRODUCTORY ESSAYS

1. Making Space in a Post-Darwinian World: Theology and Science in Apposition 3

   Stanley P. Rosenberg

2. Distinguishing Doctrine and Theological Theory: Creating Space at the Interface of Modern Science and the Christian Tradition 11

   Benno van den Toren

PART I THE IMAGE OF GOD AND EVOLUTION 27

   Michael Burdett, editor

3. Questions, Challenges, and Concerns for the Image of God 33

   J. Wentzel van Huyssteen

4. The Biblical Text and a Functional Account of the *Imago Dei* 48

   Mark Harris

5. Will the Structural Theory of the Image of God Survive Evolution? 64

   Aku Visala

6. The *Imago Dei* as Relational Love 79

   Thomas Jay Oord

v

7. The *Imago Dei* as the End of Evolution   92
   Ted Peters

   Conclusion to Part 1   107
   Michael Burdett

PART 2 ORIGINAL SIN AND EVOLUTION   111

   Benno van den Toren, editor

8. Questions, Challenges, and Concerns for Original Sin   117
   Gijsbert van den Brink

9. Augustine, Original Sin, and the Naked Ape   130
   Andrew Pinsent

10. Adam as Federal Head of Humankind   143
    C. John Collins

11. The Irenaean Approach to Original Sin through Christ's
    Redemption   160
    Andrew M. McCoy

12. Original Sin and the Coevolution of Nature and Culture   173
    Benno van den Toren

13. A Nonhistorical Approach: The Universality of Sin without the
    Originating Sin   187
    Christopher M. Hays

    Conclusion to Part 2   203
    Benno van den Toren

PART 3 EVIL AND EVOLUTION   209

   Michael Lloyd, editor

14. Questions, Challenges, and Concerns for the Problem of Evil   213
    C. Ben Mitchell

15. Can Nature Be "Red in Tooth and Claw" in the Thought of
    Augustine?   226
    Stanley P. Rosenberg

16. Theodicy, Fall, and Adam   244
    Michael Lloyd

17. The Fallenness of Nature: Three Nonhuman Suspects   262
    Michael Lloyd

18. An Irenaean Approach to Evil   280
    Richard Swinburne

19. "Free-Process" and "Only Way" Arguments   293
    Christopher Southgate

20. Non-Identity Theodicy   306
    Vince Vitale

    Conclusion to Part 3   326
    Michael Lloyd

    Bibliography   331

    Contributors   357

    Scripture and Ancient Writings Index   361

    Name Index   365

    Subject Index   371

Introductory Essays

I

Making Space in a Post-Darwinian World

Theology and Science in Apposition

Stanley P. Rosenberg

Walking south along Parks Road in Oxford, UK, one comes across a pair of buildings that set the stage for this book. These two important buildings in the Oxford landscape stand in apposition (but not opposition) across the road from each other. On the east side is the Oxford Museum of Natural History, built of stone and begun in 1855.[1] Engraved over the neo-Gothic stone-arch entry sits an angel, holding a book and a dividing cell. The book represents one or more possible uses of the book as an icon in Christian theology—representing either the Bible, the book of life, or the two books analogy (the book of nature and the book of revelation). The cell directs one's attention to the work of a scientist. Studying life is affirmed at the highest level, by an angel representing the work and message of the divine. In this building in 1860 Thomas Henry Huxley and Bishop Samuel Wilberforce held their infamous

1. For an excellent discussion of the vision behind the building of the museum and the role that reflection on the cosmos played in its design, see Carla Yanni, "Nature as Creation: The Oxford University Museum," chap. 3 in *Nature's Museums: Victorian Science and the Architecture of Display* (New York: Princeton Architectural Press, 2005).

debate about Darwin's interpretation of evolution, which for the first time gave a cogent explanation of the mechanism of evolution (the general notion of evolution was not a novel or very contentious one in the nineteenth century). A compelling idea now had explanatory power but did not possess fully verifiable evidence, and it raised massive questions about our understanding of human origins and natural history. This was not the first time such a lag between inference and evidence had occurred. Scientific progress is replete with such stories: one of the most well known of these is Galileo's inferences supporting Copernicus, which could not be proven until the early nineteenth century, when technological advancements finally achieved the ability to create sufficiently clear, powerful telescopes and verify the transit of Venus across the sun.

Oxford's Museum of Natural History offers an architectural style directly reminiscent of the great British Gothic cathedrals, with an entrance and windows in the Norman style. In addition, it has a monastic kitchen (from the abbot's kitchen at Glastonbury) built alongside to represent chemistry, and its internal structure features a grand open space with columns and carvings like a Christian basilica and other Gothic buildings.[2] The style was employed not to mock or replace the church but to be a testament to the enduring connection its designers found between the book of life and the book of nature. So, this building—presided over by an angel of God and in an architectural style emphasizing the spiritual—offered the stage for one of the oft-reported, and frequently mispresented, debates between science and religion. Or was it such a debate?

But before reaching the museum, one comes to the other building, on the west side of the street: the chapel of Keble College, Oxford. Keble College was built to commemorate John Keble, the founder of the Oxford Movement, a reform movement within the Church of England that emphasized the sacramental nature of worship, sacramental theology, and the preparation of priests for service in parishes for the urban and rural poor, which the Church of England had seemingly ignored. Soon after the college's founding, a chapel was added—full of color, life, and images of the life of the church. A side chapel, added later, houses one of the famous paintings of religious

2. In contrast to the neoclassical style of prior generations, the Victorians created Gothic buildings and used Gothic flourishes, believing the Gothic style offered something more human and spiritual. On the architects Pugin and Scott and the Gothic revival, see Alexandra Wedgwood, "Pugin, Augustus Welby Northmore (1812–1852)," in *Oxford Dictionary of National Biography*, ed. H. C. G. Matthew and Brian Harrison (Oxford: Oxford University Press, 2004), available at http://www.oxforddnb.com/view/article/22869 (subscription required); Gavin Stamp, "Scott, Sir George Gilbert (1811–1878)," in *Oxford Dictionary of National Biography*, available at http://www.oxforddnb.com/view/article/24869 (subscription required).

life from the period, *The Light of the World* by Holman Hunt. Unlike the museum across the street, built of dressed stone in the manner of Oxford's stately buildings, Keble College and its chapel are built of ordinary brick but with flourishes of design with blue and white bricks. The college's architectural design matches the vision for sacrament and beauty with the vision of serving the ordinary, the poor, and the overlooked (brickwork was viewed as ordinary and plebeian in contrast to the grandeur of stone). A college founded for the teaching of theology and the formation of priests to serve the urban poor (which quickly added the full science curriculum, to be sure), built out of a deep understanding of religious vocation, stands across the street from a natural history museum presided over by an angel of God welcoming the faithful into its exhibits. What an interesting if not ironic sense of apposition!

Yet this is not the most interesting part of the story of these two buildings. To learn more we must turn to their respective sources of funding. The Oxford Museum of Natural History was paid for by the royalties enjoyed by Oxford University Press through its sales of King James Bibles. The press's grant of £30,000, a princely sum then, provided for the building of the museum. The source of funding for Keble Chapel (begun in 1873) is equally interesting. The chapel was paid for thanks to the invention of nitrate-based fertilizer earlier in the century. The donor, William Gibbs, provided the grant to build the chapel. The funds came from the family business exporting guano mined in the South Pacific.[3] Guano was a major ingredient in fertilizer that, once discovered and exploited, enabled an agricultural revolution as well as the creation of more destructive armaments as witnessed by the horrors of World War I.

So a natural history museum built by the income from the sales of Bibles stands in apposition to a Christian chapel built by the income generated by the science of agriculture with the discovery of fertilizer and modern armaments. Elsewhere we find opposition. Our current intellectual climate illustrates the cultural, religious, and academic significance of the relationship between science and religion. Of pressing concern is the controversy and clash often sparked by cross-disciplinary interactions. Indeed, as C. P. Snow cogently identified more than fifty years ago,[4] a gulf exists between the humanities and the sciences, and evidence abounds that this has not abated in the intervening years. This gulf provides a fundamental context for interpreting some of the substantial challenges and rifts separating religion and science. Rhetorically fierce debates featuring high-profile figures abound and attract

3. "Chapel History and Treasures," Keble College, Oxford, accessed June 19, 2017, http://www.keble.ox.ac.uk/about/chapel/chapel-history-and-treasures.

4. C. P. Snow, *Two Cultures and the Scientific Revolution* (New York: Cambridge University Press, 1959); the book is based on his Rede Lecture earlier that year.

media attention, but much of the debate is not founded on scholarship and balanced argument. Metaphysical arguments and various scientisms are too often passed off as scientific arguments (by both scientists and nonscientists, religious and nonreligious alike), and assertions made about the treatment of science at the hands of the ill-minded religious still depend on ugly, partial anecdotes. Of course, examples of scientists misrepresenting, misunderstanding, or otherwise mistreating religions and religious interpretations likewise abound. Myths have also had a prominent place in the popular and academic imagination, such as the nineteenth-century romanticized canard, promulgated by Washington Irving in his biography of Christopher Columbus, that the Christian West, until the discovery of Columbus, believed in a "flat earth."[5] For counterevidence one need only look at the common use of armillary spheres in late antiquity and in the early Christian, medieval, and renaissance worlds, along with the artwork dotting churches that portrays Christ astride a globe. Another nineteenth-century myth that has had massive currency—propounded by Draper and White, who invented and popularized the "conflict thesis"[6]—is that Galileo's trial was a simple suppression of science by the church, which many scholars and the popular press still cite despite innumerable studies demonstrating otherwise.[7]

Recently, evolutionary theory has been fine-tuned and developed through discoveries in the areas of epigenetics, statistics, mathematics, and game theory, and genetic research has advanced human knowledge in remarkable ways, with hugely important implications for agriculture, forensic science, history, demography, ethics, and theology. The contributors to this book are keen to model a healthy engagement with these new scientific discoveries and interpretations—not only for reasons of public relations but also out of a belief that Christians should be open and committed to truth, pursuing it wherever it may be found and following it wherever it may lead. Following the dictum of Augustine that "all truth is God's truth, wherever it is found,"[8] Wycliffe Hall—one of the institutional partners of this volume and the institution in which all four editors have held or currently hold faculty status—restates

5. See Washington Irving, *A History of the Life and Voyages of Christopher Columbus*, 3 vols. (New York: Carvill, 1828).

6. Andrew Dickson White, *The Warfare of Science* (New York: Appleton, 1869); Andrew Dickson White, *A History of the Warfare of Science with Theology in Christendom*, 2 vols. (London: Macmillan, 1896); John William Draper, *The History of the Conflict between Religion and Science* (London: Henry S. King, 1875).

7. Among the many options see the very accessible *Galileo Goes to Jail, and Other Myths about Science and Religion*, ed. Ronald L. Numbers (Cambridge, MA: Harvard University Press, 2009).

8. Augustine, *On Christian Instruction* 2.18.28.

this as part of its own academic values, and we repeat it here as reflecting a commitment of this project and the book that has come out of it: "convinced that all such pursuit of truth will ultimately lead to, because all truth comes ultimately from, Jesus Christ."[9]

In this volume we seek to create space for honest investigation and dialogue. The science of human evolution has opened vast new pathways for exploration, brought verifiable data to bear on earlier inferences, offered new inferences, revealed new understandings of human and broader biological development, and offered significant new challenges to our self-understanding. We are now led to ask questions like, *After Darwin and the revolutions spawned in genetic research, who are we? And how do we define ourselves and find our past in light of these revolutions?* These simple questions require careful, balanced, and nuanced answers.

Ideas are often said to have a consequence, but what is sometimes forgotten is they also have a context. History and culture matter. Ideas are born in a time and place, though rarely full bodied all at once. Rather, ideas themselves are evolving products that reflect substantial development over time, are influenced by many different thinkers and issues, and are susceptible to the shape given by the context in which they are expressed and the histories on which they are constructed (often described as the geography of knowledge).[10] This is true of interpretive constructs, whether they be found among the faculty of history, theology, or the scientific disciplines. The facts may or may not alter, but their reception and the ways in which they are understood and interpreted do alter—often profoundly.

Hence we do not wish merely to tie our interpretations to contemporary scientific findings and interpretations, as those are provisional and subject to change. Churchmen working in the wake of the renaissance of the twelfth century made that mistake when they tied their theology and interpretations of the cosmos to the scientific methods and interpretations of the Aristotelian tradition. Fruitful as they found some of those theological products, the fruit ultimately proved sour, offering a scientifically and theologically limited view

9. Wycliffe Hall's Statement of Academic Values and Virtues is accessible at https://www
.wycliffehall.org.uk/data/wycliffe/downloads/WH%20Academic%20Values%20and%20Vir
tues.pdf. This paragraph is based on part of the introduction to part 3 (written by the principal
of Wycliffe Hall), which is devoted to the problem of evil in the light of evolution and modern
genetics.

10. See, e.g., the many works by David N. Livingstone, who demonstrates how local issues
and culture have shaped the reception of Darwin by different communities that otherwise
share the same creeds and theology. For an important explanation of this phenomenon, see his
Dealing with Darwin: Place, Politics, and Rhetoric in Religious Engagements with Evolution
(Baltimore: Johns Hopkins University Press, 2014).

of the solar system and broader cosmos, tied as it was to the Ptolemaic and Aristotelian imagination of the cosmos. Preoccupied with crystalline spheres and the place of God outside the lunar orbit, they could not intellectually encompass the inferences and discoveries of Copernicus and Galileo. This led both to the scientific challenges posed by Copernicus, Kepler, and Galileo, among others, and to the theological revisions posed by the Protestant Reformation.

The research group that produced this book, in examining theology in the context of contemporary science, wishes to use the discoveries and interpretations of contemporary science as a dialogue partner with historic doctrinal commitments. We are keenly aware of the bitter experience of misappropriating earlier scientific positions by overly relying upon them, or confusing prior scientific representations as theological facts. This provides a context to reflect on possible avenues for conversation—not to shut down conversation, limit the options, or tie ourselves to current interpretations that are necessarily finite and subject to change. That would demonstrate a failure to learn from our past. Most contributors to this volume participated in several colloquia in Oxford where ideas were presented and debated. Criticisms were lodged, defenses offered, judgments (however, tentative) rendered, reflection and investigation expanded, and positions defined. In this volume, you will find a variety of views and historical reflections offering differing ways of responding to scientific models and discoveries and working through key ideas attached to theological anthropology—that is, theological reflections on human nature. But it is not just scientific models that can differ; so too can theological and philosophical models that shape our vision of the world. These can differ and create differing ways of managing the science. This recognition has enabled the team—and we hope the reader as well—to explore whether differing theological traditions may have available resources, or whether there are resources from our own tradition that can be recovered, allowing us to respond to contemporary challenges.

The arguments in the ensuing chapters are not presented as necessarily offering contrasting opinions that negate one another and force the reader to choose between them. This is not a "four views" type of book presenting necessarily mutually exclusive positions. Some authors and their positions support one another, while others disagree; some positions are complementary or explanatory, while others may inherently critique each other. Rather than intentionally selecting competing viewpoints, we have assembled scholarship presenting different approaches and methods and insights, introducing a variety of models that may be considered and that just might, either individually or severally, provide a coherent path forward. So while some positions could exclude *some* other positions on a given issue, this is not necessarily the case, and the book should not be read as offering such an oppositional strategy. The editorial team, with the support of the chapter authors, has sought to leave issues open, to create mental space to explore difficult issues amid a changing landscape. That is, we have chosen an appositional (but not oppositional) strategy. Even if issues are left unsettled, these need not be unsettling, as we acknowledge the complexity of the issues and the need for individuals of goodwill to come together to discuss frankly and openly, committed to truth while not foreclosed to particular answers, recognizing the limits of knowledge, imagination, and experience that bedevil us all. Intellectual and spiritual humility require a willingness to take such risks.

In chapter 2 Benno van den Toren reflects on the difference between a settled doctrine and theological systems that attempt to make sense of that doctrine. While a doctrine is something firm—or if creedal, extremely firm—the theological systems that grow up around a doctrine are much more exploratory, interpretive, subject to a culture (denominational, institutional, etc.), and thus often more tentative. The editors and contributors have approached our subject with a firm commitment to the doctrinal core but have agreed to a certain flexibility and openness to the systems that have grown up around them. So, for example, all are committed to the notion that humans are divine image bearers. But as to what the image of God means and what its implications are for humanity, we've agreed to hold a more generous approach, seeking to engage the many ways of interpreting that statement and evaluating the various views.

Following the introductory essays, the volume is divided into three parts: part 1, edited by Michael Burdett, addresses issues surrounding the *imago Dei*, or image of God; part 2, edited by Benno van den Toren, addresses issues surrounding original sin; and part 3, edited by Michael Lloyd, addresses issues surrounding theodicy, or the problem of evil. Each part follows the same basic pattern: it begins with a brief introduction by the relevant editor, followed by a leadoff article by a prominent scholar setting out key issues with which a thoughtful response must engage. This is then followed by chapters taking up the issues and offering differing approaches: biblical, historical, systematic, and contextual theology, intellectual history, analytic and continental philosophy, and so on. Different authors come at the central questions from different angles, and each part thus provides a wide-ranging discussion of the issues at stake. The editor then concludes the part with a reflection on the main threads of the essays and provides a brief list of further readings on the topic of the respective part.

This volume was made possible by a research grant given by the BioLogos Foundation as part of its Evolution and Christian Faith project. The project team engaged with a group of theologians, biblical scholars, historians, ancient Near Eastern specialists, philosophers, physicists, geneticists, biologists, and chemists. We particularly wish to thank Ard Louis and Jonathan Doye, a biophysicist and chemist, who were members of the project team, and Emily Burdett, a cognitive psychologist, all three of whom were scientific advisers to the editorial team. Any mistakes in representing the science are our own, but these three have saved us from multiple factual errors and worked to ensure that the editors are aware of contemporary findings and interpretations. Conversation partners have been diverse and international, drawing on the British context at Oxford and the contributions from multiple colleagues from Europe, the United States, South America, and Africa. Everyone came together for the project, directed by Stanley Rosenberg and Benno van den Toren, titled Configuring Adam and Eve: Creating Conceptual Space for New Developments in the Science of Human Origins. The grant project itself was housed at Wycliffe Hall, a permanent private hall at Oxford University that focuses on ordination training for the Church of England and theological training more broadly as part of its key commitment to deeper theological engagement. The latter activity is taken up by its partner that managed the grant, Scholarship and Christianity in Oxford, or SCIO, which is the UK subsidiary of the Council for Christian Colleges and Universities. SCIO manages a visiting student program for undergraduates in partnership with Wycliffe Hall and conducts major research and pedagogical projects in science and religion and ancient texts, with grants from major funding bodies.

Did the team succeed at creating space at the interface of theological anthropology and evolutionary science? We believe it was hugely beneficial to all involved, and this volume is one of many products, along with numerous articles, that came out of it. But more importantly, the project, and this volume that came out of it, demonstrate how a group of diverse individuals reflecting varying theological traditions from the humanities and the sciences can come together to work in ways that complement, challenge, and engage one another—and not merely to win a skirmish but to seek deeper understanding and to find points of demarcation not in opposition but in apposition.

2

Distinguishing Doctrine and Theological Theory

Creating Space at the Interface of Modern Science and the Christian Tradition

BENNO VAN DEN TOREN

Various Tools for Negotiating the Relation between Faith and Science

Many Christians and non-Christians experience a profound dissonance between the Christian faith and discoveries—or purported discoveries—of science. Given the high authority ascribed to science in our culture, this may for non-Christians be a reason not even to begin considering historic Christianity as a serious option. For many Christians it may be a reason to steer clear of the world of secular science or to simply accept the need to live with these unresolved tensions. This latter approach may not be as unreasonable as it might seem at first sight. When we have apparently contradictory beliefs, it may be wiser to accept the tension than to reject beliefs for which we have

For a more extensive treatment of the issues in this chapter, see Benno van den Toren, "Distinguishing Doctrine and Theological Theory: A Tool for Exploring the Interface between Science and Faith," *Science and Christian Belief* 28, no. 2 (2016): 55–73. My thanks to the editors of *Science and Christian Belief* for permission to reproduce ideas from that article in more condensed form here.

important reasons to believe. Life is not always as neat and harmonious as we hope. Living in this tension, however, is unsatisfactory in the long run. Christians do believe that the Bible and the world of science are concerned with the same reality—this one reality in which we try to chisel out a meaningful existence and to live to the glory of God.

Where this dissonance between science and faith is most acutely felt changes from one era to the next. In the later Middle Ages in Western Europe, Aristotelian science presupposed that the universe was eternal, while the Christian faith presupposed that it had a beginning in time. In the beginning of the modern era, the move in the scientific world from a geocentric universe to a heliocentric universe was a focus of this tension. In the nineteenth century the Darwinian evolution of animal life proved one of the main foci and has been so for a significant time, at least in public discourse and in the experience of many ordinary Christians. In the last decade the spotlight has been particularly on the human species because of significant developments in the science of human evolution—for example, through the use of DNA mapping and the extrapolation of findings in the science of cognitive development to evolutionary development.

The history of the interaction between science and Christian faith teaches us important lessons. It teaches us that we should be critical of what presents itself as scientific truth. Sometimes major theories have been discarded (such as the idea that the universe in its current form is eternal), while at other times the challenges to the Christian faith came not from the science itself but from unwarranted ideological extrapolations from a sober scientific truth (such as the idea that the removal of the earth from the center of the universe means that humankind can no longer be at the center of God's creative project). History also shows us that some challenges simply will not go away. In my view, the age of the universe and the gradual development of life are examples of this. Although the last word has not been said about the nature of the evolutionary process, the evidence for an old universe, an old earth, and a gradual development of life is overwhelming and only keeps growing. It would be foolish to cite the changing scientific theories concerning the evolution of life as a reason to reject this evolution entirely. The limitations of theoretical explanations are no valid reason to keep rejecting the data that these theories try to explain. Finally, history teaches us the need for patience. It may take time to work out how we should respond to scientific developments from a faith perspective. Some issues have taken generations to settle, and hasty conclusions about which scientific theories should be rejected at all costs, or which tenets of the Christian faith can no longer be believed, have too often proved wrong.

From this short introduction one can distill a number of tools that will help to navigate the often choppy waters between science and Christian faith: the historic relativity and hypothetical nature of science, the difference between proper science and ideological extrapolations, and the need to develop an appropriate hermeneutic of both Scripture and science. While it would be unwise to suppose that one tool could do all the work that is needed to navigate these waters, in this chapter I introduce a particular tool that has been crucial to the project out of which this volume has grown: the distinction between doctrine and theological theory. I use "doctrine" here in the technical sense and according to the original meaning of the word—that is, "what the Christian community *teaches* concerning her faith." And I use "theological theory" here to denote theories that theologians have developed to explain and make sense of these doctrines, or teachings of the church.

A case in point would be the real presence of Christ in the celebration of the Last Supper, or Eucharist. Most church traditions teach that Christ is present in the celebration of the sacrament, but traditions have developed different theories to make sense of this reality. The medieval church drew on Aristotelian metaphysics and developed the theory of transubstantiation, according to which the bread and wine in reality becomes the body and blood of Christ even though the outward appearance remains that of bread and wine. In the Calvinistic tradition the real presence was understood in terms of the presence of the Holy Spirit—a view easily taken up in charismatic circles. More recently certain theologians have been exploring whether speech-act theory might provide a means for understanding the real presence of Christ.[1]

The distinction between doctrine and theological theory therefore distinguishes between levels of belief-commitments. It is an instantiation of a broader theological practice of distinguishing between different levels of the importance of beliefs in general as well as of religious and theological beliefs. My commitment to the doctrine of the Trinity is necessarily higher than my commitment to how to make sense of the metaphysical intricacies of this doctrine. Without a belief in the Trinity, the debate about how the different persons of the Trinity relate to one another does not make sense. All major Christian traditions make a distinction between beliefs that are more central and less central, between issues of church orthodoxy and those of mere private opinion, between the central confession of faith and so-called adiaphora, between gospel issues and second-order issues. We believe that we can legitimately be united in Christ even if we differ about second-order

---

1. Melvin Tinker, "Language, Symbols and Sacraments: Was Calvin's View of the Lord's Supper Right?," *Churchman* 112, no. 2 (1998): 131–49.

issues, and we also believe that in reflecting on what it means to be a Christian in this world we can be much more relaxed in changing our opinion about such secondary issues than we can about what we consider to be an issue of orthodoxy or heresy, an "article of faith by which the church stands or falls."[2]

The distinction between doctrine and theological theory is particularly relevant for the interface between science and faith. We develop this application of the distinction in what follows, first by looking into the specific role and function of doctrines in the life of the church and in Christian discipleship. We then look into the role of theological theories for Christian theology and apologetics, considering both their importance and their *relative* importance. Finally, we conclude with a reflection on how this distinction can be made fruitful for the relationship between science and faith. More specifically, we ask what the value of this distinction is for the task we have set ourselves in this volume of essays on the interface between the Christian doctrine of what it means to be human and recent developments in the sciences that explore human evolution.

The Specific Role of Doctrine

"Doctrine" is the English rendering of the Latin *doctrina*, or "teaching." Although we use "doctrine" for a wide range of Christian beliefs, it is most properly used for what the church or Christian community teaches, for the teaching it transmits from one generation to another that guides the faith and life of the Christian community and of individual Christians. Following the publication of George Lindbeck's *The Nature of Doctrine*,[3] a wide-ranging discussion ensued about the role of doctrines. Lindbeck's interlocutors have rightly criticized his tendency to downplay the role of doctrine as truth-claim. Christian doctrines have several functions, one of which is to claim something about the nature of reality. When the church teaches that "Jesus Christ is Lord," it does not only say something about how the Christian community intends to live or to symbolically express Christian experience. It also makes a truth-claim: the Christian life and Christian experience make sense only because the church believes it to be true that Christ conquered death and is now "seated at the right hand of God" (Col. 3:1) and thus shares in the highest authority over the universe.[4]

2. Theodor Mahlmann, "Articulus Stantis et (Vel) Cadentis Ecclesiae," in *Religion Past & Present: Encyclopedia of Theology and Religion*, ed. Hans Dieter Betz et al. (Boston: Brill, 2007).

3. George A. Lindbeck, *The Nature of Doctrine: Religion and Theology in a Postliberal Age* (Philadelphia: Westminster, 1984).

4. Cf. Alister E. McGrath, *The Genesis of Doctrine: A Study in the Foundations of Doctrinal Criticism* (Cambridge, MA: Blackwell, 1990), 72–78; Sue M. Patterson, *Realist Christian*

This criticism of Lindbeck's approach, however, does not invalidate that he rightly draws attention to the regulative function of doctrine.[5] Two aspects of this regulative function are of particular importance for our theme. First, doctrine sets boundaries to what is considered to be acceptable Christian language about God and his relationship to the world. A classic example can be found in the Chalcedonian Definition (AD 451) concerning the two natures of Christ. Karl Rahner has rightly pointed out that the Chalcedonian christological formulation that Jesus Christ is truly God and truly human does not intend to give a once-for-all, universal description of the nature of Christ, nor an explanation of how the relationship can be understood. The formula rather defines the *boundaries* within which future reflection on the nature of Christ needs to take place. Rather than closing off further reflection, the formula invites further exploration of a mystery that is always greater than humans can grasp.[6]

These boundaries are crucial because the Christian understanding of salvation is bound up with certain truths that cannot be denied without undermining the salvation that the gospel offers.[7] As it has been classically expressed: if Jesus Christ is not truly God, he lacks the power to save us and bring us into communion with God; if he is not truly human, he isn't able to represent us and save our humanity in its entirety. For many Christians, the doctrine of justification by faith alone holds a similar status as "an article of faith by which the church stands or falls." As Luther so persuasively argued, justification is possible only if it is by grace and through faith, for if it in any way depended on human works, it could only fail.[8] Doctrines represent certain aspects of

---

Theology in a Postmodern Age (New York: Cambridge University Press, 1999); Benno van den Toren, *Christian Apologetics as Cross-Cultural Dialogue* (New York: T&T Clark, 2011), 16–18.

5. See McGrath, *Genesis of Doctrine*, 37–52; Kevin J. Vanhoozer, *The Drama of Doctrine: A Canonical-Linguistic Approach to Christian Theology* (Louisville: Westminster John Knox, 2005), 102–10.

6. Karl Rahner, "Current Problems in Christology," in *Theological Investigations* (London: Darton, Longman and Todd, 1974), 1:149.

7. Some careful distinctions are essential: First, these doctrines do not need to be consciously understood. They may be implicit. They cannot, however, be *denied* without implicitly denying the reality of the Christian faith. Second, the fact that the reality of salvation in the Christian sense depends on the truth of these doctrines is not necessarily linked to the question of whether individuals who deny such doctrines can be saved. The first question is a question of theology and church polity; the second is a question of judgment that is better left to God.

8. Though highly debated in the time of the Protestant Reformation, a recent ecumenical agreement between the Roman Catholic Church and the Lutheran World Federation accepted "a common understanding of our justification by God's grace through faith in Christ." Lutheran World Federation and Catholic Church, "Joint Declaration on the Doctrine of Justification," 1999, http://www.vatican.va/roman_curia/pontifical_councils/chrstuni/documents/rc_pc_chrstuni _doc_31101999_cath-luth-joint-declaration_en.html.

the truth discovered in the Gospels that are essential for the Christian understanding of salvation and of our saving God. About other truths we may legitimately disagree: How many women saw the angels in the tomb on the day of the resurrection? In which year did the crucifixion take place? Is it better for the church to be led by bishops or by an assembly of elders? But particular doctrines set certain boundaries because these theological and scriptural truths cannot be denied or radically reinterpreted without putting salvation itself in jeopardy. These doctrines (sometimes called dogmas) therefore have a regulative function because they set the boundaries of what language and which truth-claims are acceptable within the community of the church.[9]

In addition to regulating language, doctrines have a second regulative function. In the language of Kevin Vanhoozer, they give guidance to Christian "performance": they regulate the life of the Christian community and the life of Christian discipleship.[10] The Chalcedonian Definition is a truth-claim that not only regulates language but also regulates Christian living. It tells us that Christ can and should be worshipped as God, a practice central to Christian worship yet abhorrent to, for example, Muslims, who have a radically different understanding of Jesus. The doctrine also teaches us that Jesus Christ can be trusted because of his divine power and his ability to represent us before God on the one hand and his ability to identify with our weakness and suffering on the other. The doctrine of justification by grace through faith alone is a doctrine that is intended to give us confidence about our salvation whatever our failings may be, and it motivates us to glorify God's grace rather than boast of our own achievements. The doctrine of the real presence of Christ in the celebration of Holy Communion encourages us to partake regularly in the communal celebration of the Last Supper as a crucial means of maintaining and growing in our relationship with Christ.

The *Relative* Importance of Theological Theories

Theological theories are important, but they are of secondary importance compared with doctrines. Our worship of Christ and our trust in Christ

9. Not all regulative doctrines are dogmas in the limited sense that they are essential to guard the salvation as proclaimed in the gospel. Others might be regulative in a more general sense—they determine the boundaries of a certain understanding of salvation that is characteristic for a certain denomination, such as the Christian and Missionary Alliance doctrine concerning the sanctifying filling of the Spirit as a progressive experience subsequent to conversion (see "The Alliance Stand," https://www.cmalliance.org/about/beliefs/doctrine). This doctrine does not have the same claim to catholicity as dogma, but it does have a similar regulative function on a more limited scale.

10. Vanhoozer, *Drama of Doctrine*, 363–97.

depend on an—explicit or possibly implicit—understanding of his full divinity in his full humanity, but they do not depend on a particular theory concerning how we should understand the relationship between his divine and human nature. Should we, for example, think of this relationship in terms of kenosis, in terms of a *communicatio idiomatum*, or in terms of a human nature encompassed by a divine nature? The doctrine does not depend on having any theory at all concerning this relationship. We may simply accept it on trust that others will work this out for us—or that this mystery is safe in the hands of God. The theological theory we develop concerning the nature of Christ's presence in the celebration of Holy Communion will have some practical implications—for example, for how we treat the leftover bread and wine after Communion. But our celebration of communing itself will not change greatly with the theory and will not even depend on our ability to formulate a theory, as many committed and sincere believers will not be able to do so. Similarly, our confidence in justification by grace alone does not depend on a specific forensic theory concerning how the righteousness of Christ is appropriated to the believer.

Likewise, the doctrines that humankind is created in the image of God, that humans are sinful from birth, and that God is not the author of evil are central to the Christian faith and to Christian living. Because all humans are created in the image of God, they are worthy of respect and protection. Because all humans are created in the image of God, God has a special calling on their lives, and they have a special calling in this world that distinguishes them from all other living species. These implications for Christian discipleship do not depend on any specific theory concerning how the image of God may be understood. The so-called functional, substantial, relational, and dynamic understandings of the image of God may still lead to roughly the same outworking in the Christian life.

Theological theories tend to be more influenced by the intellectual environment in which they grow than the corresponding doctrine. The theories for explaining Christ's real presence in the Eucharist are a case in point: medieval theologians used the Aristotelian metaphysics at hand, while contemporary thinkers are exploring speech-act theory, which is barely half a century old.[11] Similarly, Hendrikus Berkhof has pointed out that the history of the theology of the image of God should be read in close parallel with the history of philosophical anthropology: in their understanding of the uniqueness of humankind theologians have often been deeply influenced by contemporary culture

11. The groundbreaking work in this field was J. L. Austin, *How to Do Things with Words* (Cambridge, MA: Harvard University Press, 1962).

and philosophy.[12] That should on the one hand make us worried about the impact of various streams of philosophy on Christian theology, yet on the other hand it could be read as an encouragement that theologians have been able to draw on a wide variety of sources in order to develop the notion of the image of God that, through all these changes, has remained central to Christian faith and life.

I have intimated several times that the acceptance of a certain doctrine not only does not depend on a specific theological theory but *does not even depend on having any theological theory at all*. If this were a characteristic of theology alone, it might easily be used as a reason to discredit Christian theology—and sometimes it is effectively used in this way. But the fact that we know things to be true and real and yet are unable to find a viable explanation for them is a simple fact of life—and also of the sciences. Scientists were well aware of the existence of electrical current before they were able to formulate a remotely convincing theory for the behavior of electricity. They studied light long before the current theory of light as electromagnetic waves was formulated. Gravity is so much a reality of life that the change from an Aristotelian (via a Newtonian) to an Einsteinian understanding of gravity did not change the role of gravity for average earth dwellers, be they scientists or not. That an evolutionist worldview has put the uniqueness of the human species under pressure in the West has thankfully not yet led to a wide rejection of human rights; apparently the experience of the uniqueness of humankind is so strong that it can withstand a certain level of cognitive dissonance with scientific theories that place the human species on par with the rest of the animal world.

The limited importance of theological theories compared with doctrine has significant implications for the interface between science and faith. First, we should not worry too much if we are not (yet) able to produce a viable theological theory to explain a particular reality that doctrines describe and that Christians live by. If a lack of understanding of realities that we otherwise know to be real is already a common part of our understanding of the natural world, how much more should we expect this when engaging with the truth of the gospel, where we try to understand how the trinitarian Creator of the universe interacts with the created order?

Second, the relatively limited importance of theological theory means that we should be patient when we temporarily experience tension or even cognitive dissonance between our Christian doctrine on the one hand and scientific

12. Hendrikus Berkhof, *Christian Faith: An Introduction to the Study of the Faith* (Grand Rapids: Eerdmans, 1979), 179.

theories on the other. The half-life of scientific "truths" is limited. But even more importantly, we may be justified in continuing to accept a doctrine even if for the time being we are not able to formulate an adequate theory that helps us coordinate this doctrine with a scientific theory, and even if that theory may well appear to be true in the long run. It may simply take time to work out how the two should be coordinated. Just as it took time to work out how the uniqueness of humankind should be understood in the light of the realization that the earth was not at the center of the universe, it may take time to work out how the uniqueness of humankind created in the image of God should be understood given the strong evidence that humans and other species share the same ancestors and that the boundaries between *Homo sapiens* and *homo neanderthalensis* may be blurred through interbreeding.

Third, we may need to realize that the tension or even dissonance experienced between a Christian *doctrine* and a scientific theory may not be dissonance between the doctrine and the scientific theory but rather may be between a specific *theological theory* and a theory developed by one of the other sciences. For example, when we understand the uniqueness of humankind as created in the image of God in terms of the existence of a spiritual soul, we may experience tension with modern neuroscience, which makes it increasingly problematic to locate consciousness in a spiritual soul that exists independently of the physical brain. Yet when we realize that there are a number of theological theories that describe and explain the nature of the image of God, we also see that there are multiple ways to coordinate the notion of the image of God with modern neuroscience, of which the idea of a soul as a separate metaphysical entity is only one—with its specific merits and demerits.[13] This means that the debate concerning the relationship between science and faith can progress if we are aware of the secondary nature of theological theories in regard to doctrine. Yet this does not mean that theological theories are of no consequence whatsoever. Theological theories have only a *relative* importance, but they still have an *importance* of their own.

The Role of Theological Theories

Theological theories have a secondary importance in comparison with doctrine as the teaching of the church. An ordinary believer can get on well in her discipleship without an intricate understanding of all or even any theological theories. Theological theories are primarily at home in the sphere of

13. For a defense of the existence of the soul as explanation of human uniqueness, see Richard Swinburne, *The Evolution of the Soul*, 2nd ed. (Oxford: Oxford University Press, 1997).

the academy, just as other scientific theories are. But this does not make them unimportant, either in the academy or beyond. Let me explore two reasons for developing theological theories: first, the simple desire to understand and, second, the need for an internal and external apologetic of Christian faith and doctrine.

The first reason to engage in the critical development of theological theories, then, is the desire for understanding, the desire to know the truth, and the desire to explore the reality that theology has in common with the other sciences. In theology, this more general desire—classically formulated by Aristotle[14]—is linked with the specific desire to know God, an expression of our love for God. We are commanded by Jesus: "You shall love the Lord your God with all your heart, and with all your soul, and with all your mind" (Matt. 22:37). This is part of our love and worship and therefore also part of how we find our true destiny—in knowing and loving God. It is therefore an expression of the famous maxim of Anselm of Canterbury (1033–1109), *fides quaerens intellectum*, "faith in search of understanding." Faith does not need understanding in order to trust or to know what it believes, yet it desires to understand because understanding adds another dimension to our faith and love. If I am taught in the Scriptures and Christian tradition that humans are sinful from birth, I will want to understand how this process of inheritance works. In the process, I may come up with theories such as the Augustinian theory of the natural unity of the human race or the Calvinistic understanding of the federal unity of the human race. Theological understanding is valuable in itself and not necessarily pursued for any other reason,[15] just as understanding in the other sciences may be pursued for the pleasure and value of knowing itself, whatever other value it might have. It is the natural curiosity of the researcher—or of the human, if you wish—that pushes the evolutionary biologist not to stop at the simple observation that the earth and animal life have a long history but to want to understand the processes that have guided this development.

Precisely because this desire to understand is not simply an academic desire but a human and Christian desire, it will not stop at neat academic disciplinary boundaries. As a Christian theologian, I believe that the God who revealed himself in the Scriptures is also the God who created the world in which I live. I also believe that the human of whom the Scriptures speak is the same as the one studied by biology or the social sciences. I will therefore want to understand how these two aspects of human and Christian experience interrelate. The

14. Aristotle, *Metaphysics*, trans. Hugh Lawson-Tancred (New York: Penguin, 1998), sec. A1, 980a.

15. H. Berkhof, *Introduction to the Study of Dogmatics* (Grand Rapids: Eerdmans, 1985), 13–14.

same would be true for a Christian academic studying evolutionary biology, even though she would probably ask these questions differently. If I want to develop a theological theory in order to make sense of the doctrine of original sin, I will not only look at the scriptural data and theological arguments developed in the tradition of the church. I will also look at other experiences that tell me something about the relationship between the generations and at scientific insights or theories from other disciplines that may help me deepen and broaden my understanding. This does not mean that all these insights have equal weight, but it does mean that they all may contribute insights, sometimes unexpectedly. All truth is God's truth, and all aspects of this reality are aspects of the world that God has created and into which he speaks.

The second reason to engage in the formation of theological theories is an apologetic one. It concerns both internal apologetics (as part of the edification of the Christian community) and external apologetics (as part of the Christian witness to the wider world). The real or perceived dissonance between the Christian faith and scientific theories can cause severe faith-stress and thereby diminish Christian conviction and commitment, finally leading to a departure from the faith. The presumed dissonance between the Christian faith and modern science in much Western public discourse also needs attention. It is a reason for many public intellectuals to keep disparaging or even attacking the Christian faith, a reason for many people not to consider the Christian faith seriously even though there might otherwise be many factors attracting them to Jesus Christ. This characteristic of public discourse may also be a real barrier for those who seriously consider faith in Christ but feel they cannot accept him because this would amount to intellectual suicide. In all these respects the development of appropriate theological theories that help to coordinate Christian doctrine with modern science can be a significant part of the apologetic response that the Christian community provides.

We need to be careful here. In light of the above, it should be clear that the possibility of accepting or continuing to believe Christian doctrine does not *depend* on the availability of viable theological theories that help us deal with the perceived tensions. Sometimes our apologetic reasoning implicitly accepts the challenge of the wider public discourse that one cannot accept the Christian faith unless it fits neatly with current scientific understanding. Life just isn't that smooth, and intellectual life isn't either. Everyone, Christian or not, will need to learn to live with paradoxes and question marks. For me the love of God shown in Christ is so convincing and overwhelming that it is perfectly reasonable to accept these limits. At the same time, the development of appropriate theological theories will help to ease the tension. If formulations of Christian theology fly in the face of accepted science and seem to force me to accept outdated physics and metaphysics, conversion to the faith and ongoing faithfulness in it may become unnecessarily burdensome. Following Jesus always means putting ourselves under a yoke, but there is no need to burden this yoke with additional baggage that derives from tradition and cultural misunderstanding rather than from the gospel.

Looking for appropriate theological theories has two different apologetic functions. On the one hand, we may need to look for theories that are *contextually* appropriate. An understanding of the image of God in terms of an Aristotelian anthropology may have been reasonably appropriate in a context in which Aristotle's anthropology was a dominant factor in public discourse. Unless this Aristotelian anthropology is true—which it may be, but that would demand an argument by itself—it is less contextually appropriate in a world in which understandings of what it means to be human have little in common with Aristotle's understanding. Here we need to develop theological theories that link in—both critically and favorably—with anthropological notions of the current cultural climate. In that respect this apologetic engagement with Western science is simply an example of a culturally relevant contextual theology and apologetic. A theological theory in China might in the same way need to engage Confucian anthropological understandings. In this respect we need to note that scientific understandings are not the only ones that shape Western public discourse. Theological theories may equally need to engage with anthropological notions that originate from other sources, such as contemporary politics, philosophy, art, or popular culture.[16]

On the other hand, we also need to look for theological theories that engage with aspects of reality as discovered by various scientific disciplines. Most scientists believe that their scientific discoveries are not merely cultural constructs but that they say something about the nature of reality as it is independent of our theorizing.[17] There is an apologetic need for theological theories that are appropriate to the nature of reality as understood by the best available science. Such theories are needed because we want to understand reality as it is and because through science many people have a level of understanding of this reality—for example, of what it means to be human—that they have gained independently of the Christian faith. It is of crucial importance that the relationship between Christian faith and doctrine on the one hand and these scientific insights on the other be coordinated by the best theological

16. For the need of a culturally appropriate apologetic, see van den Toren, *Christian Apologetics*.

17. J. C. Polkinghorne, *Reason and Reality: The Relationship between Science and Theology* (Philadelphia: Trinity Press International, 1991), 5; Polkinghorne, *Rochester Roundabout: The Story of High Energy Physics* (New York: Freeman, 1989), 162.

theories that we can think of. We are called to develop theories that show that the Christian faith is not bound up with outdated physical or metaphysical realities but rather makes surprisingly good sense—and possibly uniquely good sense—of the best science available.

Sometimes we may be almost certain that we need to develop new theological theories to do justice to the nature of reality as uncovered by science. In other cases we may be aware that we are constructing theological theories that are merely contextually appropriate for mediating between Christian doctrine and contemporary Western perceptions of human nature and human existence. In many cases we may not know whether or to what extent it is one or the other. We ourselves may be much too bound up with our own cultural context to know the difference. Augustine was probably not consciously constructing a contextual theology when he incorporated elements of Platonism in his theological theories. He was simply using what he considered the best understanding available in his time of the nature of reality.[18] We probably do not always need to know whether we are engaging with the created reality as uncovered by science or merely with the culturally dominant perceptions of our time. If we realize that the theological theories we are formulating are just that—theories that help us understand the reality of the saving action of God revealed in Christ—we will be able to hold them with conviction yet lightly since they are not the reality on which our salvation depends.

The Task Ahead in This Project

This chapter has introduced the distinction between doctrine and theological theory as a tool that will help create space for conceptual flexibility at the interface between Christian faith and secular science. The doctrines of the image of God, original sin, and the goodness of God in the face of evil do not map directly onto scientific data. From both sides the relationship is mediated by theories that make sense of these data and of this faith. This chapter has concentrated on theological theories. The value and limits of scientific theories for this interface have been explored elsewhere.[19] The distinction at hand does indeed create space because it shows that our faith does not depend on

18. With regard to social practices, Augustine was very aware of the manner in which our own cultural location regarding appreciation of the value of practices is described in Scripture. See Augustine, *On Christian Teaching*, trans. R. P. H. Green (Oxford: Oxford University Press, 1999), 3.50–51. I am not aware of similar indications concerning his philosophical perspective.

19. E.g., Alister E. McGrath, *The Foundations of Dialogue in Science and Religion* (Malden, MA: Blackwell, 1999), 87–94; McGrath, *A Scientific Theology*, vol. 3, *Theory* (New York: T&T Clark, 2006).

the availability of viable theories and that available theories can be studied critically without necessarily putting the faith and its doctrines in jeopardy. This places before us the following opportunities and challenges when we explore the interface between theological anthropology and scientific theories concerning human evolution.

In the contributions that follow, we will explore where theological convictions are properly doctrinal and where they belong to the sphere of theological theory. That this distinction is valid does not always mean that it is easy to make. I may, for example, contend that the existence of the soul is part of a historically grown theological theory that is deeply influenced by ancient Greek philosophical anthropology and that the theory can therefore be reformulated in other terms to allow for a better understanding of the image of God in the light of contemporary science. Others may contend that the existence of a soul as a separate metaphysical substance is essential to Christian faith and doctrine. This is where the debate effectively begins, yet it is also where it can move forward in new ways by asking what is part of the doctrine and what are explorations concerning the best theoretical explanation. A complexity when engaging in these debates is that believers are often heavily invested in certain theories, particularly if they have become part of denominational and institutional identities, such as federal understandings of original sin or a direct creation of the soul.

At the same time, we will explore alternative theological theories that have been developed in a variety of theological traditions. The distinction between doctrine and theological theory is a valuable tool not only for the science-and-faith debate but also for ecumenical exchange. When encountering theological differences, it helps to ask where the differences are doctrinal and where they are located at the level of theological theories.[20] Here too we should hold on to our theories more lightly because it is the doctrines that are more directly related to faith and discipleship. This distinction therefore also allows us to explore alternative theological theories that have been developed in other theological traditions and that may prove fruitful for engaging with the challenges of contemporary science. So often theologians feel that they have little leeway in the face of issues raised by science because their theological theory is the only model they know as an expression of this central Christian doctrine. They can only think of one way of understanding original sin, the image of God, or theodicy. The doctrines therefore seem to stand or fall with

20. Cf. George A. Lindbeck, "Doctrinal Standards, Theological Theories and Practical Aspects of the Ministry in the Lutheran Churches," in *Evangelium-Welt-Kirche: Schlussbericht und Referate der römisch-katholisch/evangelisch-lutherischen Studienkommission "Das evangelium und die Kirche,"* 1967–1971 (Frankfurt am Main: Lembeck and Knecht, 1975), 263–83.

one particular theory that needs to be defended at all costs—or that, if lost, also means the loss of this doctrine.

This volume therefore brings together different theological theories for understanding the image of God, original sin, and theodicy—different models, if you wish. This approach allows us to explore whether other theological traditions may have resources that allow us to respond to contemporary challenges that are unavailable or have been lost in our own traditions. If this leads to an increased appreciation of the ecumenical breadth of the church, this is an added bonus. Our first intention is to mine these resources to serve Christian theology and witness in the face of contemporary science.

PART I

The Image of God
and Evolution

MICHAEL BURDETT, EDITOR

The doctrine of the image of God is one of the most cited teachings of the church. It has been invoked by lawyers, both explicitly and implicitly, as a basis for universal human rights. It is often referred to by bioethicists and doctors when considering proper use of new biotechnologies and in appeals to human dignity. It is even a significant topic for artists, who create images themselves and reflect the divine image through their creativity. The doctrine of the image of God has also proven to be important in recent years because of new empirical research in the evolutionary sciences. Part 1 provides an introduction to that growing dialogue between evolutionary scientists and scholars of the image of God. But before turning to the relevant science and the crux of the theological issues, let me define the four typical views of the image of God, around which part 1 is organized.

The Functional View

The image of God first arises in Genesis 1:26–28, and the functional view of it largely stems from modern biblical criticism on this passage and several others in the Hebrew Bible. The functional view claims that humans reflect God's image in the world by their role as agents of God's dominion in his creation. It is clear from modern biblical scholarship that the Genesis passages are drawing on the ancient Near Eastern (ANE) context and, specifically, the notion that ANE rulers reflected the image of the deity. The biblical text takes this notion and democratizes and universalizes it such that it is not just rulers but the entirety of humanity that reflects God. Indeed, the functional interpretation gets extended when the issue of dominion found in these passages is also placed in the ANE context. Ancient Near Eastern rulers would often place statues of themselves in remote parts of their kingdom as a way to convey their presence and power when they were physically absent. In other words, their image in this context signified their dominion: the image had the function of rulership. The Genesis texts co-opt this ANE practice and locate humanity as the divine image bearer, whose responsibility is likewise that of dominion. The functional model is captured well in the following quotation from Gerhard von Rad:

> Just as powerful earthly kings, to indicate their claim to dominion, erect an image of themselves in the provinces of their empire where they do not personally appear, so man is placed upon earth in God's image as God's sovereign emblem. He is really only God's representative, summoned to maintain and enforce God's claim to dominion over the earth. The decisive thing about man's similarity to God, therefore, is his function in the non-human world.[1]

In chapter 4 below, Mark Harris analyzes the functional view in more detail.

The Structural View

The functional interpretation of the image of God is one of the most recent interpretations in the history of the doctrine, despite its close following of the biblical text and critical biblical scholarship. The structural view is the most common view and also the earliest to appear in church history. The structural model claims the image of God refers to some quality or faculty

1. Gerhard von Rad, *Genesis: A Commentary*, trans. John H. Marks, rev. ed. (Louisville: Westminster John Knox, 1973), 60.

that is inherent in the human. It is something in human nature, something human nature possesses that makes it an image bearer. As Stanley Grenz says, the structural view understands the image of God "as referring to certain characteristics or capacities inherent in the structure of human nature. Because they resemble the corresponding qualities in God, their possession makes humans like God."[2] It is often referred to as the "substantive model" as well because "it depicts something of substantial form in human nature, a faculty or a capacity that we humans possess over against animals."[3] So we might say that some quality or component of human nature is shared with God and that this is unique to both humans and God relative to the rest of God's creation. In chapter 5 below, Aku Visala offers a helpful description and defense of the structural view.

The Relational View

Turning from the structural approach to the relational one means moving the weight of the image "from noun to verb."[4] Christian ethicist Paul Ramsey defines the relational approach this way: "The image of God is . . . to be understood as a relationship *within which* man sometimes stands, whenever like a mirror he obediently reflects God's will in his life and actions. . . . The image of God, according to this view, consists of man's position before God, or, rather, the image of God is reflected in him because of his position before him."[5] Here the image of God is rooted in the divine address, in the very relationship God has to humanity. In other words, what makes humanity in the image of God is primarily the unique relationship humanity has with God and the special way in which the human is responsible to God. Secondarily, adherents to this view sometimes assert that it isn't just our unique relationship to God that makes us image bearers but that because we are relational, as God is relational in the Trinity, we reflect God's image in the world. Human uniqueness in this model, then, is rooted first in the special relationship with God, and secondarily in humans' unique relational abilities with other humans and creatures. In chapter 6 below, Thomas Jay Oord represents the relational model in light of evolutionary science.

2. Stanley Grenz, *The Social God and the Relational Self: A Trinitarian Theology of the Imago Dei* (Louisville: Westminster John Knox, 2001), 142.

3. J. Wentzel van Huyssteen, *Alone in the World? Human Uniqueness in Science and Theology* (Grand Rapids: Eerdmans, 2006), 126.

4. Grenz, *Social God*, 162.

5. Paul Ramsey, *Basic Christian Ethics* (Louisville: Westminster John Knox, 1993), 255 (emphasis original).

The Dynamic View

The dynamic view is sometimes referred to as the christological or eschato-logical model—and for good reason. Both titles help better define what makes this view unique: its focus on both Christ and eschatology. In reference to the latter, Stanley Grenz explicitly links the image of God to eschatology when he says this model "sees the *imago dei* as humankind's divinely given goal or destiny, which lies in the eschatological future towards which humans are directed."[6] It proposes that the image of God is not something entirely held or completed at the beginning of anthropological history but is instead the *telos*, or end, of the human to be completed in the future. So instead of being a protological concept (having to do with origins), it is an eschatological concept (having to do with ends). Instead of the image of God originating and being rooted in the first Adam, it has its center of gravity in the second Adam, Christ, and in the glorification of humanity in Christ. Thus, the image of God is also a christological concept. In chapter 7, Ted Peters argues for the dynamic, or proleptic, model in the face of evolution.

Evolution and the Image of God

Why is the image of God an important doctrine when theology converses with evolutionary theory? The most significant issue Christians have with evolution relative to the image of God is the position of apparent human uniqueness or distinctiveness to the image of God. In other words, if humans are created in the image of God—and this has often been interpreted to refer to a particular set of capabilities that humans share with God that is unique to humans—what happens when the evolutionary sciences find these capa-bilities in other creatures? Because evolution posits common ancestry with other creatures, does this not make our creation less unique or distinct? Does evolution challenge the image of God—and perhaps even human dignity?

Since Darwin, the evolutionary sciences have changed our self-perception and how we relate to other creatures. In many ways, the distinction between humans and animals has collapsed or been blurred. For example, some human capabilities that in the past were thought to be special and defining are in-creasingly found in rudimentary form in other creatures. Some have claimed humans are unique in their rationality and intellectual capacities, yet the sci-ences have identified germinal but robust instances of each of these in other animals. Elephants, some higher apes, and even crows have been shown to

6. Grenz, *Social God*, 177.

exhibit impressive reasoning capabilities when given a complex task with many progressive steps that depend on the success of each prior step.[7]

Human uniqueness or distinctiveness is not the only point of contact between the image of God and evolutionary theory. In a related way the development of personhood is also a common point of dialogue. Traditionally, the human capabilities that make up the image of God are also those that make the human a person. So, when we talk about the development of rationality, self-reflection, morality and altruism, individual freedom, or creativity (just to name a few) in either single individuals or the whole human race throughout history, we are talking about the development of the person. Evolution also tracks the development of personhood because genetic and phylogenetic changes on the tree of life correspond to changing capabilities relevant to personhood. According to evolutionary theory, at some point these personally defining capabilities arose in our ancestral past. Often in discussions on the image of God and evolution, people want to identify when certain capabilities arise so as to identify or locate the first theologically recognized human (either in the singular or in a community). Creatures that bear this image of God have a special responsibility and relation to God, and studying the evolutionary record can sometimes illuminate a deeper understanding of ourselves and how we have developed personally. If the image of God in Christian theology in some sense defines the human (or at least is the paramount and distinctive feature of it), how does this relate to the apparent changes the human undergoes in history and in its lifetime? Both theology and evolutionary science agree that the human changes; how should they relate, and does the image of God provide an anchor or prism to understanding the origin or end of the human?

These are just some of the issues that take center stage when the image of God and evolution meet. All the chapters in this section touch on these topics in more comprehensive ways and with a view to assessing how particular models of the image of God (e.g., structural, relational, functional, etc.) might allow for greater illumination or conceptual space when dialoguing with evolution.

---

7. Countless videos can be found online of animals solving puzzles that even some children cannot solve. For a larger selection of such capacities, see Michael Burdett, "The Image of God and Human Uniqueness: Challenges from the Biological and Information Sciences," *Expository Times* 127, no. 1 (2015): 6–8.

3

Questions, Challenges, and Concerns for the Image of God

J. Wentzel van Huyssteen

Contemporary scholars from numerous and highly diverse fields are not only addressing the questions of what makes us human and what it means to be a self but are also seeking multidisciplinary input to inform and enhance their answers to these fundamental issues. These questions do not only pertain to empirical questions about what distinguishes humans from their hominid ancestors, but they often also refer to a very different kind of question—namely, which of our specific peculiarities give humans our distinctive "species specificity" and significance. The complex question of what it means to be human is also directly important for the Christian faith and Christian theology, where the doctrine of the *imago Dei*, or image of God, in its many shapes and forms, has for centuries directly influenced the question of what it means to be human. In this chapter we survey recent developments in evolutionary science and then consider the theological challenges and questions these developments raise.

Evolutionary Science and the Uniqueness of Humanity

The meaning, markers, and justification of human identity and status have fluctuated throughout Western academic history. Generally language has been viewed as a crucial marker for what it means to be human.[1] In addition, conceptions of humanness have lately shifted toward our capacity for "prosociality"—that is, our biocultural propensity to stay in close proximity with other humans as well as our unique propensity for imitation.[2] Also music, sexuality, and empathy are in the process of being thoroughly researched and hailed as the foundation not only of language, social norms, and morality but also of symbolic and even religious behavior.[3]

Another genuinely panhuman trait is the remarkable human capacity for seeing things from someone else's perspective, generally known as "theory of mind." Humans are indeed strongly disposed to intuitively understanding the motivations of others—so much so that we often see motivations where they do not exist.[4] This unique ability gives us adaptively valuable insight into the intentions of our friends, enemies, predators, and prey. And, ironically, both sadism and compassion are neurologically grounded in this disposition.[5]

For scientists such as Agustín Fuentes and Richard Potts, the real success of humans as a species can be attributed largely to our tendency and capacity for extreme alteration of the world around us.[6] We not only construct material items but also engage in the creation and navigation of social and symbolic structures, space and place, in a manner unequaled by other organisms. Most anthropologists agree that human identity should be seen as interactively constructed by, and involved in the construction of, a conflux of biological, behavioral, social, and symbolic contexts.[7]

1. Cf. Terrence William Deacon, *The Symbolic Species: The Co-evolution of Language and the Brain* (New York: Norton, 1997); Ian Tattersall, *The Monkey in the Mirror: Essays on the Science of What Makes Us Human* (New York: Harcourt Brace, 2002).

2. Cf. Matt Cartmill and Kaye Brown, "Being Human Means That 'Being Human' Means Whatever We Say It Means," *American Journal of Physical Anthropology* 144 (2011): 106; James M. Calcagno and Agustín Fuentes, "What Makes Us Human? Answers from Evolutionary Anthropology," *Evolutionary Anthropology* 21 (2012): 182–94.

3. Cf. Steven Mithen, *The Singing Neanderthals: The Origins of Music, Language, Mind, and Body* (Cambridge, MA: Harvard University Press, 2006); Maxine Sheets-Johnstone, *The Roots of Thinking* (Philadelphia: Temple University Press, 1990); Frans B. M. de Waal, *Primates and Philosophers: How Morality Evolved*, ed. Stephen Macedo and Josiah Ober (Princeton: Princeton University Press, 2006); Waal, *The Age of Empathy: Nature's Lessons for a Kinder Society* (New York: Harmony, 2009); Maxine Sheets-Johnstone, *The Roots of Morality* (University Park: Pennsylvania State University Press, 2008).

4. Cf. Cartmill and Brown, "Being Human," 182.

5. Cartmill and Brown, "Being Human," 182.

6. Cf. Agustín Fuentes, "A New Synthesis: Resituating Approaches to the Evolution of Human Behaviour," *Anthropology Today* 25, no. 3 (2009): 12–17; Richard Potts, *Humanity's Descent* (New York: Morrow, 1996); Richard Potts, "Environmental and Behavioral Evidence Pertaining to the Evolution of Early *Homo*," *Current Anthropology* 53, supp. 6 (2012): S299–S317.

7. Cf. Fuentes, "New Synthesis," 12; Christopher Boehm, *Moral Origins: The Evolution of Virtue, Altruism, and Shame* (New York: Basic Books, 2012).

For this reason some evolutionary anthropologists now find the distinctions "Darwinian" and "neo-Darwinian" unhelpful for many of the current evolutionary theories of interest and argue that we should recognize that there is an expansive body of research and theory that is not captured by these headings anymore.[8] Basic Darwinian theory prioritizes natural selection and sexual selection as the prime factors in evolutionary change and the emergence of adaptations.

Without discounting the important role of natural and sexual selection in biological systems, some anthropologists want to emphasize that scientists are now expanding on Darwin's contributions and invite us to focus on more recent, emerging trends in evolutionary theory. Evolutionary anthropologist Christopher Boehm, for instance, has recently pointed out how clearly Charles Darwin always implied that potentially changeable environments are continuously acting on the gene pool with significant results for evolutionary development and even speciation.[9] At the heart of Darwin's project, then, can be found what evolutionary biologists and anthropologists today are calling a process of *niche construction*, in which, in a remarkable, interactive process, potentially changeable natural environments are acting continuously on variation in the gene pools of populations, causing gene pools to be modified over generations.

Eva Jablonka and Marion Lamb's important work, *Evolution in Four Dimensions* (2005), especially calls for the renewal of evolutionary theory by arguing for "evolution in four dimensions" rather than for a focus on just one, the *genetic*. Jablonka and Lamb's basic claim is that biological thinking about heredity and evolution is undergoing a revolutionary change, and what is emerging is a new synthesis that challenges the classic gene-centered view of neo-Darwinism that has dominated biological thought for the last fifty years. Jablonka and Lamb argue for three other inheritance systems—in addition to genetics—that also have causal roles in evolutionary change: *epigenetic, behavioral*, and *symbolic inheritance* systems. Epigenetic inheritance is found in all organisms, behavioral inheritance in most, and symbolic inheritance only in humans.[10] According to this view, there is more to heredity than genes, some acquired information is inherited, and evolutionary change can thus result from instruction as well as from selection. This constructivist view moves beyond standard neo-Darwinian approaches and acknowledges

8. Cf. Fuentes, "New Synthesis," 12.
9. Cf. Boehm, *Moral Origins*, 3–4.
10. Cf. Eva Jablonka and Marion J. Lamb, *Evolution in Four Dimensions: Genetic, Epigenetic, Behavioral, and Symbolic Variation in the History of Life* (Cambridge, MA: MIT Press, 2005), 1–8; Fuentes, "New Synthesis," 13.

that many organisms transmit information via behavior; thus acquisition of evolutionarily relevant behavioral patterns can occur through socially mediated learning. Symbolic inheritance comes with language and the ability to creatively engage in information transfer that can be complex and contain a high density of information. What makes the human species so different and special—and what makes the species *human*—lies in the way humans can organize, transfer, and acquire information. The ability to think and communicate through words and other types of symbols makes humans fundamentally different. On this view, then, rationality, linguistic ability, artistic ability, and religiosity are all facets of symbolic thought and communication.[11]

On this interactionist perspective, there clearly is much more to evolution than simply the inheritance of genes. Moreover, this perspective blurs any clear prioritization in inheritance systems and thus requires a clear move away from approaches that are limited to either social or biological focuses. On this view "evolution as construction" is the idea that evolution is never only a matter of biologically developing organisms but also of organism-environment systems interacting and changing over time in a dynamic interactive process of niche construction as a significant evolutionary force alongside natural selection.[12] For an understanding of human evolution this is extremely important, and most anthropologists would agree that humans are constructed by, and involved in the construction of, contexts that are simultaneously physiological, behavioral, historical, social, and symbolic. In this sense human behavioral evolution must be seen primarily as *a system evolving* rather than as a set of independent or moderately connected traits evolving.[13] On this view, niche construction is a core factor in human behavioral evolution. The startling conclusion, however, is that we should consider the potential impacts of a diverse array of processes that affect inheritance and evolutionary change and the possibility that natural selection can occur at multiple levels and may not always be the only, or main, driver of change.[14]

In addition anthropologists have largely rejected the antiquated dichotomy of nature versus nurture in favor of dynamic, interactive understandings of social, biological, and historical complexities. Against this kind of background it should come as no surprise that, on the specific matter of human evolution, an anthropologist such as Jonathan Marks could argue that instead of seeing ourselves as "upgraded" versions of our ancestors, we should

11. Cf. Jablonka and Lamb, *Evolution in Four Dimensions*, 193–231.
12. Cf. Fuentes, "New Synthesis," 14; Michael Ruse, *The Philosophy of Human Evolution* (Cambridge: Cambridge University Press, 2012), 125.
13. Cf. Fuentes, "New Synthesis," 15.
14. Fuentes, "New Synthesis," 16.

accept that "we have evolved into biocultural ex-apes." In fact, to imagine that we are "nothing but apes" and to find human nature in apeness actually constitutes a denial of evolution. As Marks succinctly puts it: "we evolved; get over it!"[15] Evolution is indeed the interactive production of difference and novelty, and we are indeed not our ancestors anymore. What we need is an understanding of evolutionary anthropology that helps us "understand what it means to be a cultural, as well as a natural, being" with remarkable symbolic propensities.[16]

Crucial to our ability for symbolic behavior is our equally remarkable ability for imagination. From a philosophical and theological perspective, this point is where the evolution of the moral sense and of morality become crucially important. To approach and understand these defining traits, especially the propensity for religious imagination, Fuentes has suggested an important distinction: the quest for understanding the human propensity for religious imagination (and, I would add, the quest for understanding the evolution of the moral sense) can be aided and enriched by investigating more fully the core role of the evolutionary transition between *becoming human* and *being human*.[17] A distinctively human imagination is part of the explanation for this evolutionary success.

In my book *Alone in the World? Human Uniqueness in Science and Theology*, I argue from an evolutionary point of view for the *naturalness of the religious*.[18] If indeed there is an evolutionary naturalness to religious imagination, or to the propensity of religious belief, then it would be a valid question to ask *how* such an imagination as a system emerged over the course of human evolution. Against the background of a broader, more robust view of the many dimensions of evolution that include extensive, interactive niche construction, we can say that *Homo sapiens sapiens* is a species that had a hand in making itself. From this follow the central theses of evolutionary anthropologist Agustín Fuentes's work: *first*, that an evolutionary assessment of a distinctively human way of being in the world includes the capacity and capabilities for metaphysical thought as a precursor to religion and, *second*, that this can be facilitated by recognizing the increasingly central role of niche

15. Cf. Jonathan Marks, "On Nature and the Human: Off Human Nature," *American Anthropologist: Vital Forum* 112, no. 4 (2010): 513.

16. Marks, "Off Human Nature," 513.

17. Agustín Fuentes, "Human Evolution, Niche Complexity, and the Emergence of a Distinctly Human Imagination," *Time and Mind* 7 (2014): 241; cf. Steven Mithen, *The Prehistory of the Mind: A Search for the Origins of Art, Religion and Science* (London: Thames & Hudson, 1996).

18. See J. Wentzel van Huyssteen, *Alone in the World? Human Uniqueness in Science and Theology* (Grand Rapids: Eerdmans, 2006), 93–106.

construction, a niche being the structural and temporal context in which a species exists.

Following up on my own quest to understand the naturalness of the propensity for religious imagination and for our aesthetic, creative capacities, Fuentes now believes this idea can be aided significantly by investigating more fully the core role of the evolutionary transition between *becoming human* and *being human*.[19] This transition itself can be understood better by a broad assessment of hominin evolution over the last six million years. And here the focus should be on the terminal portion of that epoch, meaning the final transition from the archaic form of our genus *Homo sapiens* into the current form of *Homo sapiens sapiens*. The focus on this transition, which is a shift to a wholly human way of being in our current socio-cognitive niche, will add to our insight into how we, as humans, experience the world in the here and now. Fuentes now suggests that we can connect this emergence of a distinctly human socio-cognitive and ecological niche to existence in a meaning-laden world and to the emergence of an imagination that facilitates the capacity and capabilities for metaphysical thought. Moreover, this process is intricately connected to our success as a species.[20]

While many scholars have proposed that the origin of religion and of religious belief is either an adaptation, an exaptation,[21] or a by-product of our cognitive complexity, others suggest that it is more complicated than that.[22] In addition, Fuentes argues that evolutionary answers to the question of the origin of such systems might not lie either in the specific content of religious beliefs or only in neurological structures themselves but rather (at least partially) emerge out of the way in which humans successfully negotiated the world during the terminal stages of the Pleistocene.[23] Evolutionary epistemologist Franz Wuketits argues that metaphysical belief is the result of particular interactions between early humans and their external world and thus results from specific life conditions in prehistoric times.[24] More importantly,

19. Cf. Fuentes, "Human Evolution."

20. Fuentes, "Human Evolution," 2.

21. "Exaptation" is a term used by evolutionary biology to describe a trait that has been co-opted for a use other than the one for which natural selection has selected it.

22. Cf. Wesley Wildman, *Science and Religious Anthropology* (Farnham, UK: Ashgate, 2009); Boehm, *Moral Origins*; J. Wentzel van Huyssteen, "From Empathy to Embodied Faith: Interdisciplinary Perspectives on the Evolution of Religion," in *Evolution, Religion, and Cognitive Science: Critical and Constructive Essays*, ed. Fraser Watts and Léon P. Turner (Oxford: Oxford University Press, 2014).

23. Cf. Fuentes, "Human Evolution," 3.

24. Cf. Franz M. Wuketits, *Evolutionary Epistemology and Its Implications for Humankind* (Albany, NY: SUNY Press, 1990), 118.

within this evolutionary context one can now envision a distinctive imagination as a core part of the human niche that ultimately enabled the possibility of metaphysical thought. This component of our human niche as our way of being in the world is the central aspect of our explanation for why *Homo sapiens* has flourished while all other hominins, even members of our own genus, have gone extinct.

On this view, then, looking at human origins and the archaeology of personhood, and thus at the evolution of our lineage across the Pleistocene, it is evident that there is significant increasing complexity in the way we interface with the world: increases in the complexity of culture and social traditions, tool use and manufacture, trade and use of fire, enhanced infant survival and predator avoidance, habitat exploitation, and information transfer via material technologies, all of which have increased in intensity rather dramatically in the last four hundred thousand years.[25] All of these increasing complexities are tied directly to a rapidly evolving human cognition and social structure that require increased cooperative capabilities and coordination within human communities. Thinking of these as specific outcomes of a niche construction actually provides a mechanism as well as a context for the evolution of these multifaceted response capabilities and coordination within communities.[26]

Finally, the emergence of language and a fully developed theory of mind with high levels of intentionality, empathy, moral awareness, symbolic thought, and social unity would be impossible without an extremely cooperative and mutually integrated social system in combination with enhanced cognitive and communicative capacities as our core adaptive niche. Interestingly, on this point Fuentes himself wants to incorporate an analysis on *compassion*.[27] I believe, however, that this can be pushed even further back by tracing the deep evolutionary roots of empathy and attachment.[28] Our genus thus provides a scenario wherein we can envision a distinctively human imagination as a key part of our niche and as a part of the explanation for why our species succeeded and all other hominins went extinct. Fuentes puts it rather forcefully: the imagination and the infusion of meaning into the world by the genus *Homo* in the late Pleistocene (the geological epoch that lasted from about 2,588,000 to 11,700 years ago) are what underlies and preceded our current

25. Cf. Fuentes, "Human Evolution," 9.
26. Fuentes, "Human Evolution," 9.
27. Fuentes, "Human Evolution," 10.
28. Cf. van Huyssteen, "Embodied Faith"; Sarah Hrdy, *Mothers and Others: The Evolutionary Origins of Mutual Understanding* (Cambridge, MA: Harvard University Press, 2009), 82ff; Lee A. Kirkpatrick, *Attachment, Evolution, and the Psychology of Religion* (New York: Guilford, 2005); Sheets-Johnstone, *Roots of Morality*.

ability to form a metaphysics, which in turn eventually facilitates religious beliefs. This landscape of meaning and associated imagination is also a system that facilitates an array of other symbolic and meaning-laden aspects of human behavior and experiences that are not at the core of our current niche and lives.[29] Importantly, though, there is no single trait that explains human evolutionary success, nor is there a particular environment that created it. And part of this significant tool kit includes a robust imagination and a landscape and perceptual reality wherein everything, whether material or not, is infused with multifaceted meaning.

At the heart of these advances is the increasingly rapid and dynamic niche construction by humans, particularly as it relates to aspects of cognitive and symbolic function and social relationships, and the imaginative ability to deploy multiple modes of responding to evolutionary pressures. Fuentes agrees here with Terrence Deacon, Merlin Donald, Barbara King, Alan Barnard, and Andrew Robinson that it is our use of symbol as a core infrastructure of our perceptions dealing with the world that acts as a major hallmark of human evolution.[30]

Humans have an imagination that is part of our perceptual and interactive reality and is a substantive aspect of lived experience. Thus it is realistic to accept that at some point in the last four hundred thousand years language and hypercomplex intentionality acted to "lock in" the more-than-material as our permanent state of being and so laid the groundwork for the evolution of morality, the possibility of metaphysics, aesthetic inclinations, religious imagination, and the propensity for religious belief as crucial parts of the uniquely human experience.[31] Now existing in a landscape where the material and social elements have semiotic properties, and where communication and action can potentially be influenced by representations of both past and future behavior, implies the possession of an imagination and even something like "hope"—that is, *the expectation of future outcomes beyond the predictable.*[32] The assertion here is that this interactive process occurs as a component of the human niche as it moves dynamically through the Pleistocene as part of the emerging human tool kit.

29. Cf. Fuentes, "Human Evolution," 11.

30. See Deacon, *Symbolic Species*; Merlin Donald, *A Mind So Rare: The Evolution of Human Consciousness* (New York: Norton, 2001); Barbara King, *Evolving God: A Provocative View on the Origins of Religion* (New York: Doubleday, 2007); Alan Barnard, *Genesis of Symbolic Thought* (Cambridge: Cambridge University Press, 2012); Andrew Robinson, *God and the World of Signs: Trinity, Evolution, and the Metaphysical Semiotics of C. S. Peirce* (Boston: Brill, 2010). Cf. Fuentes, "Human Evolution," 12.

31. Cf. van Huyssteen, *Alone in the World?*

32. Cf. Fuentes, "Human Evolution," 13.

On this view, imagination—and therefore religion—is not just an exaptation, a spurious by-product of evolution, but is crucial to the process of human evolution and incorporates behavioral processes and a sense of hope that would, and did, increase the likelihood of innovation and successful responses to evolutionary challenges.[33] This view also implies that human distinctiveness may have emerged not through the ascent of a hierarchy of semiotic competence, of which symbolic competence was the pinnacle, but rather through the entrance of what Andrew Robinson refers to as the *semiotic matrix*.[34] In the Upper Paleolithic in Europe, and probably earlier in Africa, anatomically modern humans crossed a new cognitive threshold into a semiotic realm, a threshold of semiotic competence that allowed for the combination of remarkable new forms of symbolic communication.[35]

This brief review of human origins and human evolution demonstrates the path and substantive impact of changes in behavior, life histories, and bodies of our human ancestors and in the human species itself. It is clear, then, that these changes in the Upper Paleolithic would lead to the unambiguous appearance of art and symbol, now also combined with the evolution of empathy and compassion and deep caring for others.[36] It should therefore not be surprising that a distinctively human imagination is part of the explanation for human evolutionary success and can be seen as one of the structurally significant aspects of the transition from earlier members of the genus *Homo* to human beings.

A better understanding of cooperation, empathy, compassion, the use of and engagement with materials, symbols and ritual, and the notion of a semiotic landscape in which humans and their immediate ancestors exist or existed does indeed move us along in our analysis of what it meant to become human. And the understanding of all of this is indeed a true interdisciplinary process: the insights we gain via the fossil and archaeological record and via behavioral, neurological, and physiological systems provide a more robust understanding of how humans perceive and experience the world. And it is this process that creates the possibility for an imaginative, potentially metaphysical, and eventually religious experience of the world.[37]

For Christian theologians this provides an exciting bottom-up view of the spectacularly complex way in which God has shaped and prepared our

33. Fuentes, "Human Evolution," 14.
34. Cf. Robinson, *God and the World of Signs*, 150–51.
35. Cf. van Huyssteen, *Alone in the World?*, 217–70.
36. Cf. Boehm, *Moral Origins*; Fuentes, "Human Evolution"; van Huyssteen, "Embodied Faith."
37. Cf. Fuentes, "Human Evolution," 17.

species to be physically, mentally, and spiritually "ready" for faith. I believe that my original intuition that there is a naturalness to human imagination, even to religious imagination, that facilitates engagement with the world in some ways that are truly distinct from those in other animals—even closely related hominins—thus becomes even more plausible.[38]

Evolutionary Science and the *Imago Dei*

As a Christian theologian interested in human origins and the controversial issue of human distinctiveness or uniqueness, I have been increasingly drawn to the contributions of scientists and other scholars to the challenging problem of what it means to be human. In my own recent work I have been deeply involved in trying to construct plausible ways for theology to enter into this important interdisciplinary conversation. An interdisciplinary approach, carefully thought through, can help us to identify these shared resources in different modes of knowledge so as to reach beyond the boundaries of our own traditional disciplines in cross-contextual, cross-disciplinary conversation. It can also enable us to identify possible shared conceptual problems as we negotiate the porous boundaries of our different disciplines.

One such shared interdisciplinary problem is exactly the concern for what makes us human, for human distinctiveness, for what it means to be a self or a person—and how that may, or may not, relate to human origins and the evolution of religious awareness. It is, therefore, precisely in the problem of human distinctiveness that theology and the sciences clearly find a shared, interdisciplinary research trajectory. In the interdisciplinary conversation between theology and the sciences, the boundaries between our disciplines and reasoning strategies are indeed often shifting and porous; however, deep theological convictions cannot be easily transferred to philosophy or to science to function as data in foreign disciplinary systems. In the same manner, interdisciplinary reasoning does not imply that scientific data, paradigms, or worldviews can be transported into theology to set the agenda for theological reasoning. Interdisciplinary reasoning does mean that theology and science can share concerns and converge on commonly identified conceptual problems such as the problem of human distinctiveness. Yet these mutually critical tasks presuppose the richness of the transversal moment in which theology and anthropology or paleoanthropology may find amazing connections and overlapping intersections on issues of human origins and uniqueness.

38. Cf. van Huyssteen, *Alone in the World?*

I believe that the most responsible Christian theological way to look at human nature requires, first, a move away from esoteric, abstract notions of human distinctiveness and, second, a return to radically embodied notions of humanness, where our sexuality and embodied moral awareness are tied directly to our embodied self-transcendence as creatures who are predisposed to religious belief. I would further argue that, from a paleoanthropological point of view, human distinctiveness has emerged as a highly contextualized, embodied notion that is directly tied to the embodied, symbolizing minds of our prehistoric ancestors as physically manifested in the spectacularly painted cave walls and portable art of the Upper Paleolithic. This opens up not only the possibility for converging arguments from both theology and paleoanthropology for the presence of imagination and religious awareness in our earliest Cro-Magnon ancestors but also the plausibility of the larger argument: since the very beginning of the emergence of *Homo sapiens*, the evolution of those characteristics that made humans uniquely different from even their closest sister species—characteristics such as consciousness, language, imagination, moral awareness, symbolic minds, and symbolic behavior—has always included a general tendency for religious awareness and religious behavior.

The idea that religious imagination might not be an isolated faculty of human rationality—and that mystical or religious inclinations can indeed be regarded as an essentially universal attribute of the human mind—has recently also been taken up in interdisciplinary discussion by some theologians.[39] Colleen Shantz has offered a fascinating and entirely plausible account of religious experience and religious ecstasy as not only a significant feature of the apostle Paul's life but also as part of a strong argument for the epistemological relevance of religious experience. Her argument for the universal significance of religious experience and of alternate states of consciousness is first of all an argument against a completely disembodied exegesis that is restricted, and epistemically limited, to the analysis and comparison of biblical texts. But, second, it is an argument for forms of cognition that go beyond linguistic dominance: the human self and its embodied experience includes elements that are known apart from language, elements that are still essentially human.[40] In this exciting interdisciplinary project her discussion partners are cognitive neuroscientists, textual exegetes, and social anthropologists, and the point is to argue not that God is generated by the brain but rather that God cannot be known apart from the brain, the embodied person.[41]

39. Cf. Colleen Shantz, *Paul in Ecstasy: The Neurobiology of the Apostle's Life and Thought* (Cambridge: Cambridge University Press, 2009).

40. Cf. Shantz, *Paul in Ecstasy*, 9–10.

41. Shantz, *Paul in Ecstasy*, 15.

I suggest that a theological appropriation of these rich and complex results of science at the very least should inspire the theologian carefully to trace and rethink the complex evolution of the notion of human distinctiveness, or the *imago Dei*, in theology. A reconception of personhood in terms of embodied imagination, symbolic propensities, and cognitive fluidity may enable theology to revise its notion of the *imago Dei* as an idea that does not imply superiority or a greater moral value for humans over animals or earlier hominids but that might express a specific task and purpose to set forth the presence of God in this world.[42] In theology I would, therefore, call for a revisioning of the notion of the *imago Dei* in ways that would not be disembodied or overly abstract but that would instead acknowledge our embodied existence, our close ties to the animal world and *its* uniqueness and to those hominid ancestors that came before us, while at the same time focusing on what our symbolic and cognitively fluid minds might tell us about the emergence of an embodied human distinctiveness, consciousness, and personhood, and the propensity for religious awareness and experience.

In my own recent work I have argued that theologians should be intensely aware of how interpretations of the *imago Dei* have varied dramatically throughout the long history of Christianity.[43] Interdisciplinary theologians are now challenged to rethink what human distinctiveness might mean for the human person, a being that has emerged biologically as a center of embodied self-awareness, identity, and moral responsibility. This notion of self or personhood, when reconceived in terms of embodied imagination, symbolic propensities, moral awareness, and cognitive fluidity, will enable theology to revise its notion of the *imago Dei* as emerging from nature itself. In this kind of interdisciplinary conversation, theology can help to significantly broaden the scope of what is meant by human distinctiveness, or the notion of self or personhood. However, *Homo sapiens* is not only distinguished by its remarkable embodied brain, a stunning mental cognitive fluidity expressed in imagination, creativity, linguistic abilities, and symbolic propensities. As real-life, embodied persons, humans are also affected by hostility, arrogance, ruthlessness, and cunning and therefore are inescapably caught between good and evil. This experience of good and evil—and theological distinctions between evil, moral failure, sin, tragedy, and redemption—lies beyond the empirical scope of the fossil record and therefore beyond the scope of science.[44] Our evolutionarily developed bodies are the bearers of human distinctiveness, and this embodied

42. Cf. Philip Hefner, "Biocultural Evolution and the Created Co-Creator," in *Science and Theology: The New Consonance*, ed. Ted Peters (Boulder, CO: Westview, 1998), 88.

43. Cf. van Huyssteen, *Alone in the World?*

44. Van Huyssteen, *Alone in the World?*, 325.

existence is precisely what confronts us with the realities of vulnerability, sin, tragedy, and affliction. Here, then, theology has a special task: in terms of the complexity of the history of human niche construction, theology may now provide a rather unique key to understanding the profound tragic dimensions of human existence—and also why religious belief has provided humans and their distant ancestors with dimensions of hope, redemption, and grace.

Rethinking the *imago Dei* theologically in a bottom-up, historical way, as *emerging from nature*, opens up theology to the interdisciplinary impact of the fact that the potential arose in the embodied human mind to undertake science and technology, to create art, and to discover the need and ability for religious belief. It is in this sense that we cannot understand early human behavior, or human personhood itself, if we do not take the evolution of this fundamental religious dimension into account.

Conclusions

We conclude with four observations from our preceding discussion. First, the strong interdisciplinary convergence between theology and the sciences on the question of what it means to be human implicates arguments from both evolutionary anthropology and paleoanthropology. Since the very beginning of the emergence of *Homo sapiens*, the evolution of those characteristics that make humans distinct from even their closest sister species—characteristics like consciousness, language, imagination, moral awareness, and symbolic minds and behavior—most probably always included some form of religious awareness and religious behavior. Embedded in this argument, however, is the remarkable degree of adaptability and versatility of the human species. *Homo sapiens* emerged as a result of its ancestral lineage, having persisted and changed in the face of dramatic environmental variability and having coped so successfully with interactive niche construction. This versatility gives new depth to the kind of human symbolic capacities that Jablonka and Lamb as well as Fuentes have highlighted in their recent work and that archaeologist Richard Potts has called the "astonishing hallmark of modern humanity."[45]

Second, in thinking about the emergence of religion or of spirituality in prehistory, and in considering the historical human self as *Homo religiosus*,

45. Cf. Jablonka and Lamb, *Evolution in Four Dimensions*; Fuentes, "New Synthesis"; Fuentes, "Human Evolution"; Fuentes, "On Nature and the Human: Introduction," *American Anthropologist: Vital Forum* 112, no. 4 (2010): 512; Fuentes, "On Nature and the Human: More than a Human Nature," *American Anthropologist: Vital Forum* 112, no. 4 (2010): 519; Richard Potts, "Sociality and the Concept of Culture in Human Origins," in *The Origins and Nature of Sociality*, ed. Robert W. Sussman and Audrey R. Chapman (New York: Walter de Gruyter, 2004).

we should not expect to discover some clearly demarcated, separate domain that we could identify as "religion" as such. What this means is that we should avoid making easy and uncomplicated distinctions between the natural and supernatural or between the material and spiritual when trying to understand the long history of the prehistoric self as it hovers between *becoming human* and *being human*. The history and archaeology of the human self demands a more interactive, holistic approach where not just special artistic objects and artifacts but also daily material life itself must have been deeply infused with imagination and spirituality. This approach implies that theologians, along with evolutionary anthropologists and archaeologists, can recognize the spiritual or religious in early time periods only through the material legacy of the people of that time. Imagery, sculptures, paintings, other artifacts, and mortuary practices may not always be exclusively religious but nevertheless certainly point to normal living spaces and practices as possible symbolic, religious realms.

Third, at the heart of the idea of being created in the image of God we find as the deepest intention of the Genesis texts the conviction that the mythical "first humans" should be seen as the significant forerunners of humanity that define the special relationship between God and humans. Being created in God's image in a very specific sense highlights the extraordinary importance of humans as walking representations of God—in no sense superior to other animals yet with an additional call to responsible care and stewardship to the world and to our sister species in this world. The multileveled meaning of the notion of the *imago Dei* in the ancient biblical texts was transversally integrated into the dynamics of one crucial text: in Genesis 3:22 we read: "Then the LORD God said, 'See, the [human] has become like one of us, knowing good and evil.'" Here, in the emergence of an embodied moral awareness and a holistic, new way of knowing, lies the deepest meaning of the notion of the image of God. Moreover, the theme of the image of God in the texts of the New Testament reflects a remarkable continuity with the Old Testament texts, Jesus now being identified as the one who, like the primal human before him, defines the relationship between humanity and God. This notion of the *imago Dei* is as contextual and embodied as that of the "first Adam": what we know of God, we know only through the story of the suffering and resurrection of the embodied person of Jesus, the Jewish peasant. Against this background, the notion of the *imago Dei* still functions theologically to express a crucial link between God and humans and should give Christian theologians *intra*disciplinary grounds for redefining notions of evil, sin, and redemption within Christian theology.

Fourth, feminist theology has crucially influenced contemporary rethinking of the *imago Dei* and has unequivocally shown that this doctrine has traditionally functioned as a source of oppression and discrimination against women.[46] Any attempt to revise the powerful resources of the *imago Dei* should, therefore, specifically uncover the fact that this important theological symbol gives rise to justice and thus exemplifies a root metaphor for understanding the human person. Such an understanding should ground further claims to human rights because all humans are equally created in the image of God. In his vision for an intercultural theology, George Newlands has argued in similar fashion for the radical ethical dimension of all interdisciplinary work in theology and science, developing the same strong ethical dimension implicit in the idea of humans created in the image of God and applying it directly to theological anthropology and interdisciplinary theology.[47] On this view, now enhanced by Christology, Newlands argues that a theology (and science, for that matter) that does not build communities in ways that enhance humanity fails as Christian theology.[48] Newlands goes even further and claims that an ethics of care and solidarity implies care for, and solidarity with, the marginalized at a fundamental, interdisciplinary level. Thus Newlands opens up a creative way to help us recognize that the issue of human personhood and human rights belongs at the heart of any discussion of the *imago Dei*.

In sum, rethinking theologically the *imago Dei* as emerging from nature opens theology to the interdisciplinary impact of the fact that the potential arose in the embodied human mind to undertake science and technology, to create art, and to discover the need and ability for religious belief. It is in this sense that we cannot understand early human behavior, or human personhood itself, if we do not take this fundamental religious dimension into account.

---

46. Cf. van Huyssteen, *Alone in the World?*, 126–32.
47. Cf. George Newlands, *The Transformative Imagination* (Aldershot, UK: Ashgate, 2004).
48. Cf. George Newlands, *Christ and Human Rights* (Aldershot, UK: Ashgate, 2006).

4

The Biblical Text and a Functional Account of the *Imago Dei*

MARK HARRIS

The idea that humans are made in the image of God, or *imago Dei* (Latin), is as rare in the Bible as it is ubiquitous in modern Christian culture. Admittedly, the idea first appears at the high point of a passage of momentous importance—the Genesis 1 creation narrative (Gen. 1:26–27)—but the simple fact that it crops up thereafter in the Hebrew Bible only once (Gen. 9:6; twice if you include Gen. 5:1–3), and a handful of times in the New Testament (significantly connecting the image of God with Christ; e.g., 2 Cor. 4:4), suggests that it should be used with more care than is often the case. There is surely some truth in the wry observation of systematic theologian David Fergusson that "the creation of human beings in the image of God is a theological platitude."[1] Moreover, the need to scrutinize the content of such biblical "images" is particularly urgent in light of the encounter between Christian faith and the natural sciences, not least because the traditional "structural" interpretation of the *imago Dei* (see chap. 5) is especially vulnerable to challenges from evolutionary biology.

---

1. David Fergusson, "Humans Created according to the *Imago Dei*: An Alternative Proposal," *Zygon* 48 (2012): 439.

This chapter explores the main areas of nuance in the biblical texts under-lying the *imago Dei* motif, looking especially at the difficult critical problems of translating and interpreting these texts, before setting out the dominant solution (the "virtual consensus")[2] among biblical scholars. This so-called functional interpretation reads the *imago Dei* as a divinely instituted role for humans, the ambassadorial exercise of God's "dominion" over other creatures (Gen. 1:26).

It is important first to realize that the functional interpretation is *histori-cal*, in that biblical scholars believe it to be (most probably) the view of the original biblical authors. The question of whether it is still the best view *to hold for today* is another kind of issue, and one that biblical scholars tend not to concern themselves with professionally, judging that to be a question for the theologians. Hence, I will leave it to other chapters in this book to do the heavy theological lifting, although I would like to make some points in favor of continuing to hold the functional interpretation today. In addition to its probable historical authenticity, the functional view offers two advantages over other interpretations of the *imago Dei* in the contemporary science-and-religion debate. First, the functional interpretation emphasizes human stewardship of the earth. It is surely no accident that this view has grown in popularity in recent decades alongside an emerging awareness of ecological crisis and of the ways in which modern humans have failed to be good stew-ards. The functional interpretation highlights our urgent need to revisit the divine command to "be fruitful and multiply, and fill the earth and subdue it" (Gen. 1:28), given that our very literal multiplying and subduing has become problematic for both our own flourishing and that of other creatures on this planet.[3] Second, unlike the structural and relational interpretations of the *imago Dei*, the functional view does not rely on the presence of a *uniquely* human trait that might then render it vulnerable to a challenge from evolution-ary biology; from that point of view, the functional interpretation is neutral in the debate between science and religion. While these two advantages have little bearing on what the *ancient* authors of the biblical texts thought, it is hard to deny that they are important in *modern* thinking on the matter. Any theological appropriation of the *imago Dei* for our times would therefore need to take account of these two advantages conferred by the functional interpretation as well as modern biblical scholars' belief that it is the *histori-cally authentic* view. There is, however, much more to consider, as I hope to demonstrate through close study of the biblical texts.

2. J. Richard Middleton, *The Liberating Image: The* Imago Dei *in Genesis 1* (Grand Rapids: Brazos, 2005), 25.
3. Philip Hefner, *The Human Factor: Evolution, Culture, and Religion* (Minneapolis: Fortress, 1993), 9.

The *Imago Dei* in the Hebrew Bible

The relevant biblical passages are few and appear in a highly specific literary setting. With the exception of Psalm 8 (which is of indirect relevance anyway), the *imago Dei* motif is only found in the primeval history (Gen. 1–11), in the sections usually assigned to the Priestly author or editor—and in just a handful of verses (Gen. 1:26–27; 5:1–3; 9:6). Moreover, the author makes little attempt to define the *imago* terminology beyond qualifying "image" (*tselem* in Hebrew) by the addition of "likeness" (*demuth*) in Gen. 1:26 (and 5:3), an enigma in itself. Straightaway, then, we see the importance of understanding the literary and historical contexts of the *imago* passages before any theologizing takes place; to focus on the *imago* motif distinct from its setting is to commit an act of biblical cherry-picking.[4] A related point is the need to avoid reading the *imago* passages with an incautious degree of literalism compared to their settings; this is not so different from the young earth creationist's tendency to read the six days of creation literally as a scientific datum, while other aspects of Genesis 1 (notably the solid "firmament" of 1:6 RSV) are treated loosely.[5] In short, the *imago* passages should be considered as inseparable from the wider literary unit in which they are embedded.

So what do we know of the historical, literary, and theological contexts of these passages? For much of its history over the last two centuries, biblical scholarship has been fairly united in the belief that the Pentateuch (Genesis, Exodus, Leviticus, Numbers, and Deuteronomy) was composed from four source documents stemming from different historical periods. These sources were interwoven over time to make the text we now possess. One of those documents was the Priestly source (usually referred to as P), which reflected the theological interests of an exilic or postexilic school of clergy. Although scholarly confidence in this "documentary hypothesis" has steadily eroded in recent decades (and by no means represents any kind of consensus now), it is still commonplace for scholars to refer to the P passages of Genesis 1–11 as though they in some sense belong together in historical, literary, and theological terms.[6] For our purposes, the significant P-designated passages in Genesis 1–11 are the Genesis 1 creation text, the genealogy of Genesis 5, and various parts

---

4. A very common practice in popular use of the Bible, cherry-picking is the act of establishing a view by lifting suitable terms, motifs, and passages selectively out of their context. This is often done without regard to potentially conflicting evidence that might be present. Prooftexting is a related practice of similarly dubious merit.

5. Mark Harris, *The Nature of Creation: Examining the Bible and Science* (Durham, UK: Acumen, 2013), 43.

6. It is important to bear in mind that some scholars are agnostic about such a P source, notably Middleton (*Liberating Image*, 141). I myself share Middleton's agnosticism, although

of the flood story (including God's covenant with Noah; 9:1–17). Each of these three P-designated passages contains an instance of the *imago Dei* motif.

By far the most frequently cited *imago* passage is the first, Genesis 1:26–27, and I will focus on it extensively here. Since it contains the main interpretive problems, I will bring the other passages in as they are relevant for understanding this one. The wider context of the first *imago* passage is the P creation story (Gen. 1:1–2:3). Scholarly and popular discussion of the P creation story is gargantuan in scope, and it is impossible to summarize it. Nevertheless, important themes that emerge from critical biblical scholarship for understanding the *imago* motif are as follows:[7]

- its primary focus on the nature and being of God in the mode of creating, over against the details of creation itself;
- its use of (and reaction to) mythological elements from other ancient Near Eastern (ANE) cultures;
- its likening of the creation of the universe to God fashioning and hallowing a cosmic temple;
- its establishment of an intricate network of relationships between animate and inanimate creatures and their Creator; and
- its description of the special responsibility of humans as creatures made in God's image and possessing dominion over other living creatures.

These themes are far from exhaustive. The P creation story is extraordinarily rich for such a relatively short text, and many of its theological themes are explored through layers of metaphor and allusion. It is therefore hardly surprising that the *imago Dei* passage should—like all other parts of the P creation story—be so spare in literal terms but so richly enigmatic in interpretive terms. One point is especially worth noting: given the signs that the P creation story is in part a polemical reaction against other ANE creation stories and polytheistic ideologies,[8] it is not "value free." The same can be said of the *imago* motif: it has an agenda (as we shall see).

The immediate context of the *imago* passage is the sixth day of P's creation story in Genesis 1, where humans are made at the end of the sequence of all living things. Unlike all other creatures, which come into being at God's spoken invitation ("Let there be . . ."), humans are created directly by God speaking

---

I find the terminology of a P source or editor convenient in encapsulating the thematic links between Gen. 1 and other chapters in the primeval history.

7. Harris, *Nature of Creation*, 35–50.

8. Gordon J. Wenham, *Genesis 1–15*, Word Biblical Commentary (Waco: Word, 1987), 8–9.

in the first person ("Let us make . . ."), are said to come in two genders ("male and female"), and are commanded to "subdue" the earth and to have domination over other living creatures. The creation of humans is therefore climactic.

Turning now to the crucial *imago* passage itself (Gen. 1:26), outstanding difficulties immediately come into focus around individual terms, difficulties that have been discussed countless times over the millennia. As with Genesis 1 as a whole, it is impossible to summarize the wealth of material here adequately (since it would constitute the entire history of Christian anthropological thought), but it is at least possible to draw attention to the main sticking points in the text, which we can do by going through its main components in turn. For reference, here are two popular translations of the main phrases (with key Hebrew words shown):

> "Then God [*elohim*] said, 'Let us make humankind [*adam*] in our image [*tselem*], according to our likeness [*demuth*]; and let them have dominion over . . .'" (NRSV)

> "Then God [*elohim*] said, 'Let us make mankind [*adam*] in our image [*tselem*], in our likeness [*demuth*], so that they may rule over . . .'" (NIV)

"Let Us Make"

The outstanding question here is why God's self-exhortation to make humans should be voiced in the plural ("Let us make . . .") rather than in the singular ("Let me make . . ."). There have been six main alternative proposals to explain whom God's "us" is referring to:[9]

1. a mythological interpretation, where the passage is said to have stemmed from an originally polytheistic background but was not entirely purified of all polytheistic references before being included in Genesis 1, in which case the "us" would therefore refer accidentally to the polytheistic pantheon that is otherwise unrecognized by P;
2. God is speaking as Father, Son, and Holy Spirit (i.e., the Trinity of Christian tradition) or in some kind of early recognition of plurality within the Godhead;
3. God is speaking in the "plural of majesty," just as an earthly monarch, when speaking formally, might use "we" for "I" (e.g., Queen Victoria's infamous line, "We are not amused");

---

9. These alternatives are discussed in all of the main scholarly commentaries on Genesis. See Victor P. Hamilton, *The Book of Genesis: Chapters 1–17*, New International Commentary on the Old Testament (Grand Rapids: Eerdmans, 1990), 133–34.

4. God is using the idiomatic plural of deliberation, rather as in modern English, where I might muse aloud to myself, "Let's see now . . .";

5. God is speaking cooperatively to the earth to join him in bringing forth humans (as the earth brought forth living creatures in v. 24);

6. God is speaking to the other divine beings (*elohim*), such as angels, in the heavenly court—a well-attested notion in the Hebrew Bible (e.g., 1 Kings 22:19–22).

There is no scholarly consensus here; it is possible to find supporters for each viewpoint. This lack of certainty has implications for how the *imago Dei* is to be interpreted, since humans are made in the image of the "us" whose identity is so uncertain. For instance, if we adopt (6), then humans are made in the image of angels (*elohim*) as much as of God, a proposition very different from that implied by (2) as a counterexample. And if we adopt (5) instead, then humans are made in the image of the earth as well as of God (or divine beings), a very different kind of proposition again.[10] Each of these alternatives carries different implications for solving the *imago Dei* problem (especially in the structural and relational interpretations), but the functional interpretation is relatively immune to them since its weight falls on the *what* of the function being exercised rather than on the *who* who gives it.

"In Our Image, according to Our Likeness"

The main *imago* terms "image" (*tselem*) and "likeness" (*demuth*) are paired so closely in 1:26 that it implies they are nearly synonymous. But what do they really mean, and what is the difference between them?

Elsewhere in the Hebrew Bible, the word *tselem* mostly refers to a physical representation of some kind, such as a statue (e.g., Num. 33:52), an idol of a deity (e.g., 2 Kings 11:18), or a physical replica or model of another physical object (e.g., 1 Sam. 6:5). When this meaning of *tselem* is stood alongside the usual translation of *demuth* as "likeness," we get the sense of an almost tangible similarity between humans and God, such that humans represent God by means of a physical resemblance. Indeed, there is other evidence to support such a conclusion. The *imago* text in Genesis 5:3, which describes Adam's son Seth as being in Adam's "image" (*tselem*) and "likeness" (*demuth*), presumably refers to the physical, or visual, resemblance between a father and son. It might even be said that the frequent anthropomorphisms in the

---

10. Because humans reflect a joint creative enterprise between God and "nature" in this interpretation, there is scope here for making a theological gloss on the evolutionary account of human origins. However, care should be taken to negotiate the anachronism involved.

Bible could be added to this evidence, whereby God is said to have human characteristics and features such as an ear (e.g., Ps. 17:6), eyes (e.g., 2 Kings 19:16), a finger (e.g., Exod. 8:19), a face (e.g., Gen. 33:10), and a back (e.g., Exod. 33:23). Moreover, God can be encountered on face-to-face terms (Gen. 32:22–30; Exod. 24:9–11). In the same way, if we assume that the "us" of "Let us make . . ." includes both God and angels—as in interpretation (6) above—then the implication is that there is some kind of heavenly appearance shared by all of the *elohim* (God and angels) with which humans (uniquely among earthly beings) have been gifted.[11] The occasions when angels are mistaken for humans in the Hebrew Bible might be added as support (e.g., Gen. 19): humans and *elohim* look physically alike.

However, before getting carried away it is important to recognize that there are indications in the biblical text that the *imago* terminology should *not* be read with such a strong emphasis on the physicality of humans as representative of God. There are, for instance, two notable occurrences in the Psalms where *tselem* refers not to a physical representation but rather to something extremely insubstantial: a dream, shadow, or vapor (Pss. 39:6 [v. 7 in the Hebrew]; 73:20).[12] Moreover, while God is frequently anthropomorphized in the Hebrew Bible, there are texts that speak of God's incorporeality and invisibility (e.g., Deut. 4:15–16)[13] and the illegitimacy of seeing God (Exod. 33:20) or of representing God (or anything else for that matter) in physical terms (20:4). In other words, standing against the anthropomorphisms of the Hebrew Bible are biblical signs that God should not be thought of as in any sense having a physical form for humans to resemble or represent.[14] In any case, it might be noted that P is often said to avoid anthropomorphism.[15] If these latter indications are taken as the key for understanding the *imago Dei*, then instead of the sheer physical presence of the human body we might instead look to more ethereal human capacities as representative, such as cognition or spirituality. Indeed, Christian tradition for centuries after Augustine saw the image of God in such structural (rather than functional) terms as the human intellect or the human soul (see chap. 5).

When we turn to the word usually translated as "likeness" (*demuth*) in Genesis 1:26, the situation becomes yet more uncertain. Although *demuth*

---

11. John F. A. Sawyer, "The Meaning of בְּצֶלֶם אֱלֹהִים ('in the Image of God') in Genesis I–XI," *Journal of Theological Studies*, n.s., 25 (1974): 423–24.

12. Hamilton, *Genesis: Chapters 1–17*, 134–35.

13. Wenham, *Genesis 1–15*, 30.

14. D. J. A. Clines, "The Image of God in Man," *Tyndale Bulletin* 19 (1968): 59; H. H. Rowley, *The Faith of Israel* (London: SCM, 1956), 75–79.

15. Wenham, *Genesis 1–15*, 30.

appears to have been intended as a qualifier for *tselem* in 1:26, it is unclear how. Is *demuth* intended to solve the embarrassing association of *tselem* with idols elsewhere in the Hebrew Bible, by toning down the physicality of *tselem*, so that humans are *not* to be seen as exact replicas of God?[16] If so, then the addition of *demuth* might imply that the image is only to be taken as an abstract resemblance, as in the theophany scenes of Ezekiel 1–10, where *demuth* indicates the metaphorical nature of the prophet's vision and "deliteralizes" the images he uses (e.g., Ezek. 1:5; 10:21–22).[17] On the one hand, this reminds us that *demuth* can mean "likeness" in the loose sense of "analogy" or "similarity." But on the other hand, it must be admitted that the *imago* texts in Genesis 1:27 and 9:6 show no such sensitivities, since *tselem* appears alone, without *demuth* to qualify it. And Genesis 5:1–3 appears to use *tselem* and *demuth* interchangeably, as though there were no great nuances in their meaning. And, finally, in 5:3 both terms imply a *physical* resemblance. In other words, if *demuth* is a qualifier of *tselem*, we do not know how.

As if this confusion were not enough, there is also uncertainty about the prepositions before *tselem* and *demuth* in 1:26: *be* and *ke*, respectively. *Be* is often translated as "in," while *ke* is frequently translated as "according to" or "after." However, since these prepositions are interchanged in 5:3 (i.e., *ke* goes with *tselem* and *be* with *demuth*), many scholars conclude that there is no significant difference between them.[18] This is probably why the NIV translates both prepositions as "in" in 1:26 ("Let us make mankind in our image, in our likeness . . ."). Yet David Clines has famously argued that the *be* before the all-important *tselem* ("image") of 1:26 should be read in a more specialized sense (as a *be* "of essence"), indicating that humans are made "as" or "to be" the divine image.[19] If he is right, then we should understand the *imago Dei* not as a divine blueprint located in heaven after which (or "in" which) earthly humans are fashioned but as *the actual identity humans themselves have on earth*. Humans *are* the *imago Dei* themselves. This conveys a massive difference in meaning from the conventional rendering, as we can see by retranslating 1:26: "Let us make humankind to be our image." In this translation humans are themselves "pictures" of God, representing God concretely in what they are or what they do on earth. Ironically, although

---

16. Sawyer, "Meaning of בְּצֶלֶם אֱלֹהִים," 421–22.

17. Hamilton, *Genesis: Chapters 1–17*, 135–36; Middleton, *Liberating Image*, 46.

18. Gerhard von Rad, *Genesis: A Commentary*, trans. John H. Marks, rev. ed. (Louisville: Westminster John Knox, 1973), 58; Claus Westermann, *Genesis 1–11: A Commentary*, trans. John J. Scullion (Minneapolis: Augsburg, 1984), 47–48; Wenham, *Genesis 1–15*, 29; Hamilton, *Genesis: Chapters 1–17*, 136–37; Middleton, *Liberating Image*, 47–48.

19. Clines, "Image of God," 75–80.

Genesis commentators have been reluctant to adopt Clines's argument here,[20] many of them still support it in effect. As we shall see in the next subsection, many scholars liken the *imago Dei* to ANE statues or "images" of earthly kings and thereby (wittingly or not) emphasize the physicality of the image as a concrete and visible representation.

In summary, the situation is highly complex. The results of this kind of detailed exegetical study of the *imago Dei* terms—based squarely within the text of the Hebrew Bible—are inconclusive.[21] Progress can only be made by looking at the rest of 1:26 and by bringing in the ANE context. It is this latter feature in particular that provides the decisive key to unlocking the functional interpretation.

"Let Them Have Dominion Over / Rule Over"

The key starting point here concerns the question of how God's self-exhortation of 1:26 to make humankind in the divine image and likeness relates to the second exhortation in the verse for them to "have dominion" or to "rule" over living creatures. Is having dominion the primary content of the "image," or is it a secondary consequence (or are the two entirely unrelated)? Although Genesis commentators often claim that dominion is a secondary consequence of the image,[22] the predominance of the functional interpretation among biblical scholars means that exercising dominion comes close to being the primary content of the image. This becomes apparent when we ask how "dominion" or "rule" is to be understood.

The Hebrew verb *radah* in 1:26, translated as "have dominion" (NRSV) or "may rule" (NIV), can refer to various kinds of overseeing relationships in the Hebrew Bible: a master over servants, an administrator over employees, a king over subjects, one nation over another, or a shepherd over a flock.[23] Clearly, there is a fair degree of latitude here, but translators of 1:26 going back to the Septuagint (LXX) have opted in favor of a specifically regal solution by choosing words such as "dominion" or "rule." Psalm 8 offers strong support since, although it does not use the *imago* terminology of "image" or "likeness," its

---

20. See J. Maxwell Miller, "In the 'Image' and 'Likeness' of God," *Journal of Biblical Literature* 91 (1972): 296; C. L. Crouch, "Genesis 1:26–7 as a Statement of Humanity's Divine Parentage," *Journal of Theological Studies* 61 (2010): 9.

21. Middleton, *Liberating Image*, 44.

22. John Skinner, *A Critical and Exegetical Commentary on Genesis* (Edinburgh: T&T Clark, 1930), 32; Rad, *Genesis*, 59; Westermann, *Genesis 1–11*, 153; Wenham, *Genesis 1–15*, 31–32; C. John Collins, *Genesis 1–4: A Linguistic, Literary, and Theological Commentary* (Phillipsburg, NJ: P&R, 2006), 66.

23. Hamilton, *Genesis: Chapters 1–17*, 137.

language is strongly reminiscent of Genesis 1. What is more, Psalm 8 describes humans as gifted with the status of kingship: crowned with glory and honor and made to rule the living creatures (vv. 5–8 [6–9 in Hebrew]).

Evidence from the ANE context of the Hebrew Bible has been unearthed that indicates decisively that translators have been right to see *radah* in royal terms.[24] Egyptian and Assyrian texts have been found that speak of the pharaoh, or king, as the "image" of a deity. This ANE evidence also strengthens the possibility discussed in the previous subsection that the *imago* motif refers to humans as physical representations of God. An Assyrian text gives an excellent example, where the seventh-century king Esarhaddon is addressed by his astrologer as the image of the deity Bel: "The father of the king, my lord, was the very image [*salmu*] of Bel, and the king, my lord, is likewise the very image of Bel."[25] In texts such as these we see the king (or sometimes other high-level functionaries such as priests) described as the physical representative of a deity on earth. That the "image" of the deity in ANE texts was so often seen to be conferred through *royalty* provides the crucial link between the *imago* language and God's conferral of "dominion" on humans (Gen. 1:26).

While drawing on these parallels extensively, biblical scholars have also not been slow to point out the crucial difference between a king being *imago Dei* (ANE texts) and all of humankind being *imago Dei* (Genesis). In line with the other suspicions that P's creation story reacts polemically against ANE polytheistic culture, in the *imago* texts P appears to have *democratized* the ANE idea of the monarch representing a deity. Genesis radicalizes the ANE contention so that every human represents God physically on earth.[26]

A related piece of evidence from the ANE context is also frequently cited as support for the physical-representative reading of the *imago* motif—namely, the ANE practice of the monarch placing statues of himself in remote corners of his kingdom to stand for his presence there. The most spectacular example came to light in 1979, when a ninth-century statue of an Assyrian ruler, Hadad-yis'i, was discovered at Tell Fekheriye in Syria.[27] This statue bears an inscription in Assyrian, with a translation in Aramaic, giving the text of a dedicatory prayer of the king to Hadad the storm god, followed by

24. Middleton, *Liberating Image*, 93–145.
25. Cited by Clines, "Image of God," 83.
26. Clines, "Image of God," 93; Wenham, *Genesis 1–15*, 31; Hamilton, *Genesis: Chapters 1–17*, 135; Middleton, *Liberating Image*, 121, 204–14, 219.
27. A. R. Millard and P. Bordreuil, "A Statue from Syria with Assyrian and Aramaic Inscriptions," *Biblical Archaeologist* 45, no. 3 (1982): 135–41; W. Randall Garr, "'Image' and 'Likeness' in the Inscription from Tell Fakhariyeh," *Israel Exploration Journal* 50 (2000): 227–34.

a series of baroque curses on anyone who might damage the statue. Clearly, the statue is intended as a concrete reminder of the authority of both the god and king. But what is most interesting about the text on the statue is that it includes Assyrian and Aramaic terms cognate to the crucial Hebrew words for "image" and "likeness" (*tselem* and *demuth*, respectively). The Assyrian text, for instance, describes the statue throughout as an "image" (*salmu*). This close parallel to Genesis 1:26—together with the ANE evidence cited above of human kings being seen as the "image" of a deity—has convinced many scholars that we need look no further than these ANE practices for the answer to the riddle of the *imago Dei*. Gerhard von Rad's well-known words, written long before the discovery of the Tell Fekheriye statue, now appear to be even more apt: "Just as powerful earthly kings, to indicate their claim to dominion, erect an image of themselves in the provinces of their empire where they do not personally appear, so man is placed upon earth in God's image as God's sovereign emblem. He is really only God's representative, summoned to maintain and enforce God's claim to dominion over the earth. The decisive thing about man's similarity to God, therefore, is his function in the non-human world."[28]

Here we see the so-called functional interpretation of the *imago Dei*, supported by biblical scholars, expressed in a nutshell: humans have been given the task of putting God's kingship over the living creatures of the earth into practice, and it is this function that constitutes the "decisive thing" about the image.

The Functional Interpretation

The *imago* texts of Genesis amount to a mere handful of verses in the Hebrew Bible and revolve around a handful of words within them, but, as we have seen, their interpretation is immensely convoluted. The options have been simplified by the dominance of the functional interpretation in biblical studies throughout much of the twentieth and twenty-first centuries, but there are still unsolved questions—not least *whether the functional interpretation has a clearly defined content*. Let me explain.

The functional interpretation suggests that we should see the all-important *imago* passage of Genesis 1:26–27 within the context of P's polemic against neighboring cultures: God's regal power is to be exercised by all humans alike, not by a king, and not represented in the form of an idol or statue. This polemical context provides a possible explanation of why the *imago* terminology is not adopted elsewhere in the Hebrew Bible. It has always been

28. Rad, *Genesis*, 60.

a puzzle why the *imago Dei* is localized to Genesis 1–11, given its immense attractiveness, but if the *imago* is understood as part of P's polemical response to his own specific polytheistic surroundings, then its particularity becomes more understandable. Since most commentators down the ages have supposed that Genesis 1:26–27 is a universal statement about human nature,[29] they have missed the point that it is primarily a statement about God as the sole and benevolent Creator; the wider Genesis 1 context to the *imago* passage makes this abundantly clear. And we could justifiably bring this point to the fore by subtitling the functional interpretation the "monotheistic-democratic-dominion" view to highlight its various nuances.

There are, however, additional nuances to bear in mind, which come to light when we consider three special problems within the functional interpretation. (1) Despite protestations to the contrary (noted in the previous subsection), it is hard to avoid concluding that the "dominion" is the virtual content of the "image" (its "decisive thing") and not just its consequence.[30] But this leads to a fundamental inconsistency, because in the ANE evidence that gives the functional interpretation its persuasive power, the content of the "image" is not a function ("dominion") but a physical object (a statue or human king). This point leads to two further issues. (2) Scholars may express misgivings about Clines's rendering of the traditional "Let us make humankind in our image" as "Let us make humankind to be our image," yet the functional interpretation effectively achieves just that by relying on ANE statues and texts about kings as its decisive evidence, since they imply that humans must be the "image" themselves. (3) This reliance on ANE evidence—where the "image" is something concrete, a statue or a king, acting in a representational capacity—inevitably suggests that human *physicality* is significant in representing God functionally. In short, the functional interpretation has a hard time freeing itself from the structural interpretation. To indicate the complexities beyond the "monotheistic-democratic-dominion" subtitle that I coined above, the functional interpretation could be additionally nuanced as the "physical-representative-functional" interpretation.

My enthusiasm for qualifying the functional interpretation with further clauses and shades of meaning is not unusual. Few biblical scholars profess to hold the functional view in an uncompromisingly full-blooded form; instead, they continue to emphasize complexity within it. It would be safe to conclude that the *imago Dei* problem has not quite been solved yet. In any case, there is still the New Testament to consider.

29. E.g., Westermann, *Genesis 1–11*, 155–56.
30. As Middleton concludes in *Liberating Image*, 54–55.

The New Testament

The intertestamental literature (often referred to as "Apocrypha") shows little more interest in the *imago Dei* than does the Hebrew Bible, since we only find three references to it (Wisdom 2:23; Sirach 17:3; 4 Ezra 8:44).[31] There is a possible tendency toward a structural view, but it is not decisive. The first text (Wisdom 2:23) suggests that God originally made humans in the divine image so that they would be eternal like God (a structural interpretation?); the second (Sirach 17:3) connects the *imago* with God-given "strength" over other creatures as well as knowledge and intellect (a structural interpretation); the third (4 Ezra 8:44) offers no clear view of the *imago Dei* other than that it simply makes humans "like" God.

With the New Testament, though, a distinctive development comes into focus that illustrates that we would be wrong to assume that there is one fixed, biblical meaning to the *imago Dei*. The functional interpretation might gain traction in Genesis 1:26–27, but it does not hold in the New Testament.[32] Found mostly in the Pauline corpus of letters, the *imago* terminology of the New Testament is used quite fluidly. Significantly, the *imago Dei* loses the inclusivity of Genesis 1 and begins to refer to subsets of the human race. While one text uses the *imago* terminology to refer to all people (the non-Pauline text of James 3:9), another restricts it only to male humans (1 Cor. 11:7), and three others restrict it only to members of the church (2 Cor. 3:18; Col. 3:10; Eph. 4:24).[33] Best known are the two texts that speak of Christ alone *as* the divine image (i.e., Christ is not made *in* the divine image, but he *is* the image of God):

> . . . Christ, who is the image of God (2 Cor. 4:4)

> He [the Son] is the image of the invisible God, the firstborn of all creation. (Col. 1:15)

The latter passage is also of note in that it connects the Son with the making of the original creation. This text is surely alluding to Genesis 1, which is why it can say that the divine Son of God *is* the divine image, consistent with humans being made *in* the Son's image (a christological reinterpretation of Gen. 1:26). A related idea is expressed in 1 Cor. 15:49:

31. Wisdom of Solomon 7:26 is a possible fourth text but does not concern the divine image in *humans*.

32. The Greek term for "image" (in LXX and the New Testament) is *eikōn*, from which we derive our word "icon." "Likeness" is *homoiōsis*.

33. Related to these are passages that describe believers as possessing the image of Christ (Rom. 8:29; 1 Cor. 15:49).

Just as we have borne the image of the man of dust [i.e., Adam], we will also bear the image of the man of heaven [i.e., Christ].

Here Paul uses the *imago* motif allusively to suggest that although we might currently be mortal, frail, and fallible like the first humans (Adam and Eve), we will be transformed into the image of Christ in the eschatological fullness of time.

These Pauline texts form the basis of the eschatological interpretation of the *imago Dei*, which holds that the image is not protological in its anthropology (i.e., it is not concerned with the first creation of humans) but eschatological (i.e., it is concerned with the anthropology of the new creation). The risen Christ, as the first human of the new creation, is the eschatological divine image, which we hope to attain ourselves in the fullness of time.[34]

Conclusions

For all its scarcity, the biblical *imago Dei* motif is astonishingly difficult to interpret, and a secure solution to the many problems it poses has proved elusive. As one looks across all the relevant biblical texts, no clear interpretive picture emerges for the *imago Dei*. The functional interpretation is held in great respect by Hebrew Bible scholars, but this is largely because of the strength of the ANE background to Genesis 1:26–27 rather than any great certainty stemming from exegesis of those biblical texts themselves. As we have seen, exegesis is largely inconclusive. But as we have also seen, the ANE evidence is a mixed blessing, since it brings problems of inconsistency. In any case, the functional interpretation is largely localized to the *imago* texts in Genesis 1–11, since it hardly applies to the New Testament *imago* texts. These latter texts display a quite different series of patterns—the most celebrated being Christ as the *imago Dei*.

In spite of these weaknesses, in a *historical* and *critical* sense the functional view undoubtedly makes the most sense of the decisive *imago* text in Genesis 1:26–27, as its widespread dominance in biblical scholarship demonstrates. The functional view also poses relatively few problems in the modern evolutionary paradigm. By contrast, the structural interpretation, in relying on a unique human trait (such as advanced cognition), must always negotiate the difficult challenge from evolutionary biology that humans are different in degree, not in kind, from other animals. By majoring on God's theological vocation for humankind rather than on any evolved particularity of the human race, the

34. Chapter 7 below by Ted Peters explores this idea more fully.

functional view is much less vulnerable to the challenge from science. It is worth remembering, however, that in its reliance on ANE evidence the functional interpretation is unable to escape biology altogether. In particular, the *physical presence* of humans on earth (as effective "statues") is arguably integral to their functioning in the *imago Dei*. Thus, the functional interpretation cannot avoid the evolutionary question that the other *imago* interpretations face: At what point in their long and complex evolutionary history did creatures in the genus *Homo* begin to reflect the *imago Dei*? Responses will vary according to which interpretation is adopted.

The structural and relational interpretations must answer this question by identifying the stage in evolutionary history at which decisive *imago* traits emerged. This task is fraught with uncertainty and ambiguity, but it is necessary for the coherence of each interpretation. The functional interpretation avoids the difficulties here simply by noting the evolution of human physicality *in general*—that the *imago Dei* is reflected in the appearance of *Homo sapiens* as an entire species. Hence, the functional interpretation is probably the interpretation that sits most easily with the evolutionary view of human origins.

A more challenging issue for the functional interpretation is this question: What exactly is the function that constitutes *Homo sapiens* in the *imago Dei*? Answers tend to focus on the exercise of God's "dominion," and it is commonplace to see this described as good "stewardship of the earth," where nurture and restraint are emphasized as correctives to our current *domination*. One sophisticated (and evolutionary) version of this approach sees humans as God's "created co-creators," who act in freedom "to birth the future that is most wholesome for the nature that has birthed us."[35] However, it is unlikely that the ancient biblical authors would have understood "dominion" in these ways: such "totalizing" and planetary perspectives are decidedly modern and anachronistic, reflecting contemporary reaction to the worldwide ecological crisis.[36] Instead, an authentic functional interpretation would begin with the ancient Israelite view of nature. More work is needed to establish this view clearly,[37] but it must have diverged enormously from our own. Subsistence farming and hunting, together with elementary forestry and mining, would have forged a view of nature that was, of necessity, lived out more precariously, intimately, and "locally" than our own. Arguably, in such a context, a call to exercise dominion would be seen more as an encouragement to tame

35. Hefner, *Human Factor*, 27.

36. Richard Bauckham, *Bible and Ecology: Rediscovering the Community of Creation*, Sarum Theological Lectures (Waco: Baylor University Press; London: Darton, Longman and Todd, 2010), 6.

37. Harris, *Nature of Creation*, 83–90.

nature than to tame ourselves. Hence, the domestication of animals, a key agricultural development in the Neolithic, might be seen to provide a possible historical peg for the "content" of the functional interpretation. This is a tempting interpretation, but we should again be cautious before reading a modern idea (this time from paleoanthropology) into an ancient text. For one thing, pegging the dominion to the historical domestication of animals hardly captures the full scope and force of the biblical passage, which embraces *all* living creatures (i.e., not just the domesticated ones such as cattle but all fish, birds, and "creeping things" too; Gen. 1:26). Therefore, we find that, in spite of its virtual consensus among biblical scholars, the functional interpretation remains frustratingly vague when we attempt to cash it out.

It is possible that our attempts to see the functional interpretation in concrete terms are frustrated precisely because the weight of the Genesis 1 *imago* text falls not on the human exercise of function but on the heavenly call to humans. Hence, the functional interpretation should be seen primarily in the theological realms of *grace* and *vocation* (from God to humans) rather than in terms of naturalistic, or scientific, prescriptions for how those theological gifts are to be realized (from humans to other living creatures). In other words, we should be careful not to make the same error as the creationist with the six days of creation, assuming that Genesis 1:26–28 can only be interpreted in scientific, literalistic ways. Quite simply, the *imago Dei* is a statement about God's grace to creation and not about human self-ability.[38]

The New Testament resonates with this assessment. I have been most concerned with the *imago* traditions of Genesis in this discussion, but my insistence on seeing the functional interpretation in terms of *vocation* means that the New Testament's christological *imago* passages also come into view. The early church's practice of typological exegesis is helpful here, where an earlier text (e.g., Gen. 1:26–28) might be read as a prototype of a later text (e.g., the New Testament *imago* texts) while still retaining its own integrity. Seen this way, the *imago Dei* evolves typologically: the description of the human vocation to exercise God's dominion in Genesis 1 comes to its sharpest point of focus in the historical person and work of Christ but is incomplete or embryonic in the rest of humankind until the eschatological fullness of time. In this way, the functional interpretation merges imperceptibly with the eschatological interpretation.

---

38. A related argument is made by Joshua Moritz with his "election" model of the *imago Dei*. See Joshua M. Moritz, "Evolution, the End of Human Uniqueness, and the Election of the *Imago Dei*," *Theology and Science* 9, no. 3 (2011): 307–39.

5

Will the Structural Theory of the Image of God Survive Evolution?

Aku Visala

Traditionally, Christian theology has assigned humans a special place in creation and salvation history. Humans are the only beings in creation who have been formed in the *imago Dei*, or image of God. This uniqueness has often been understood in terms of each human having been endowed with a soul that provides a unique personality and a set of mental capacities. There are a number of different ways to understand what souls are and how they function, and I will return to these views in more detail below. The view that being the image of God consists of being a person with certain mental capacities that reflect, or are somehow analogous to, God's capacities is what we here call the structural theory of the image of God (STIG).[1] Unlike other views of the image of God, such as the relational and functional theories, the structural theory identifies the image of God in humans with the soul and the set of capacities that the soul endows each person with.

In this chapter, I will examine the kinds of challenges that an evolutionary understanding of humans might produce for STIG and suggest that a properly modified version of STIG will have the resources to deal with them—or at

1. Sometimes it is also called the substantial theory or the soul theory.

64

least that it is just as capable of meeting the challenges posed by evolution as any of the other theories of the image of God.[2]

The Structural Theory of the Image of God

STIG, or some variant thereof, was the default position of Christian theologians and philosophers for the majority of Christian history until the twentieth century.[3] Augustine, Thomas Aquinas, Martin Luther, and John Calvin all held versions of STIG. According to STIG, the image of God is some shared feature of divine and human nature such that humans reflect God's nature by having this shared feature. As mentioned above, these features are often associated with personhood and certain mental capacities, such as the capacities for abstract thought and moral autonomy. This reflection is far from perfect, but there is an analogy between God's being and human being. Theologians have usually assumed that the special relationship derived from this shared feature is unique to humans and God, though there have been theological debates from time to time about whether, for instance, angels (who seem to have personhood and abstract thought) qualify as images of God as well. In what follows, I will put the question of angels aside and focus on God, humans, and nonhuman animals.

According to STIG, humans reflect God by having certain kinds of capacities that are uniquely human. Traditionally these capacities have been associated with rationality and intellect. These capacities not only make rational action possible but also make it possible for humans to grasp abstract and universal truths and respond to the revelation of God in the life of Christ. By virtue of their intellect and rationality, humans become free, morally responsible persons, who transcend their animal nature and, in so doing, can relate to God in a special way.[4]

On this account, then, the image of God relates to the development of personhood. There are many ways to fill in the details regarding the metaphysics

2. For contemporary defenses of STIG, see, e.g., Aku Visala, "*Imago Dei*, Dualism and Evolutionary Psychology," *Zygon* 49, no. 1 (2014): 101–20; Joshua Farris, "A Substantive (Soul) Model of the *Imago Dei*: A Rich Property View," in *The Ashgate Research Companion to Theological Anthropology*, ed. Joshua R. Farris and Charles Taliaferro (Farnham, UK: Ashgate, 2015), 165–78. For a more comprehensive defense, see J. P. Moreland, *The Recalcitrant* Imago Dei: *Human Persons and the Failure of Naturalism* (London: SCM, 2009).

3. The following discussion is based mostly on Marc Cortez, *Theological Anthropology: A Guide for the Perplexed* (London: T&T Clark, 2010), 18–19, 37–40. See also J. Wentzel van Huyssteen, *Alone in the World? Human Uniqueness in Science and Theology* (Grand Rapids: Eerdmans, 2006), chap. 3.

4. Olli-Pekka Vainio, "*Imago Dei* and Human Rationality," *Zygon* 49, no. 1 (2014): 121–34.

of personhood.[5] Traditionally, structural theories have been committed to either substance dualism (the Augustinian tradition) or compound dualism (the Thomistic tradition). According to both forms of dualism, the nonphysical soul is the seat of reason and intellect. Here the analogy between the nonphysical nature of the intellect and God's mind comes into play. God is a perfectly rational and free person, and by virtue of their nonphysical, intellectual souls, humans also have intellect and freedom that are analogous to those of God.

Although physicalism—the view that minds and persons consist solely of basic physical parts (such as atoms, brains, and bodies)—is the dominant view in current analytic philosophy, defenses of dualism occur frequently. There is room for dualist accounts today, and critiques of strong forms of physicalism are now more common than ever.[6] In addition, there are good responses to the standard critiques of dualism, such as the interaction problem.[7] Indeed, Christians have more resources (and reasons) to defend dualism than their non-Christian colleagues.

Regarding the scriptural basis of STIG, the tradition takes the Genesis narrative as a starting point. However, twentieth-century biblical scholarship has argued that the Genesis account should be interpreted in a more functionalist way. The image of God is to be found in God's special calling and aim for humanity as a whole. This is one of the main reasons many contemporary theologians reject STIG.[8] Yet, as Mark Harris's chapter in this book on the functional theory of the image of God suggests, the "physical" likeness of God and humans does indeed play some role in the Genesis account. This supports the conclusion that the "image" language of Genesis cannot be completely detached from the idea of "likeness." Furthermore, John Cooper has argued extensively that although biblical anthropology is clearly more holistic than dualist Greek and Roman accounts, basic scriptural commitments to, say, life after death imply something like persons existing without their physical bodies. Hence, dualism and STIG might be more endemic to the biblical witness than is often claimed.[9]

5. For an accessible overview of the development of *imago Dei* doctrine, see Dominic Robinson, *Understanding the "Imago Dei": The Thought of Barth, von Balthasar and Moltmann* (Farnham, UK: Ashgate, 2011), chap. 1.

6. See, e.g., Benedikt Paul Göcke, ed., *After Physicalism* (Notre Dame, IN: University of Notre Dame Press, 2012). An accessible critique of physicalism can be found in Thomas Nagel, *Mind and Cosmos: Why the Materialist Neo-Darwinian Conception of Nature Is Almost Certainly False* (Oxford: Oxford University Press, 2012).

7. For a nice defense of dualism by a well-known physicalist philosopher, see William Lycan, "Giving Dualism Its Due," *Australasian Journal of Philosophy* 87 (2009): 551–63.

8. See, e.g., Joel Green, *Body, Soul, and Human Life: The Nature of Humanity in the Bible* (Bletchley, UK: Paternoster, 2008).

9. See John Cooper, *Body, Soul and Life Everlasting: Biblical Anthropology and the Monism-Dualism Debate* (Grand Rapids: Eerdmans, 1989).

STIG also makes sense of a number of other theological doctrines and commitments. For instance, it solves how individuals can survive their bodily deaths and become embodied in new, incorruptible bodies. Moreover, it is built on an idea of personhood that is closely connected to central Christian doctrines such as the Trinity and incarnation.[10] The main motivation behind STIG, however, is that it explains why only humans have a special relationship with God. According to STIG, humans are *Homo religiosus*, a religious species that seeks God.[11]

In twentieth-century theological anthropology, many have become critical of STIG and suggested a number of alternatives, such as relational and functional accounts of the image of God.[12] However, it seems to me that especially the functional and relational accounts are not really alternatives to STIG because, as with STIG, they also seem to entail, or at least to strongly imply, something like uniquely human capacities for reason and intellect.[13] Let me explain.

One central criticism of STIG is its alleged ethical problem. If an individual somehow lacks basic rationality and intellect (because of a disability, for instance), this person seems to reflect God less than a fully functioning individual. Although this objection is often wielded against STIG, it also cuts against the functional and relational theories. In the functional theory, the *imago Dei* is to be located in God's call and task: humans are to participate in taking care of the creation. It seems to me that this view implies that humans are indeed capable of, first, hearing and responding to God's call and, second, participating in this work with God. How is this possible? I think a good case could be made that it is the capacities that STIG describes (e.g., intellect and moral judgment) that make it possible for humans to understand and respond to God and to freely participate in the venture that God is calling them to.

The same applies to the relational theory, according to which the *imago Dei* in humans is based on the kinds of relational properties (relationships with God and other humans) that humans possess. Being able to have meaningful personal and moral relationships requires something like personhood and the

10. See Anne Marmodoro and Jonathan Hill, eds., *The Metaphysics of the Incarnation* (New York: Oxford University Press, 2011).

11. Theologians disagree about how the fall altered the image of God. All agree that sin has corrupted some of the capacities of the soul (will and desire), but defenders of STIG usually maintain that reason and intellect were not lost in the fall. Their operation might be impaired in a number of different ways because of the disordering of other faculties, but our fallen human intellect nevertheless largely reflects God's image.

12. For reasons see Cortez, *Theological Anthropology*, 18–21; Oliver Crisp, "A Christological Model of the *Imago Dei*," in Farris and Taliaferro, *Ashgate Research Companion*, 217–32.

13. This is also suggested by Mikael Stenmark, "Is There a Human Nature?," *Zygon* 47 (2012): 895; Crisp, "Christological Model of the *Imago Dei*."

basic communicative and intellectual capacities associated with it. This leaves the relational account, as with the functional account, open to the same ethical objection as STIG in this case. There are plenty of people who do not have the necessary capacities to engage in taking care of creation, responding to God's call, or participating in personal relationships with other humans and God in any explicit way. If defenders of the functional or relational theories appeal to the possibility of such individuals potentially having these capacities or reflecting the image of God as parts of the human community, these defenses should be open to STIG as well: people lacking fully developed intellects are images of God because they have the potential to develop such capacities, have human souls, and belong to a community of humans. STIG is in no way worse off in this respect than the functional and relational theories, which are entirely dependent on the structural model for their own coherence.

To recap, the distinctive features of STIG are human uniqueness and mind-body dualism—namely, that humans are endowed with a supernatural soul. The human soul shares with God features that make it a person, such as rationality or intellect. According to STIG, humans are distinguished from nonhuman animals by possessing a set of capacities that nonhuman animals seem to lack.

Two Evolutionary Challenges

STIG has fallen out of favor in theological circles in the last century, and this is due in part to evolutionary accounts of humanity. Evolution challenges STIG in two ways. First, it seems that the capacities for intellect and moral autonomy that in STIG ground the imaging relation between God and humans can now be given a naturalistic, evolutionary explanation. We can now, so the argument goes, explain the emergence of such human capacities without any recourse to supernatural causes or explanations. Evolutionary psychologists, for instance, are exploring the evolution of our cognition, cultural forms, and behavioral patterns. Writers such as Steven Pinker maintain that the basic architecture of the human mind consists of a number of different mechanisms that developed to solve problems in our ancestral environments. Our capacity for moral behavior and moral emotions, for instance, is a product of the selective pressures toward increased cooperation and collaboration. Similarly, our capacity for abstract reasoning is a product of our need to co-ordinate behavior in ever-expanding human groups.[14] In sum, if evolutionary

14. See Steven Pinker, *How the Mind Works* (London: Penguin, 1997). For an overview of theories and hypotheses, see Agustín Fuentes, *Evolution of Human Behavior* (New York: Oxford University Press, 2009).

psychology indeed succeeds, there is no need for a supernatural explanation of human mental capacities.

Second, human uniqueness can be challenged by invoking the ubiquitous evidence we have about the evolutionary roots of the human species. The evolutionary sciences claim—and I agree—that humans did not appear from nothing but share a history and a set of basic cognitive and biological capacities with other living beings. Therefore, there is no clear dividing line between human and nonhuman animals.

In what follows, I explain these two problems in more detail and offer an account of STIG that will solve them.

Dualism, Evolution, and the Brain

It might seem that, if it is indeed the case that humans have evolved, this casts doubt on the claim that humans have souls (or are souls), as STIG entails. Evolution might call dualism into question in at least two different ways. First, the general plausibility of dualism is called into question in light of evolutionary explanations of our mental capacities. Second, if one looks at the archaeological record, one sees no evidence of souls being put into human organisms in some supernatural way. We do indeed see occasional leaps of evolution: after long periods of stability we often observe a burst of change in culture and behavioral patterns. However, there seems to be no single, empirically identifiable point where souls are added into the historical mix.

There are several ways in which the defender of STIG could deal with these worries. I think the best way would be to look more carefully at what souls are and what they actually do. Although it might be possible to defend a version of STIG that would entail the creation of souls from nothing, I suggest that we should give this up and adopt a more moderate form of dualism in which souls are forms of bodies or emergent substances.

First, we need to do some groundwork on basic concepts.[15] Let us distinguish property dualism from substance dualism. Property dualists think that only physical substances exist but that some properties that these substances have are more or less nonphysical. Against this, substance dualists believe that in addition to physical substances there are nonphysical substances. There is a distinction to be made here between substances (individuals existing in

15. In this section I mostly follow Dean Zimmerman, "Three Introductory Questions," in *Persons: Human and Divine*, ed. Dean Zimmerman and Peter van Inwagen (New York: Oxford University Press, 2007), 13–28. For a more comprehensive treatment, see Aku Visala, "Persons, Minds, and Bodies: Christian Philosophy on the Relationship of Persons and Their Bodies, Part I," *Philosophy Compass* 9 (2014): 713–22.

their own right) and the properties of those substances. In property dualism, there are only physical substances, such as human bodies, trees, and stones. Some properties that these substances have (e.g., being of a certain shape, color, or softness) are physical properties in the sense that they are organizations of simple physical properties posited by contemporary theories of physics (atoms, forces, etc.). But some properties are nonphysical, such as mass and force. Mental properties are here understood as properties such as "believing that it will rain tomorrow" or "thinking about one's lost love." For the property dualist, mental properties are nonphysical properties.

Opposed to property dualism, substance dualists maintain that in addition to material substances such as bodies and brains, there are mental substances as well. Together these are what is traditionally called the soul: essentially a thinking thing. There are many different versions of substance dualism, but they all share two features: (1) for every thinking person, there is such a thing as a soul that lacks most physical properties of the body and other nonthinking substances; and (2) this soul is essential to the person and to a large extent responsible for the person's mental life.[16]

Substance dualism takes the mental substance as the essential mark of personhood: persons are essentially mental beings. More precisely, human persons are identical to essentially nonphysical souls and only contingently have physical bodies. Contrary to this, a third form of dualism, compound dualism, does not identify persons with a nonphysical mental substance but rather describes persons as composites of form (soul) and matter (body). In other words, the compound dualist would resist identifying the person with the mental only. Body and soul are both required for human persons to exist and function.[17]

No dualist would deny the close connection between the soul and the brain. All contemporary dualists accept the idea that physical changes in the brain affect mental functioning. The brain and the soul are not insulated from each other, but rather there is a close dependency in terms of function. Although classical compound dualists believe that higher-level mental functions—such as rational reflection—cannot be performed by any purely physical system, they nevertheless insist that the kind of mental functions that neurosciences

16. For defenses of dualism, see Mark C. Baker and Stewart Goetz, *The Soul Hypothesis: Investigations into the Existence of the Soul* (New York: Continuum, 2011).

17. This does not mean that all theories of personhood are "mentalistic" or "psychological." Defenders of animalism argue that to be a human person is to be identical with a human animal (human organism). See Eric Olson, *What Are We? A Study in Personal Ontology* (New York: Oxford University Press, 2007).

and cognitive sciences study (perception, memory, language skills, emotion, attention, etc.) are rooted in and performed by the body.[18]

Those who hold to a view known as emergent dualism, such as William Hasker, argue that the soul is indeed a mental substance of its own right and contributes to thinking more extensively than simply shaping the body; however, as Hasker describes, they hold that the soul is not supernaturally created but emerges from the central nervous system after it reaches a certain level of complexity. The soul is thus a part of the natural order of things in the world. The soul has a location within the human body and depends on the functions of the body for its existence and functioning. As with other dualists, Hasker thinks that the substantial soul is what makes human bodies persons: the soul is the seat of the first-person perspective and activity, guaranteeing the unity of the person and consciousness.[19]

We can now see how contemporary dualists could answer the evolutionary challenges presented above. First, they could maintain that evolutionary psychologists and other scientists are indeed making progress in finding out how human cognition works but that this does not mean that the scientific picture completely explains human mental life. Being in the image of God is not an explanation that competes with the evolutionary story for basic human mental capacities. Souls do a different explanatory job from evolutionary explanations. Evolutionary psychologists seek to explain why our perceptual, conceptual, and emotional systems work the way they do in terms of their selective advantages in our ancestral environments. In contrast, souls are responsible for mental processes that do not map onto the physical in any systematic way. Souls account for phenomena such as the existence of the person and self-consciousness, the unity of consciousness, the qualitative aspects of consciousness, intentionality, human dignity and value, and survival after death. In this sense, evolutionary psychology explains the raw material of our mental life but not the first-person perspective that our mental life presumes.

Second, dualists have no particular problem responding to the challenge from the continuity of the archaeological record. Dualists readily admit that souls are emergent and depend on the function of the body and the brain. When bodies and brains evolve, various capacities emerge and get shaped by

18. Aquinas is an example of a compound dualist, and his view has been understood in a number of different ways. See Brian Leftow, "Souls Dipped in Dust," in *Soul, Body and Survival: Essays on the Metaphysics of Human Persons*, ed. Kevin Corcoran (Ithaca, NY: Cornell University Press, 2001), 120–38; Eleonore Stump, "Non-Cartesian Substance Dualism and Materialism without Reductionism," *Faith and Philosophy* 12 (1995): 505–31.

19. William Hasker, *The Emergent Self* (Ithaca, NY: Cornell University Press, 1999); Hasker, "Souls Beastly and Human," in Baker and Goetz, *Soul Hypothesis*, 202–21.

the environment. What souls add to the mix is the existence of the person: self-consciousness where the outputs of cognitive systems come together. STIG entails that there must be a point where the first human soul emerges—a point in time before which there were no human souls (images of God) and after which there were human souls. The dualist can still maintain that such a point would not necessarily leave a clear mark in the archaeological record, since the organism in question could exhibit basic cognitive capacities both before and after this point. It would follow from this that we might not be able to clearly pinpoint the exact time in evolutionary history when humans finally became persons and images of God. Nevertheless, such a point could exist.

Human Uniqueness Regained

Many theologians think that STIG entails a sharp dividing line between humans and nonhuman animals such that humans are unique. The dividing line is located between those with thought and selfhood and those incapable of it. The problem is that if the Darwinian view of species is correct, there is no clear dividing line between organisms that are capable of thought and selfhood and those that are not.

The issue of human uniqueness is far from simple. First, there are different ways of understanding what "uniqueness" means exactly. One way to understand the notion is to talk about the uniqueness of human performance. This is the most uncontroversial notion of uniqueness. I do not think anyone in their right mind could deny that humans can do things that nonhumans cannot (speak Klingon, invent the internet, build oil tankers, etc.). What is more controversial is whether human performance is based on unique cognitive capacities. It is clear that humans share most of their capacities with many other animals (perception, basic forms of reasoning, etc.). Uniqueness comes in degrees. All species are clearly unique in the sense that they are different from one another. However, it might be that human capacities differ from those of other animals but are plausibly of the same type or kind or have similar evolutionary histories. There seems to be no clear-cut way of determining at what point a quantitative distinction becomes a qualitative one.[20]

In what follows, I suggest that the evolutionary human sciences indeed point toward a certain degree of human uniqueness and that this should be enough for STIG. I have no space to outline in any detail the state of the debate in evolutionary sciences concerning the boundary between human and nonhuman animals. Primatologists and psychologists are conducting comparative

20. See Michael Burdett, "The Image of God and Human Uniqueness: Challenges from the Biological and Information Sciences," *Expository Times* 127, no. 1 (2015): 3–10.

studies of our species and our closest relatives—such as chimpanzees, bonobos, and great apes—and our understanding is expanding rapidly. It is clear that the cognitive, moral, and social capacities of our closest relatives and other nonhuman animals might have been significantly underrated in the past. Capacities that were previously thought to be uniquely human—such as symbolic language, reasoning, morality, and consciousness—have protoforms or at least rudimentary antecedents in our currently living relatives (and in the now-extinct *Homo* species). For example, our relatives do seem to have various social emotions and instincts that in our case form the basis of our morality. In *Homo sapiens*, these enablers of morality have become much more complex as human groups have gotten bigger and the need for coordination has increased, but they are nevertheless based on the kinds of mechanisms that our close relatives have. This is also the case with language and reasoning.

These results do not mean that the boundary between *Homo sapiens* and nonhuman animals and extinct *Homo* ancestors is somehow indistinguishable or nonexistent. Most scholars working in the area acknowledge some level of human uniqueness: the evolutionary human sciences do not demonstrate equality between *Homo sapiens* and other animals. It is clear that humans are descendants of nonhuman animals, but this fact does not mean that humans are "just animals," similar to nonhuman animals or not really unique in any way. Indeed, to deny the uniqueness or distinctiveness of *Homo sapiens* is to deny evolution altogether: descent does not imply identity or similarity.[21] As biological anthropologist Jonathan Marks puts it succinctly, humans are "biocultural ex-apes."[22] Our ancestors were apes, but we are not our ancestors.[23] Cognitive neuroscientist Michael Gazzaniga adds that "most human activity can be related to antecedents in animals. But to be swept away by such a fact is to miss the point of human experience. . . . Although we are made up of the same chemicals, with the same physiological reactions, we are very different from other animals. . . . Even though we have all of these connections with the biologic world from which we came, and we have in some instances similar mental structures, we are hugely different."[24] Similarly, Michael Tomasello, who has spent years doing comparative work on humans and great apes,

21. This point is forcefully made by Conor Cunningham in his *Darwin's Pious Idea: Why Ultra-Darwinists and Creationists Both Get It Wrong* (Grand Rapids: Eerdmans, 2010).

22. Jonathan Marks, "On Nature and the Human: Off Human Nature," *American Anthropologist: Vital Forum* 112, no. 4 (2010): 513.

23. Agustín Fuentes and Aku Visala, *Conversations on Human Nature* (Walnut Creek, CA: Left Coast, 2015), 116–30.

24. Michael Gazzaniga, *Human: The Science behind What Makes Your Brain Unique* (New York: HarperCollins, 2009), 2–3.

argues that humans are a "hypersocial" species and that human thinking is uniquely social: humans can think about the intentions of others and can create and regulate social and moral norms. These capacities make it possible for humans to inhabit a shared world of language and cooperation, in turn giving rise to abstract thought, art, religion, music, and science.[25]

The description above does not do justice to the wealth of extremely complex theories and interesting evidence we are now getting from comparative studies. It seems that the sciences indeed point toward many differences not just in cognitive capacities but in the forces that shaped human evolution. Many researchers think that the evolution of our lineage exhibits some unique characteristics that mostly have to do with the extensive interactions between genes and culture as well as a phenomenon called niche construction.[26] Human cognition makes it possible to contribute to culture and technology and to be shaped by it in extremely flexible ways. Via culture, we make our own environment, which in turn feeds into our biological evolution. In this sense, human evolution takes place in the context of culture and technology: our species responds to pressures not only by developing biological adaptations but also by cultural and technological innovation.[27]

The ability of biology and psychology to explain how the aforementioned capacities for morality, sociality, and abstract thought arose via biological evolution is not a problem for STIG because giving a biological explanation of our mental capacities would threaten STIG only if STIG entails that our mental capacities are nothing like our physical capacities and are performed solely by the immaterial soul. But as has become clear, dualists need not think this way. Instead, as I have proposed, dualists can affirm that most of our mental capacities are grounded in our evolved bodies, cultures, and social environments.

Human Uniqueness and Anti-Essentialism

Evolution presents another deep challenge to human uniqueness that is somewhat more conceptual in nature and has to do with the natures, kinds, and essences of all evolved species. It seems that STIG is committed to the position that there are essential—that is, necessary—features of human nature.

25. Michael Tomasello, *A Natural History of Human Thinking* (Cambridge, MA: Harvard University Press, 2014).

26. For more on niche construction, see chap. 3 above by J. Wentzel van Huyssteen.

27. See Jonathan Marks, *Tales of the Ex-Apes: How We Think about Human Evolution* (Oakland: University of California Press, 2015); Kim Sterelny, *The Evolved Apprentice: How Evolution Made Humans Unique* (Cambridge, MA: MIT Press, 2012); Tomasello, *Natural History*.

The problem is that the evolutionary approach to the human species (and to all species) undermines this assumption. According to evolutionary science, species membership is not defined in terms of essential and immutable traits or features.

Evolutionary history is a history of gradual changes in the population of particular organisms. If we accept this, there is no principled way to say where one species ends and another begins. Philosophers Paul Griffiths and Kim Sterelny write:

> There is no such thing as the "genetic essence" of a species. A central aspect of modern evolutionary biology is *population thinking*. . . . Each population is a collection of individuals with many genetic differences, and these differences are handed on to future generations in new combinations. . . . Contemporary views on species are close to a consensus in thinking that species are identified by their histories. According to these views, Charles Darwin was a human being not by virtue of having field marks—rationality and an odd distribution of body hair—described (in Alpha Centaurese) in *A Guide to the Primates of Sol*, but in view of his membership in a population with a specific evolutionary history.[28]

It follows from this that, if Darwinism is the correct way to understand species, there were no first *Homo sapiens*, and thus biology gives us no set of features or traits that constitute essential human nature.

There are a number of ways to meet the anti-essentialism of Darwinian thinking. One is to admit that, given naturalism, the argument does indeed hold, but then to contend that this should not cause too much worry for theists because they are not naturalists. For naturalists, the guide for thinking about species essence is first and foremost evolutionary biology. For Christian theists, however, the essential features of humans need not be entirely derived from a naturalistic point of view. Even if there were no naturalistically identifiable essence to *Homo sapiens*, theologians have more resources at their disposal. I see no reason why STIG need entail that "human being" in the theological sense must be identical to the biological category "*Homo sapiens*" or why the essential features of "human beings" would have to be scientifically transparent. In this sense, essential features could involve something like having a human soul or a God-given purpose and a goal to be with God in the eschaton.[29] This move would, however, have some practical consequences.

28. Paul Griffiths and Kim Sterelny, *Sex and Death: An Introduction to the Philosophy of Biology* (Chicago: University of Chicago Press, 1999), 7–8.

29. I have argued this at length in the context of both science and theology in Jonathan Jong and Aku Visala, "Three Quests for Human Nature: Some Philosophical Reflections," *Philosophy, Theology and the Sciences* 1 (2014): 146–71.

One is that we would not have a clearly delineated set of biological and psychological features to point to in order to discern who counts as a human and who does not. This could have serious ethical consequences. We have made serious mistakes in the past regarding who might qualify as fully human (e.g., slaves were considered subhuman); so, given that there are no unambiguous empirical criteria (most cases would be easy, but there would be borderline cases), we should aim to be as inclusive as possible.

Another way is to face the argument head-on, to keep the categories of "human beings" and "*Homo sapiens*" coextensive but maintain that there are indeed features of *Homo sapiens* that could be considered essential or semi-essential in some meaningful sense of the word. Mikael Stenmark, for instance, argues that once we give up the idea that essential features must be present universally across space and time, we can identify some essential features of *Homo sapiens*: "It seems as if human beings do have a species nature. The properties of our species nature include, at least, being animals with a bipedal walk, an erect posture, and a large brain, who are able to produce fertile offspring only with other humans, and who are toolmakers capable of rational and moral thinking, linguistic and artistic expression. . . . We do possess a transhistorical core of being."[30] Stenmark is not alone in this insistence: there is an interesting debate about human nature and natural kinds going on in the philosophy of biology as well. Although most participants want to avoid strong essentialist notions of human nature, there are a number of convincing accounts that appeal to human nature even under Darwinian assumptions.[31]

Animal Souls and the Pervasiveness of Mentality

As I pointed out above, mentality—that is, basic intellectual capacities for language, thinking, perceiving, emotion, and sociality—is not a uniquely human phenomenon. All nonhuman animals exhibit various levels of mentality. There are great differences between, say, mollusks and the great apes, but it nevertheless seems that cognition goes far beyond the *Homo* lineage. But this raises the question: If it is indeed the case that mentality is associated with personhood (as STIG implies) and that mentality in its basic forms is not a *Homo sapiens* phenomenon (as the evidence suggests), will this not destroy the uniqueness of the God-human relationship? Recall that in STIG the imaging relationship between God and humans is supposed to be unique.

30. Stenmark, "Is There a Human Nature?," 895.
31. For an excellent collection of classic and contemporary papers on the issue see Stephen Downes and Edouard Machery, eds., *Arguing about Human Nature* (New York: Routledge, 2013). A more accessible look is Fuentes and Visala, *Conversations on Human Nature.*

If the imaging relationship is grounded in mentality, and if mentality is everywhere, then these facts seem to suggest that souls are everywhere in the animal kingdom too. And if the soul is the seat of the *imago Dei*, then it might appear that nonhuman animals are images of God as well.

From the point of view of emergent dualism and compound dualism, there is no problem in attributing souls to nonhuman animals. Indeed, many explicitly acknowledge the existence of different kinds of souls—human souls and animal souls. Even dualists such as Swinburne think that animals have souls to the extent they possess mental life. Given the fact that we share many of our cognitive capacities and brain structures with nonhuman animals, it seems reasonable for the dualist to assume that nonhuman animals also have a mental life somewhat similar to humans', which would entail that nonhuman animals have souls as well. Animal souls might come in many varieties and differ from human souls, but they would still be souls, nonphysical mental substances that anchor certain mental properties.[32]

Given the possibility of nonhuman animal souls, the defender of STIG should be more specific and say that being the image of God is not identical to just having a soul of any kind; instead, being in the image of God is having a specifically human soul. One way to solve the problem is to modify STIG and admit that since cognitive uniqueness is on a spectrum instead of clear-cut, some nonhuman animals that are relatively similar to humans could participate in the imaging relationship with God in a manner similar to how humans participate in that relationship. There might be some scriptural, ethical, and theological reasons to accept this view.[33] In this modified STIG, there would be no clear-cut divide between reflecting God and not reflecting God; rather, being the image of God would be a gradual matter. Humans would indeed reflect God by having certain mental capacities to a higher degree than other species, but this is not necessarily so and could change over time. The image of God is as much about becoming as it is about being. Consequently, if some other species were to develop capacities similar to those of humans, they would, at least to some extent, develop human-like souls (i.e., personhood) and be images of God as well.[34]

Although I am rather sympathetic to this move myself, there might be ways in which one could preserve the commitment to the uniqueness of the God-human relationship as reflected in the *imago Dei*. One could, for instance,

32. Richard Swinburne, *The Evolution of the Soul*, 2nd ed. (Oxford: Oxford University Press, 1997), chap. 10.

33. See Celia Deane-Drummond, *The Wisdom of the Liminal: Evolution and Other Animals in Human Becoming* (Grand Rapids: Eerdmans, 2014).

34. See chap. 7 below by Ted Peters.

emphasize that in STIG the image of God is not simply identical to having some measure of mental life (which we now know many species have) but is instead to have the intellectual, moral, and social capacity for religious thinking and behavior—that is, to use theologian Robert Jenson's terminology, to be able to be addressed by God and to respond to him.[35] At least according to current science, the capacity for religion is rooted in uniquely human cognitive capacities, and thus no other living species shows anything like religion.[36]

Conclusion

What I have tried to suggest in this chapter is that a properly modified version of STIG can withstand the central challenges arising from the evolutionary account of humans. I began by outlining STIG and its commitment to human uniqueness and dualism and suggested that STIG is just as capable of responding to the challenges of evolution as other interpretations of the image of God, such as the functional and relational theories. I then looked at how the two central commitments of STIG come under fire from the evolutionary study of humans and argued that contemporary forms of dualism are not proven false or superfluous by evolutionary approaches to the mind. Furthermore, I argued that some form of human uniqueness could indeed be maintained even if standard accounts of the evolution of *Homo sapiens* turn out to be true. So it seems to me that STIG is compatible with an evolutionary view of humans and thus presents a viable way of understanding the image of God today.

35. See Robert Jenson, *Systematic Theology*, vol. 2, *The Works of God* (New York: Oxford University Press, 1999), 60–63. Although Jenson rejects STIG, the point he makes is compatible with it. See also Vainio, "*Imago Dei* and Human Rationality."

36. Cognitive and evolutionary study of religion suggests that religion is not only natural for humans but also uniquely human. See, for example, Ara Norenzayan, *Big Gods: How Religion Transformed Cooperation and Conflict* (Princeton: Princeton University Press, 2013); Scott Atran, *In Gods We Trust: The Evolutionary Landscape of Religion* (New York: Oxford University Press, 2012).

6

The *Imago Dei* as Relational Love

THOMAS JAY OORD

The idea that we are created in God's image is largely a blank canvas onto which Christians paint a wide variety of portraits. The portrait that each Christian finds most attractive invariably connects with that person's deepest intuitions and interpretations of God, creatures, the Bible, and the world. In this essay, I argue that understanding the image of God—*imago Dei*—as relational love provides the best portrait, all things considered, of how we are related to God, our status as creatures, and how we ought to act.

We Are like God

Most Christians ponder how humans might be both different from and similar to God. To say creatures are created in the image of their Creator typically means, at minimum, that the Creator and creatures are similar, resemble each other, or correspond in some way. What this similarity entails has been understood variously. The Bible offers no definitive answer regarding precisely what the *imago Dei* entails.[1] Most scholars who wrestle with Scripture, especially

---

1. Claus Westermann is among many biblical scholars who note the lack of clarity surrounding the meaning of the *imago Dei*. See Westermann, *Genesis 1–11: A Commentary*, trans. John J. Scullion (Minneapolis: Augsburg, 1984), 147–55.

Genesis 1:26–28, appeal to nearby phrases or the general biblical context when arguing for the meaning they find most plausible.[2]

A few Christians have suggested that the human form identifies humanity as bearers of God's image, though most Christians have resisted this idea, citing biblical passages that speak of God as a spirit, as bodiless, and as without form. Many biblical passages say God does not have a human-like body.

Saying that God is a bodiless spirit, however, need not mean that God has no physicality whatsoever, nor need it mean that the physical dimensions of creatures are unimportant or evil.[3] As an omnipresent spirit, God may have physical dimensions not perceptible by our five senses.[4] But with the exception of the Latter-Day Saints,[5] most Christians have said God does not essentially possess a localized physical body.[6]

Christians typically look to nonphysical capacities or capabilities as the essence of the *imago Dei* found in humans. This is often called the structural view of the image of God.[7] Christians who believe God's supreme attribute is intelligence, for instance, typically understand the *imago Dei* in terms of intellect. Humans express the image of God when they think intelligently. Christian theologians such as Augustine and Thomas Aquinas make this argument, and they often say that rational souls and power of choice differentiate humans from other animals.[8]

Throughout the centuries, Christians have located the essence of the *imago Dei* in other attributes or capabilities or in other ways in which God and

2. See chap. 4 above by Mark Harris for an in-depth account of the image of God in Scripture.

3. A number of scholars work to avoid the dualism that separates the mind or soul from the body. While they do not claim that God has a localized physical body, they argue that creatures with such bodies can express the *imago Dei* through their whole person.

4. The speculation that God's omnipresent being has a physical dimension is important for questions of divine action, revelation, and more. One of the more sophisticated metaphysical proposals seeking to understand God as possessing both spiritual or mental and physical dimensions is offered by Alfred North Whitehead in *Process and Reality: An Essay in Cosmology*, ed. David Ray Griffin and Donald W. Sherburne, corrected ed. (New York: Free Press, 1978; first published 1929).

5. Scholars debate whether the Latter-Day Saints, or Mormons, are rightly considered orthodox Christians. I will not address that debate here.

6. One possible exception to the idea that God has no form is Jesus of Nazareth. But most Christians argue that God is essentially without a localized body and in doing so distinguish between God's temporary incarnation in Jesus and God's essential nature and being.

7. For more on the structural view, see chap. 5 above by Aku Visala.

8. See Augustine, *The Literal Meaning of Genesis*, trans. John H. Taylor, SJ, Ancient Christian Writers 41 and 42 (New York: Paulist Press, 1982), 6, 12, 22; Thomas Aquinas, *Summa Theologica*, trans. Fathers of the Dominican Province, 5 vols. (Westminster, MD: Christian Classics, 1948), I.93.1–6. Stanley Grenz offers a helpful historical overview of this position, highlighting also the influence of Irenaeus, in Grenz, *The Social God and the Relational Self: A Trinitarian Theology of the Imago Dei* (Louisville: Westminster John Knox, 2001), 142–61.

humans are similar.[9] If God's primary attribute was thought to be creativity, the *imago Dei* was regarded in terms of the ability to create.[10] If morality was God's primary characteristic, those creatures with the capability to make moral decisions—typically thought to be only humans—were considered to have been made in God's image. If God's primary activity was thought to be communication, those who communicate reflect the image of God. Many other human capabilities have been said to be the essence of the *imago Dei* in Christian history: purposiveness, self-awareness, and even the capacity for religion.

Some theologians have criticized the practice of identifying any attribute or capability that allegedly God and humans share. This practice strikes them as anthropomorphic projection: we project on God what we think most noble in humans. From this point of view, our language about God corresponds with our idea of God because God is simply a bigger version of us. Ludwig Feuerbach makes this point powerfully, arguing that theology is nothing but anthropology.[11] But as Feuerbach sees it, the God described in this projecting doesn't actually exist.

I mention anthropomorphic projection because I believe theologians often overreact to the worry of anthropomorphism. In their overreaction, some try to think about God in categories entirely dissimilar or disanalogous to creatures. God is not in *any* way like creatures, according to them, and God and creatures share no metaphysical resemblance whatsoever. "We cannot grasp what God is," says Thomas Aquinas when advocating this approach, "but only what He is not."[12] This is a negative, or apophatic, way of doing theology.

Apophatic theology does not offer a satisfactory theology in general or a satisfactory understanding of the *imago Dei* in particular. Most Christians believe Scripture and the natural world reveal *something* true about God. If we are created in the image of God, we as creatures must be like God in some way, and the Creator must be similar to creatures to some extent. Creator-creature analogies must be bidirectional if they are to make sense.[13] In sum,

---

9. See Anthony A. Hoekema, *Created in God's Image* (Grand Rapids: Eerdmans, 1994).

10. See Gordon D. Kaufman, *In the Beginning . . . Creativity* (Philadelphia: Fortress, 2004). Philip Hefner expands this idea by arguing that creatures can be co-creators with God in *The Human Factor: Evolution, Culture, and Religion* (Minneapolis: Fortress, 1993).

11. Ludwig Feuerbach, *The Essence of Christianity*, trans. George Eliot (Buffalo: Prometheus Books, 1989), chap. 3.

12. Thomas Aquinas, *Summa contra Gentiles* 1.30.4, trans. the English Dominican Fathers, vol. 1 of 2 (London: Burns, Oates and Washbourne, 1923).

13. For my criticism of the negative theology found in Aquinas and others and my insistence on bidirectional analogies, see Thomas Jay Oord, *The Nature of Love: A Theology* (St. Louis: Chalice, 2010), chap. 3.

there must be some resemblance, some analogy, some similarity between God and creation if God acts in relation to creatures and creatures are to act like God (e.g., Eph. 5:1).[14]

The structural definition of the *imago Dei* is speculative, and no consensus exists among Christians on which capability God and creatures share in common. Consequently, some set this view of the *imago Dei* aside and think rather of the image of God as a calling, function, or role. Humans are called to function or act in a particular way, according to this view, and that's what it means to be created in God's image.[15]

The Genesis passage in which we first encounter the concept of the image of God talks about humans having dominion over, or care for, other creatures.[16] Because theologians typically think God has ultimate dominion and exercises ultimate care, some suggest the *imago Dei* consists of this calling or function. When humans cooperate with God's rule or reign in creation, they show that they have been made in God's image.

This view of the *imago Dei* says that humans fulfill their roles as bearers of the divine image when they exercise proper dominion over or care for creation. "Just as powerful earthly kings . . . erect an image of themselves in provinces of their empire where they do not personally appear," says Gerhard von Rad in support of this view, "so [humans are] placed on earth in God's image as God's sovereign emblem."[17] Instead of the image of God pointing to a particular attribute God and humans share, the functional understanding of the image of God focuses on what humans do.[18]

Still other theologians set aside speculation about shared attributes or callings. They simply use the "image of God" label to express the value and dignity of the human person. Humans should be afforded fundamental rights,

14. Throughout the history of Christianity, many theologians have distinguished between the divine image and the divine likeness. They usually argue that humans retain God's image but, because of sin, have lost the likeness to God. This argument represents the theologian's own theological vision, however, and extends well beyond anything specific to the biblical text. Most contemporary biblical scholars say Scripture does not demand any distinction between the image and likeness, and many believe the repetition of image and likeness in Genesis simply reinforces one idea rather than making two distinct points. See J. Richard Middleton, *The Liberating Image: The* Imago Dei *in Genesis 1* (Grand Rapids: Brazos, 2005), 44–48.

15. For more on the functionalist view, see chap. 4 above by Mark Harris.

16. For analysis of the Genesis statements about the *imago Dei* in relation to ancient Near Eastern and Mesopotamian thought, see Middleton, *Liberating Image*, chaps. 3–5, and chap. 4 above by Mark Harris.

17. Gerhard von Rad, *Genesis: A Commentary*, trans. John H. Marks, rev. ed. (Philadelphia: Westminster John Knox, 1973), 60.

18. Middleton claims that this understanding of the *imago Dei* dominates among Old Testament scholars working in the last century. See Middleton, *Liberating Image*, 24–29.

this argument goes, because humans are created in God's image. All humans have value, and they should be cared for properly and honored as having worth. This approach is useful for emphasizing human dignity, especially when noting the intrinsic value of disabled humans, those suffering from lack of mental health, or members of marginalized groups.[19] Too often such people and groups are treated as less valuable.

I will later argue that the *imago Dei* as relational love accounts well for the best in all of these views. At this point, however, I want to note that several understandings of the image of God have been proposed, but no consensus exists among Christians regarding precisely what it means to be created in God's image.

We Are like Other Creatures

The writers of Genesis refer only to humans as having been made in God's image, and the majority of Christians throughout history have thus assumed the *imago Dei* is unique to humans. Most Christians would agree with John Walton, for instance, when he says that "the image of God distinguishes us from all creatures" and that the *imago Dei* is "a direct, spiritually defined gift of God to humans."[20] Many throughout the centuries have used the *imago Dei* to elevate humans above, or to distinguish humans from, nonhuman creatures.

But there are good reasons to wonder whether Christians are warranted in thinking only humans bear the *imago Dei*. The Genesis text doesn't say humans are the *exclusive* bearers of God's image. It is silent on whether animals also bear the image. The argument from silence does not make a strong case either for or against animals being made in God's image.

Several aspects of the Genesis account suggest closer connections exist between humans and other creatures than what many are accustomed to thinking. For instance, the writers of Genesis say God created humans on the same day as other land animals. Humans are not special, in other words, in the sense of having their own day of creation. In addition, the creation story in Genesis 2 says God creates humans and every animal in the field and every bird of the air out of the dust of the earth. Humans are not made with special materials. And later in Genesis we find God making a covenant not just with humans, as the earlier chapters might suggest, but with all creation. Humans are not God's only covenant partners.

19. This is a major theme in John F. Kilner, *Dignity and Destiny: Humanity in the Image of God* (Grand Rapids: Eerdmans, 2015).

20. John Walton, *The Lost World of Adam and Eve: Genesis 2–3 and the Human Origins Debate* (Downers Grove, IL: IVP Academic, 2015), 193, 194.

Science has played a significant role in discovering similarities between humans and other creatures. Evolutionary theory, for instance, suggests that vast continuity exists between humans and other creatures. This continuity persists not only in the gradual evolutionary changes between species over long periods of time. It is not only in the evolutionary relationships and shared history between humans and other creatures. Humans also share vast genetic similarities with other animals.

Perhaps the strongest reason to wonder whether nonhuman animals also bear the image of God comes from observing the capabilities of animals themselves. For instance, many animals—especially dogs, dolphins, bonobos, elephants, and many species of birds—are far more intelligent than what was previously thought. Those who, like me, were raised on a farm, have had a close family pet, or have spent significant time hiking in the wilderness know firsthand how smart animals and birds can be. If being intelligent or using reason identifies one as bearing God's image, many creatures must be made in the image of God.[21]

The similarities between humans and other creatures go beyond intelligence. Many animals seem to make choices, for instance, as numerous laboratory experiments with animals show. Many are creative, building complex structures with inanimate objects and complex social systems. Many creatures express emotions, including empathy and fear. Some highly complex animals, such as wolves, possess a moral sense.[22] Birds and animals communicate with one another in fairly sophisticated ways, which means communication is not a characteristic exclusive to humans. In sum, traits that at one time were thought uniquely human are now known to be present among other creatures, although often in a different or diminished form.[23]

In his massive multidisciplinary work on the *imago Dei* and contemporary science, J. Wentzel van Huyssteen explores how humans might be different from other creatures. With a special focus on evolution and paleoanthropology, van Huyssteen concludes that "there is no single trait or characteristic that adequately captures the notion of human uniqueness." However, humans are "clearly distinguished from other animals on this planet" because they "share an identifiable and peculiar set of capacities and

21. See G. Roth and U. Dicke, "Evolution of the Brain and Intelligence," *Trends in Cognitive Sciences* 9 (2005): 250–57.

22. Oliver Putz, "Moral Apes, Human Uniqueness, and the Image of God," *Zygon* 44, no. 3 (2009): 613–24.

23. For a helpful article on the subject, see Nancy R. Howell, "Relations between *Homo sapiens* and Other Animals: Scientific and Religious Arguments," in *The Oxford Handbook of Religion and Science*, ed. Philip Clayton and Zachary Simpson (Oxford: Oxford University Press, 2006), 945–61.

propensities."[24] This set includes language, self-awareness, consciousness, and the capacity for symbolism, ritual, and mythology.[25]

Notice that the capacities van Huyssteen lists are complex expressions of more general capacities found among other creatures in less complex forms. For instance, humans may be the only creatures capable of speaking multiple languages. But many species possess the capacity for communication in general, the broader category in which language is a complex form. Or take self-reflection, which is a complex form of the more basic capacity of awareness through perception. Many creatures possess an awareness of others and themselves in at least a minimal form. Even highly abstract capacities that seem distinct to humans, such as symbolic reasoning, seem to be only a difference in degree and not in kind. Other animals may not be able to think symbolically, but some possess significant cognitive capacities.[26]

The capability differences between humans and other creatures seem finally to amount to differences of degree and not kind.[27] The differences among creatures pertain to complexity. There are good reasons to believe humans share basic attributes with other creatures.

On realizing that humans share much in common with other creatures, Christians may decide the *imago Dei* is mostly about the calling, function, or role humans have been given. After all, in the same passage of Genesis in which God says humans are made in the divine image, God asks humans to have dominion over or care for other creatures. The calling to have dominion over or care for others, however, seems also shared by other creatures. God's specific calls to humans are likely appropriate to their unique abilities. But loving care is not the domain of humans alone. Most birds and animals care for and have dominion over their young.

Recent work in sociobiology and related disciplines documents the capacity for altruism and cooperation in many species. Many creatures act for the good of their offspring, fellow species, in-group, or those who can help in return. Some sociobiologists, however, argue that *all* altruistic action is aimed at the

---

24. J. Wentzel van Huyssteen, *Alone in the World? Human Uniqueness in Science and Theology* (Grand Rapids: Eerdmans, 2006), 288.

25. Van Huyssteen, *Alone in the World?*, 317.

26. See, for instance, Kristin Andrews, *The Animal Mind: An Introduction to the Philosophy of Animal Cognition* (New York: Routledge, 2015); Michael Burdett, "The Image of God and Human Uniqueness: Challenges from the Biological and Information Sciences," *Expository Times* 127, no. 1 (2015): 3–10.

27. See Helen De Cruz and Yves De Maeseneer, "The *Imago Dei*: Evolutionary and Theological Perspectives," *Zygon* 49, no. 1 (March 2014): 135–56; Joshua Moritz, "Evolution, the End of Human Uniqueness, and the Election of the *Imago Dei*," *Theology and Science* 9, no. 3 (2011): 307–39.

altruist's own genetic heritage. In other words, what *looks* like self-sacrifice or cooperation for the sake of the other is *really* done for the good of oneself or kin.[28] This "selfish gene" view has been roundly criticized, especially as it pertains to describing human activity well.

A growing field of scientific research indicates that humans and other creatures care for, nurture, or protect those outside their own species. Dogs sometimes care for deer; goats sometimes care for horses; cats sometimes care for ducklings.[29] Nonhuman creatures can be genuinely altruistic. This suggests that those animals that promote the well-being of others can fulfill the general function, role, or calling humans fulfill when they promote the well-being of creation and its creatures.[30]

Acknowledging that humans share much in common with other creatures— both capabilities and general callings—should prompt Christians to think anew about what it means to be made in God's image. Perhaps other creatures also bear the image of God. Using Philip Hefner's notion that creatures can be "co-creators" with God,[31] Jason Roberts argues this point: "The shared evolutionary history of all living species makes them all created co-creators to some extent and makes interspecies relationships constitutive of the image of God. While the divine image may be borne by humans in distinct ways, it is shared with the rest of creation in at least this sense."[32]

28. The literature on sociobiology, altruism, and "selfishness" is large. Some of the more influential texts include Richard Dawkins, *The Selfish Gene* (London: Granada, 1978; repr., New York: Oxford University Press, 1989); Lee Alan Dugatkin, *Cheating Monkeys and Citizen Bees: The Nature of Cooperation in Animals and Humans* (Cambridge, MA: Harvard University Press, 1999); W. D. Hamilton, "The Evolution of Altruistic Behavior," *American Naturalist* 97, no. 896 (1963): 354–56; Elliot Sober and David Sloan Wilson, *Unto Others: The Evolution and Psychology of Unselfish Behavior* (Cambridge, MA: Harvard University Press, 1998); Edward O. Wilson, *On Human Nature* (1978; repr., Cambridge, MA: Harvard University Press, 2004). Among the massive literature integrating altruism, sociobiology, and morality, see Philip Clayton and Jeffrey Schloss, eds., *Evolution and Ethics: Human Morality in Biological and Religious Perspective* (Grand Rapids: Eerdmans, 2004); Thomas Jay Oord, *Defining Love: A Philosophical, Scientific, and Theological Engagement* (Grand Rapids: Brazos, 2010).

29. The ways in which creatures in one species care for those of another species vary, and the examples are numerous. One of the best collections of video clips noting such cross-species care is "Animal Odd Couples," *Nature*, PBS, November 7, 2012, http://www.pbs.org/wnet/nature /animal-odd-couples-full-episode/8009/. For a more scholarly presentation of this widespread phenomenon, see Lee Alan Dugatkin, *Cooperation among Animals: An Evolutionary Perspective* (Oxford: Oxford University Press, 1997).

30. I explore the capacity for love and altruism in humans and other creatures in my book *Defining Love*. For a more accessible book on the subject see my *The Science of Love* (Philadelphia: Templeton, 2005).

31. Hefner, *Human Factor*, chap. 15.

32. Jason Roberts, "'Fill and Subdue?' Imaging God in New Social and Ecological Contexts," *Zygon* 50, no. 1 (2015): 52.

The relational-love view of the *imago Dei* is open to the possibility that other creatures reflect the *imago Dei*. But we must address one more aspect of the *imago Dei* to round out the argument that the relational-love view of God's image is preferable to other views.

We Can Be like Jesus

Theologians often note that "image of God" language is found only three times in the Old Testament, each time in Genesis.[33] Christians have given much ink (and word-processing time) to pondering the *imago Dei* based largely on these few Old Testament references. But theologians also note that the phrase and its variations return in the New Testament, especially in relation to God's image found in Jesus Christ. An adequate understanding of the *imago Dei* must include christological dimensions.

New Testament writers argue that Jesus of Nazareth reveals God to creation because in some way Jesus is the unique image of God. In his letter to Christians in Colossae, for instance, the apostle Paul calls Jesus "the image of the invisible God" (Col. 1:15). In his letter to the church in Corinth, Paul says Christ is "the image of God" (2 Cor. 4:4). The writer of Hebrews says Jesus is "the exact imprint of God's very being" (Heb. 1:3). "Whoever has seen me has seen the Father," John quotes Jesus as saying, a quotation complementing the image motif (John 14:9).

New Testament writers also say that humans bear God's image. Some writers state this in a matter-of-fact way, suggesting that the image of God pertains to some capability already present in humans (e.g., James 3:9). But other New Testament passages use "image" to speak about how we can or should become like Jesus Christ. For instance, the apostle Paul calls on Christians in Rome to be "conformed to the image of [God's] Son" (Rom. 8:29). He tells Christians in Corinth that they can be "transformed into the same image" as Jesus (2 Cor. 3:18). The church plays a key role in this process, according to Paul (2 Cor. 3:18; Eph. 4:22–23; Col. 3:10). In sum, the consistent witness of the New Testament is that humans ought to become Christlike.

All of this naturally leads us to wonder about the connection between Jesus as the image of God, creatures being made in the image of God, and the goal or process of being transformed into the image of God. The connection between these important themes seems to be a central theme in Scripture.

---

33. Depending on the meaning one gives the *imago Dei*, of course, the meaning of the phrase might be said to be present in numerous other Old Testament passages.

The argument I find most compelling, given its role in Scripture and Christian life, is that love is the central theme and primary connection linking various statements about the image of God in Jesus and creatures. "God is love," the apostle John tells us (1 John 4:8, 16). Jesus reveals that God's nature is kenotic: a self-giving, others-empowering love for all (Phil. 2:5–11).[34] "This is how we know what love is," John says: "Jesus Christ laid down his life for us." Consequently, "we ought to lay down our lives for our brothers and sisters" (1 John 3:16 NIV). Or as the apostle Paul puts it, we should "be imitators of God, as beloved children, and live in love, as Christ loved us" (Eph. 5:1–2). Imitating God by living a life of love as Christ did seems the essence of conforming to the image of God's son.

The connection between God's love, Jesus's revelation of love, and the call for us to love is crucial, I believe, for understanding well what it means to be made in the image of God. With these New Testament passages in the background, I conclude that, all things considered, relational love provides the key to the image of God.

We Express the Image of God When We Love in Relationship

The relational-love view of the *imago Dei* says creatures live out the image of God when they love. They image (verb) the divine image (noun) when they lovingly reflect the image of God's son. The "relational" aspect of the view reminds us that love comes in the context of give-and-receive relationships. God makes creaturely love possible, and creatures join with God's reign of love when they love God, others, and themselves.

The relational-love view partially embraces the effort Christians have made throughout history to identify some attribute or capacity that God and creatures share.[35] The attribute God and creatures share is the capacity to love. Jesus more than any other reveals God to be the loving *abba* of all. To use a popular expression, love is the heart of God. Given this christological witness, the overall drift of Scripture, and the evidence from other sources,

34. I argue that a particular understanding of God's kenosis—what I call "essential kenosis"— makes the best sense of God's providence in a world of evil and randomness. See my book *The Uncontrolling Love of God: An Open and Relational Theory of Providence* (Downers Grove, IL: IVP Academic, 2015).

35. A number of Protestant theologians in the last four centuries have argued that the *imago Dei* as a relational category focuses on the righteous or unrighteous relationship humans have with God. Martin Luther, John Calvin, John Wesley, Karl Barth, and Emil Brunner all generally take this approach, with important distinctions among them about the nature of the relationship. Stanley Grenz explores this in *Social God*, 161–82.

the relational-love view argues that love is God's primary or chief attribute. Consequently, it makes sense to begin with love when speculating what it means to be made in God's image.

The relational-love view says God expresses love for others and empowers creatures to love God and other creatures in response. God created humans and (perhaps) other creatures with the ability to choose love. If God's chief attribute is love, and God's chief desire is that love be expressed throughout creation, love should be placed at the core of what it means to be made in, and to reflect, God's image.

One may think the "relational-love" label could easily be shortened to the "love" view of the *imago Dei*. After all, most people assume that love is inherently relational. But given the history of theology, there are important reasons to add "relational" to this view's name.

Several twentieth-century theologians argued that the *imago Dei* requires a relational component.[36] Emil Brunner, for instance, considered the image of God to be the human capacity for "responsible existence, responsive actuality."[37] Paul Ramsey argued that the *imago Dei* is "a relation of response to God in which man may, and should, live."[38] Stanley Grenz emphasizes this relational aspect in his view that the image of God points to a "social self" that is reflected in the church.[39]

As I'm using the phrase, however, "relational love" sees relationship not just as creatures responding to God. The phrase also affirms that God responds to creatures. Relational creatures can image the God whose relational love involves both giving to and receiving from others. In opposition to theologies that depict God as impassible and unaffected by creatures, the relational-love view assumes that God is not an impassible deity. An *analogia relationalis* exists between God and creatures, which includes real relations of giving and receiving.[40]

The biblical record is replete with narratives depicting God in give-and-receive relationship with creatures. The most obvious instances of such give-and-receive relationships come from interactions between God and human

36. Some point to Karl Barth as an important voice in this twentieth-century emphasis. See Karl Barth, *Church Dogmatics* III/1, *The Doctrine of Creation*, ed. G. Bromiley and T. F. Torrance (Edinburgh: T&T Clark, 1958).

37. Emil Brunner, *Christian Doctrine of Creation and Redemption*, trans. Olive Wyon (Philadelphia: Westminster, 1952), 60.

38. Paul Ramsey, *Basic Christian Ethics* (New York: Scribner, 1950), 278.

39. Grenz, *Social God*, esp. chaps. 7–8.

40. A large number of contemporary theologians argue against the view that God is impassible and unchanging. I agree with them and add my own take on these matters in *Nature of Love*.

individuals or groups (e.g., Israel). We find such instances often throughout the Old Testament.[41]

God's give-and-receive relational love appears many times in the first chapters of Genesis. For instance, God hovers over the deep when creating and then says "let there be" multiple times in the creating process. Each time God speaks, creation responds, and God calls the result "good" (Gen. 1:4, 10, 12, 18, 21, 25, 31). God's creating is best understood as relational and not unilateral. As Richard Middleton writes, God "does not command so much as *invite* creatures to respond to his will." The Creator whose image we can express, says Middleton, "is generous with power, sharing it with creatures, that they might make their own contributions to the harmony and beauty of the world."[42]

A number of theologians—notably including Karl Barth[43]—note that immediately following the famous *imago Dei* passage in Genesis 1, God creates humans male and female (1:27). Many argue that God's making both genders illustrates well the relationality inherent in the image of God. Others also point to the Trinity or God's heavenly court designated as "us" in the passage as a prime example of relationality meant to be reflected in creation.[44]

The human narratives in other chapters of Genesis illustrate the importance of right relationship. "It is not good that the man [*adam*] should be alone," says God, after discovering that the other animals were not sufficient relational partners (Gen. 2:18). So God reacts to the situation by creating Eve, and God does so using material from Adam's body.

When Adam and Eve eat forbidden fruit, God responds by seeking to restore the relationship. In seeking reconciliation with those estranged, God walks in the garden and asks, "Where are you?" (Gen. 3:9). This is a question only a God whose love involves giving and receiving would ask.

The Genesis stories also tell us that God calls on creatures to be rightly related to one another. After Cain murders Abel, for instance, the Lord asks, "Where is your brother Abel?" Cain's question in response, "Am I my brother's keeper?" is about relational accountability among creatures (Gen. 4:9). Numerous stories throughout Scripture answer Cain's question with a resounding, *Yes! You are your partner's keeper. In fact, you are to care for all creation!*

---

41. Terence Fretheim is one Old Testament scholar who recognizes and embraces this relationality. For instance, see Fretheim, *God and World in the Old Testament: A Relational Theology of Creation* (Nashville: Abingdon, 2005); Fretheim, *The Suffering of God: An Old Testament Perspective* (Philadelphia: Fortress, 1984).

42. Middleton, *Liberating Image*, 289.

43. Karl Barth, *Church Dogmatics* III/1, 194–97.

44. Grenz explores this in *Social God*.

The overriding themes of the biblical witness are that creatures ought to be rightly related to God, to other creatures, and to themselves.

The idea that all humans are made in the image of God is especially emphasized in Genesis 9:1–7, a passage that explicitly uses the phrase. This text prohibits the shedding of human blood because every human is created in God's image. Out of love for those to whom we are related, we grant dignity and value. The relational-love view of the *imago Dei*, therefore, agrees with those who say that the *imago Dei* reminds us of the basic dignity and worth of God's creatures, including those sometimes regarded as without value. Just as God tends to, cares for, and values all creation, we are called to tend to, care for, and value God, other humans, and all creation.

If the core meaning of the *imago Dei* is relational love, and if humans share so much in common with other creatures, we may be justified in believing other creatures can also image their Creator. The relational love expressed by elephants, dogs, dolphins, hens, wolves, and more will likely differ from the relational love humans express. But these are differences in degree or complexity rather than differences in general kind. Because of their increased capacities, God will ask humans to care for others in specific ways that will differ from the ways God asks other animals to care for others. While relational love in general may be possible for multiple species, the specific calling of each species and each creature will vary.[45]

The relational-love view is an inherently missional view of how creatures are created in God's image. It presupposes that creatures can participate in God's mission of love for the world (John 3:16). Creatures are able to imitate God's love (*imitatio Dei*) because they are made in God's image (*imago Dei*). Being made in the image of God makes it possible to represent God's loving care for creation. One might call this the eschatological dimension of the *imago Dei* because it provides the hope and *telos* of creation.

In sum, the relational-love view of the *imago Dei* says creatures can image God's creative reign of love when they love in response to God's leading. Rather than dominating and abusing others, the God of relational love tenderly cares for creation. Creatures can join in this *shalom* activity because they are made in God's image.

---

45. I elaborate on the idea that God's general call for love never varies—but the specific call to each creature takes into account that creature's situation, history, and capacities—in *Uncontrolling Love*, 165–66.

7

The *Imago Dei* as the End of Evolution

TED PETERS

The word "end" can have two related meanings. First, "end" can refer to the *terminus*, or conclusion, of a story. Second, it can refer to the story's goal, purpose, meaning, destiny, or *telos*. In Christian eschatology, "end" entails both conclusion and goal, both *terminus* and *telos*. Looking forward, we expect a transformation from old creation to new creation. We expect to see the divine image, the *imago Dei*, in its fullness. The *imago Dei* is the divine call forward, a call we hear and respond to now but that draws us toward transformation into a future reality.

This means that human nature is not done yet. Like bread rising before it is put into the preheated oven, the human race is not yet fully baked. If we look at ourselves through evolutionary lenses, we can forecast that our descendants will continue to evolve and perhaps even give birth to a posthuman species. If we look at ourselves through eschatological lenses, we can perceive that we are on the way to becoming transformed into the *imago Dei*, into the new humanity. Do evolution and eschatology complement each other? Is it reasonable to think of the *imago Dei* as the end of evolution?

In this chapter we will experiment with an affirmative answer to these questions: yes, the flourishing of the divine image in the human race is the end of evolution. We will measure the adequacy of this answer using two criteria:

(1) Is it faithful to Scripture? (2) Is it consonant with what modern science has discovered about hominid evolution?

In order to pursue this line of inquiry, we will give special attention to human nature. Traditionally, the topic of human nature within Christian anthropology includes two subtopics: the *imago Dei* and the fall into sin. In addition, Christian believers have assumed the *imago Dei* came first and the fall into sin came second. But in order to be consonant with evolutionary theory, we may have to reverse this relationship. Sin will come first, and the *imago Dei* will come second. Instead of placing God's image into the biological past of the human race, we will experiment with placing it in the future. The full flourishing of the image of God in humans is a promise to hope for.

Although all theologians read the same Bible, their interpretations vary like the size and ripeness of peaches on a peach tree. Some interpretations are juicier than others, even if the taste is generically the same. The ripe peach we offer here is a proleptic model of the *imago Dei* within an eschatological version of theistic evolution.

How Does the New Testament Introduce the Proleptic *Imago Dei*?

The Easter Christ is the proleptic *imago Dei*. According to Scripture, in the eschatological new creation, each of us will don Christ's image, which is God's image.

If we work solely with Genesis 1:26–27, where the human is described as the "image and likeness" of the divine, we might be tempted to look backward to our origin to find the *imago Dei*. The Septuagint translated "image" (*tselem*) with εἰκών (*eikōn*), and "likeness" (*demuth*) with ὁμοίωσις (*homoiōsis*). These appear in the New Testament with their Old Testament meanings (1 Cor. 11:7; James 3:9), yet something new and decisive is added. What is new to the New Testament is the central role played by Jesus Christ, who is the image of God, the εἰκὼν τοῦ θεοῦ. For Paul, Christ "is the image of the invisible God, the firstborn of all creation" (Col. 1:15). Elsewhere he writes, "In their case the god of this world has blinded the minds of the unbelievers, to keep them from seeing the light of the gospel of the glory of Christ, who is the image of God" (2 Cor. 4:4).

Christ is the new Adam or, better, the renewed Adam and Eve. "Thus it is written, 'The first man, Adam, became a living being'; the last Adam became a life-giving spirit. But it is not the spiritual that is first, but the physical, and then the spiritual. The first man was from the earth, a man of dust; the second man is from heaven" (1 Cor. 15:45–47).

Temporal firstness does not equate to conceptual firstness. Even though the biblical Adam and Eve predate Jesus Christ, the latter takes precedence. Christ provides the image that defines the human race in relation to heaven, in relation to God. Adam anticipates Christ, but Christ provides the definition of what is truly Adam. "For Christ who seems to come second, really comes first," writes Karl Barth, and "Adam who seems to come first really comes second. . . . Our relationship to Adam depends for its reality on our relationship to Christ."[1] In short, to view the *imago Dei*, look first to Christ and then to Adam and Eve.

The eschatological reversal of the *imago Dei* is most forcefully presented in Paul's letter to the Romans. Adam and Christ are two versions of the one image of God, but the former draws its reality from the latter. Included in Christ's version is redemption from sin and rescue from death. Theological anthropology includes the move from redemption to creation. As Paul writes to the church in Rome: "If, because of the one man's trespass, death exercised dominion through that one, much more surely will those who receive the abundance of grace and the free gift of righteousness exercise dominion in life through the one man, Jesus Christ. Therefore just as one man's trespass led to condemnation for all, so one man's act of righteousness leads to justification and life for all" (Rom. 5:17–18).

Barth drives the nail home with a Pauline sledgehammer: "Our relationship to Adam is only the type, the likeness, the preliminary shadow of our relationship to Christ. The same human nature appears in both but the humanity of Adam is only real and genuine in so far as it reflects and corresponds to the humanity of Christ. . . . Adam's humanity is a *provisional copy* of the real humanity that is in Christ."[2] To ask about genuine humanity is to ask about the *imago Dei*, and the first place a Christian theologian goes to ask about the *imago Dei* is Jesus Christ.

The Christ of whom Paul and Barth speak is primarily the Easter Christ, the risen Christ, the firstfruits of those having fallen asleep (1 Cor. 15:20, 48), the advent of the new creation. Who Adam and Eve were and who we will be can be seen when viewing the Easter Christ.

The term "prolepsis" implies this: as Christ rose on Easter, so will we rise into the everlasting kingdom of God, into God's promised new creation. It is the eschatological future that completes God's work of renewal begun in Christ's Easter resurrection and, thereby, retroactively defines present reality along with our evolutionary past.

The significance for our topic is this: how we as humans are defined is conditioned more by our future than by our past. The human reality is still one of

1. Karl Barth, *Christ and Adam*, trans. T. A. Smail (New York: Collier, 1952), 74–75.
2. Barth, *Christ and Adam*, 46–47.

becoming. Our nature was not fixed at creation, not indelibly determined by the first humans to walk on our planet. Who we are now anticipates who we will be eschatologically. Between now and God's final future, we can experience growth in Christlikeness. As Paul writes to the Corinthians: "And all of us, with unveiled faces, seeing the glory of the Lord as though reflected in a mirror, are being transformed into the same image from one degree of glory to another; for this comes from the Lord, the Spirit" (2 Cor. 3:18).

How Does the Proleptic Model of the *Imago Dei* Interpret Human Nature?

The proleptic model of the *imago Dei* synthesizes creation with redemption. When the world is finally redeemed, it will be created. Right now, we and the world around us are in a phase of becoming. Who we are today will be retroactively determined by who we will be eschatologically. Only when the world becomes redeemed will God say, "Behold, it is very good" (cf. Gen. 1:31). To live today out of the power of the eschatological tomorrow is to live proleptically.

The proleptic model begins with Jesus Christ, not Adam and Eve. Accordingly, we begin with the resurrected Christ and then retroactively incorporate Christ's *imago* into ourselves through faith, hope, and love. According to Stanley Grenz, "Paul argues not only that Christ's resurrection stands at the heart of the gospel but also that this proleptic event guarantees the eschatological resurrection."[3] The Easter Christ as the divine image is our prototype. We live now as the *imago Dei* insofar as we live in him, insofar as we participate in the reality of the eschatological resurrection into the new creation.

The proleptic model includes an ontological component. It is the being of God's future that determines the being of all that has happened in past nature and history. Writing in a different context, Michael Burdett gets it right: "The future is God's future and must be set within the interpersonal nature of a promissory triune God who brings new possibilities to the world."[4] It is not the past that defines us, but rather God's promise of newness.

The proleptic model includes an ethical component as well. We may define ethics as human action aimed at making tomorrow better than yesterday. The Christian ethicist begins with a vision of God's future and then seeks to work creatively to transform present reality in light of this vision. N. T. Wright

3. Stanley J. Grenz, *The Social God and the Relational Self: A Trinitarian Theology of the Imago Dei* (Louisville: Westminster John Knox, 2001), 234.

4. Michael S. Burdett, *Eschatology and the Technological Future* (New York: Routledge, 2015), 2.

grounds proleptic ethics in our vision of God's future when he says, "The Christian task in the present is to anticipate this eschatology, to borrow from God's future in order to change the way things are in the present, to enjoy the taste of our eventual deliverance from evil by learning how to loose the bonds of evil in the present."[5] The future new creation is already present within the present creation via the incarnation in Christ, by God's abiding providence, and by Christ's disciples, who today anticipate in their pursuit of justice the reality of God's eschatological future.

In light of the ecological crisis that is gripping our planet, many Christian eco-ethicists lift up a vision of God's promised new creation and then engage in the creative moral action this vision prompts. Nick Spencer and Robert White, for example, claim that "Christians are called to live in a way that announces the future kingdom of God, and to model the reality that, at least in part, the kingdom of God is here already, while realizing that it will only be brought about completely by the decisive intervention of Christ's return."[6] A proleptic eco-ethic means that the *imago Dei* within us—that is, the dominion that the human race has been given—will be employed to bring justice to the needy and sustainability to the biosphere and thereby anticipate the consummate whole toward which we are being drawn.

Our task now is to fold this theological anthropology into a version of theistic evolution that demonstrates consonance with Darwinian evolution. This may be challenging due to the implications of evolutionary theory for human nature. As we will see, our evolved human nature requires redemption.

What Does the Theory of Evolution Tell Us about Human Nature?

When Charles Darwin published his watershed book *On the Origin of Species by Natural Selection*, in 1859, his theory of evolution sought to explain one thing: How do new species develop? His answer was simple: random variations in inheritance are selected in (or selected out) by the natural environment. Some inherited traits survive to be passed on to the next generation. Other traits do not survive; they die out or go extinct. The natural niche—predation, food supply, disease, climate, drought, flood, and such—determines which traits survive and which go extinct. Gradually, over long periods of time, one species dies out or transforms into another. That, in short, is the origin of a new species.

---

5. N. T. Wright, *Evil and the Justice of God* (London: SPCK, 2006), 96.
6. Nick Spencer and Robert White, *Christianity, Climate Change, and Sustainable Living* (London: SPCK, 2007), 94–95.

Like the axle on a wheel, the center around which the entire theory of evolution revolves is natural selection. Nature selects which inherited traits will survive and which will go extinct. This selection takes place at the moment of reproduction. Selection takes place when those individuals who are fitted to their environment give birth to a new generation that will carry on their traits. The notorious phrase "survival of the fittest" is equivalent to "natural selection" and refers solely to reproductive fitness, to the capacity to reproduce progeny that will carry inherited traits on to future generations. In Darwin's words, "If variations useful to any organic being ever do occur, assuredly individuals thus characterized will have the best chance of being preserved in the struggle for life; and from the strong principle of inheritance, these will tend to produce offspring similarly characterized. This principle of preservation, or the survival of the fittest, I have called Natural Selection."[7]

Darwin could not explain why children are not duplicates of their parents nor why variations in inherited traits occur. A century later, the field of molecular biology arrived at an explanation—namely, genetic variation and mutation. DNA copying in the reproductive process is not precise. Variations appear frequently and normally during it. Even without this genetic knowledge, Darwin was still able to propose an elegant theory regarding speciation that has proved to be very useful and productive. The fertility of Darwin's theory of evolution has generated new research with enormous benefits in expanded food production and in combating viral and bacterial infections by medical science.

Darwin's theory has nothing to say about life's origin. Recall the title of his major work: *Origin of Species*. He tells us how a species originates but not how life originates. In *Origin of Species*, Darwin says about four times that he has no idea how life first emerged from nonlife. He can only explain how life, once present, evolves. I heartily recommend that when we use the term "evolution" that we limit its application to speciation, excluding the still-unanswered question of life's origin.

The neo-Darwinian synthesis—the synthesis of Darwin's original theory of evolution combined with genetics—saturates our science, our society, and our worldview today. "No serious biologist today doubts the theory of evolution to explain the marvelous complexity and diversity of life," contends Francis Collins, director of the US National Institutes of Health.[8] One of today's leading evolutionary biologists, Francisco J. Ayala, adds: "The message has always been twofold: (1) evolution is good science and (2) there need not be

7. Charles Darwin, *The Origin of Species by Means of Natural Selection*, 6th ed., Harvard Classics (New York: Collier, 1909; London: John Murray, 1872), 141.

8. Francis S. Collins, *The Language of God* (New York: Free Press, 2006), 99.

contradiction between evolution and religious beliefs."[9] The theistic evolutionist celebrates both.

Is Evolution Blood Red in Tooth and Claw?

As we have seen, the axle around which the Darwinian theory of evolution revolves is natural selection. Slight random differences in biological heredity will dispose some individuals more than others to withstand the threats and challenges of the environment. Those who survive to the age of reproduction will pass on their heritable characteristics. The genomes of those who die before they can reproduce will disappear into the oblivion of nature's evolutionary history. The genes that survive we call "adapted." They are the fit. They have been selected by nature to advance.

Darwin's theory of natural selection seems to unwrap and expose the drama of the long trail that life has traversed over deep time. He could wax eloquent about the complex beauty of nature as well as the advance of higher intelligence: "Thus, from the war of nature, from famine and death, the most exalted object which we are capable of conceiving, namely the production of the higher animals, directly follows. There is grandeur in this view of life . . . from so simple a beginning endless forms most beautiful and most wonderful have been, and are being evolved."[10] Darwin shines light on nature's grandeur. But a shadow accompanies this light. It is the shadow of travail, suffering, death, and extinction. New life depends on the death of the old. New species require the extinction of their predecessors and even their progenitors. In the words of Alfred Lord Tennyson's poem *In Memoriam*, the natural process by which we arrive at this grandeur is blood "red in tooth and claw." The grandeur of evolved life seems to require the wanton sacrifice of discarded living creatures.

Darwin observed that nature produces far more offspring than can survive to reproductive age. Nature is profligate, almost planning for widespread death to feed the voracious appetite of selection. Because more individuals are produced than can possibly survive, there must in every case be a struggle for existence: one individual with another of the same species, with the individuals of competitor species, or with the physical conditions of life. This means that early death is scheduled for large numbers of those creatures who are born. Nature has no intention to draw each individual life toward fulfillment,

9. Francisco J. Ayala, *Darwin's Gift to Science and Religion* (Washington, DC: Joseph Henry, 2007), 5.

10. Darwin, *Origin of Species*, 528–29.

toward actualizing its inborn potential. If suffering befalls the less than fully fit, nature sheds no tears. Nature is pitiless.

The demand of the predator to kill and devour its prey is a ubiquitous part of this universal struggle. Reproducing requires living. Living requires eating. Eating requires killing. And the form that killing takes seems cruel and harsh and unnecessary. "Natural selection does not look at all like the kind of mechanism a wise and benevolent God would institute to bring about adaptive evolution," observes Peter Bowler.[11] This observation haunts the theologian with the question of theodicy: Why would a God of grace build a machine that unceremoniously chews up and spits out its sentient children?

Exeter theologian Christopher Southgate asks what is at the heart of the problem of evil. Is it pain? No, he answers. The sensitivity to pain we and other higher animals have is necessary for a richer experience. Is it death? No, again. Death is a thermodynamic necessity. Further, we cannot say death is evil if it follows a fulfilled life. Rather, says Southgate, the heart of the problem is that so many creatures are cut down mercilessly before they can experience the richness of a fulfilled life. Think of the newly born impala torn apart and devoured by the hyena. We cannot count the number of the sufferers of predation and parasitism, including organisms for which life seems to contain no fullness, no expression of what it is to reach the potential inherent in being a creature. Indeed, nature's wastefulness in producing far more offspring than we could expect to survive means that snuffing out individuals long before fulfillment is the mass victimage perpetrated by evolution.[12]

The theologian must conclude: this is not the creation Genesis 1:1–2:3 describes as "very good." If we assume the accuracy of evolutionary theory in describing our biological past and prospects for the near future of life on earth, then we must ask: How does evolution fit within a biblically based vision of God's creative and redemptive work? This is the task the theistic evolutionist must take up.

Are We Hopeless Killers?

Evolutionary biology tells theologians what they already know—namely, that all living creatures on earth are related. "The unity of life reveals the genetic

11. Peter J. Bowler, *Monkey Trials and Gorilla Sermons: Evolution and Christianity from Darwin to Intelligent Design* (Cambridge, MA: Harvard University Press, 2007), 21.
12. Christopher Southgate, "Creation as *Very Good* and *Groaning in Travail*: An Exploration in Evolutionary Theodicy," in *The Evolution of Evil*, ed. Gaymon Bennett, Martinez Hewlett, Ted Peters, and Robert John Russell (Göttingen: Vandenhoeck & Ruprecht, 2008), 53–85. See Southgate's treatment of the theodicy problem in chap. 19 below.

continuity and common ancestry of all organisms," emphasizes Ayala.[13] This means that humans are fully embedded in the natural domain. By observation we see that other creatures exhibit at least a rudimentary level of human endowments we prize, such as rationality, communication, and altruistic love. *Homo sapiens* are as fully natural as are all other species of living critters. The implication for theological anthropology is this: we can draw no sharp line between humans and nonhumans regarding any traits we might identify as unique and hence divine.

In addition, human embeddedness in nature includes the struggle for existence and all its bloodshed. When we look at the archaeological record, we see humans have been engaged in violent if not genocidal behavior for as far back as evidence provides. In his own indirect way, Harvard's Steven Pinker reminds us that *Homo sapiens* have never lived without sin:

> Buried in the ground and hidden in caves lie silent witnesses to a bloody prehistory stretching back hundreds of thousands of years. They include skeletons with scalping marks, ax-shaped dents, and arrowheads embedded in them; weapons like tomahawks and maces that are useless for hunting but specialized for homicide; fortification defenses such as palisades of sharpened sticks; and paintings from several continents showing men firing arrows, spears, or boomerangs at one another and being felled by these weapons.[14]

This suggests that our human propensity for violence is rooted in our evolutionary history. More than merely killing to eat, our human ancestors committed murder. Was there ever a time when *Homo sapiens* were without sin?

Once Darwinian evolution is taken on board, the theistic evolutionist can no longer locate paradise or prefallen humanity in the past. Rather, paradise or sinless humanity belongs to the future, to eschatological redemption. Right now, within evolutionary history, we must live with ambiguity, with a mixture of sin and grace.

How Will the Theistic Evolutionist Face the Challenge?

Christian theistic evolutionists will want to absorb into their religious vision this evolutionary picture of the human race and to allow the theory of evolution to influence Christian anthropology. The platform on which theistic

13. Francisco J. Ayala, "Molecular Biology: Darwin's Precious Gift," in *The Cambridge Encyclopedia of Darwin and Evolutionary Thought*, ed. Michael Ruse (Cambridge: Cambridge University Press, 2013), 398.

14. Steven Pinker, *The Blank Slate: The Modern Denial of Human Nature* (New York: Penguin, 2002), 306.

evolutionists construct their scheme includes one necessary plank: through evolutionary history God is creating the world.

According to "theistic evolution," writes Robert John Russell, founder and director of the Center for Theology and the Natural Sciences, "God creates the world *ex nihilo* with certain fundamental laws and natural constants, and God acts everywhere in time and space as continuous creator (*creatio continua*) in, with, and through the processes of nature. God's action is trustworthy and we describe the results through these laws of nature. The result is the evolution of life. In essence, evolution is how God is creating life."[15]

The school of theistic evolution is by no means the only option for tackling questions raised by Darwinian theory. There are rival schools of thought, to be sure. Atheistic materialism, for example, would deny the existence of a creating and redeeming God; similarly, it would deny that evolutionary development includes a *telos*, purpose, meaning, or end. Creationism in both its biblical and scientific forms would affirm belief in God while denying that Darwinian evolutionary theory provides a complete or final description of the human condition. Intelligent design would similarly deny that Darwinian theory adequately explains the human condition, adding that the presence of design in nature testifies to purpose and meaning.[16]

In contrast to these alternatives, the theistic evolutionist begins by granting respect to Darwinian theory and credence to Christian claims regarding God. Any theologian wishing to incorporate evolutionary history must deal with some difficult problems: (1) Where can we find *telos* or purpose in blind, pitiless evolution? (2) Does God favor the fit or the unfit? (3) When does the *imago Dei* appear—the past, present, or future?

Where Do We Find Purpose in Pitiless Evolution?

"Science . . . has no need of purpose, has detected no sign of it, and finds that it can go about its business in its absence," contends biologist and atheist Peter Atkins.[17] When we look at nature through scientific lenses, no purpose, direction, meaning, *telos*, or end can be discerned.

15. Robert John Russell, *Cosmology, Evolution, and Resurrection Hope: Theology and Science in Creative Mutual Interaction*, ed. Carl S. Helrich (Kitchener, ON: Pandora, 2006), 28.

16. For the agenda of the theistic evolution school in relation to other schools—atheistic materialism, creationism, and intelligent design—see Ted Peters and Martinez Hewlett, *Evolution from Creation to New Creation: Conflict, Conversation, and Convergence* (Nashville: Abingdon, 2003); Peters and Hewlett, *Can You Believe in God and Evolution?* (Nashville: Abingdon, 2009).

17. Peter Atkins, "Atheism and Science," in *Oxford Handbook of Religion and Science*, ed. Philip Clayton and Zachary Simpson (Oxford: Oxford University Press, 2006), 128.

Meaninglessness is intolerable for Christians. Purpose is required for the cosmos to be thought of as God's creation. The theistic evolutionist needs to affirm purpose *for* nature even if purpose cannot be discerned *within* nature. We can think of divine purpose in the analogy of a human person devising purposes for things in the surrounding environment. God has a purpose for the long history of evolution, to be sure; but that purpose comes from God in redemptive interaction with the world. For theistic evolutionists to perceive an end to evolution, they must anticipate God's end for creation.

In sum, the proleptic theologian does not expect to find purpose revealed within the course of natural events themselves. Rather, we must wait for eschatological revelation. Then we will see the wolf lie down with the lamb (Isa. 11); then we will see the elimination of crying and pain (Rev. 21–22). The *terminus* will reveal the *telos*. The end will determine the end, so to speak. In this limited way, the theistic position remains consonant with evolutionary biology. The theologian does not require the scientist to see God's end in nature's processes.

Does God Favor the Fit or the Unfit?

Our temptation might be to interpret biological evolution as progressive, as leading to more complex and higher forms of life. The risk is that the theologian will mistakenly identify God's providence with fitness, with the winners in the struggle for existence. But this would betray what is revealed in Scripture—namely, that God sides with sinners right along with the losers, the victims, and the unfit.

Celia Deane-Drummond formulates the problem that the theistic evolutionist must address:

> Those creation theologies that focus simply on the return to a state of blessedness in the beginning fail to consider in sufficient depth the horror of creaturely suffering that has become known to us through an understanding of evolution. One alternative might be simply to accept such suffering as part of the process. . . . Yet the cross challenges any such acceptance; rather we are left with an image of a co-suffering God who identifies with the victims of such a process, rather than the process itself.[18]

Here the theology of the cross becomes relevant. The theology of the cross derives from Martin Luther and has become expanded in recent generations by some theistic evolutionists. Luther writes, "The manifest and visible things of God are placed in opposition to the invisible, namely, his human nature,

---

18. Celia E. Deane-Drummond, *Creation through Wisdom: Theology and the New Biology* (Edinburgh: T&T Clark, 2000), 236.

weakness, foolishness. . . . It does [a theologian] no good to recognize God in his glory and majesty, unless he recognizes him in the humility and shame of the cross. . . . 'Truly, thou art a God who hidest thyself' (Isa. 45:15)."[19] The theology of the cross entails two components. First, God's redemptive work is hidden. It is not obvious. Second, God is present to "human nature, weakness, foolishness . . . humility and shame." The truth of God is not found at first in glory but in humility. Once we have grasped the humility, then the glory becomes visible.

The proleptic theistic evolutionist applies to the natural world what we have learned about God through the cross and resurrection. According to the theology of the cross, God identifies with the victims of the predator-prey competition, not the victors. God identifies first with the losers, the outcasts, the poor, and the unfit.

Applying the theology of the cross has led some theistic evolutionists to amend traditional theology with the notion of *deep incarnation*, a nonanthropocentric version of incarnation. "God's incarnation also reaches into the depths of material existence," contends Niels Henrik Gregersen.[20] The idea of deep incarnation implies that in Jesus Christ God enters the domain of physicality—including evolutionary biology—with grace for all the losers in the struggle for existence. As Elizabeth Johnson writes, "God's own self-expressive Word personally joins the biological world as a member of the human race [and] enters into solidarity with the whole biophysical cosmos of which humans are a part. This deep incarnation of God within the biotic community of life forges a new kind of union."[21]

Note what is going on here methodologically. God's presence through deep incarnation within nature is not visible through the lenses of the microscope or telescope. Therefore, the theologian must interpret biological evolution through biblical lenses. Jeffrey Schloss makes this clear: "The Gospel's affirmation [is] that in God's cruciform economy he graciously turns death into life. . . . Not that we learn the principle of redemption from evolution, but having learned it elsewhere, we see it there."[22] Johnson succinctly summarizes the implications of deep incarnation for the *imago Dei*: "Christ is the firstborn of the dead on Darwin's tree of life."[23]

19. Martin Luther, "Heidelberg Disputation," in *Luther's Works*, vol. 31, *Career of the Reformer I*, ed. Harold J. Grimm and Helmut T. Lehmann (St. Louis: Concordia, 1957), 52–53.

20. Niels Henrik Gregersen, "Deep Incarnation: Why Evolutionary Continuity Matters in Christology," *Toronto Journal of Theology* 26, no. 2 (2010): 174.

21. Elizabeth A. Johnson, *Ask the Beasts: Darwin and the God of Love* (London: Bloomsbury, 2014), 198.

22. Jeffrey P. Schloss, "Evolutionary Theory and Religious Belief," in *Oxford Handbook of Religion and Science*, ed. Philip Clayton (Oxford: Oxford University Press, 2008), 203.

23. Johnson, *Ask the Beasts*, 209.

When Does the Garden of Eden Appear?

If we look at the human condition through evolutionary lenses, there never was a time in the past when our ancestors were not already fallen. Sin, suffering, and evil were always with us. Our fallen state is equiprimordial with our appearance in biological history.

This means we cannot locate the *imago Dei* in the past. "Evolutionary science . . . has shown clearly that no paradisal period of perfection ever existed in nature's past," writes Georgetown University theologian John Haught.[24] A historical interpretation of the garden of Eden in Genesis 2–4 cannot be confirmed by evolutionary theory. Yet this is no reason to surrender our biblical belief in the *imago Dei*. Harvard astronomer Owen Gingerich adds, "If the early chapters of Genesis are not historical, it does not mean they are false or unimportant with regard to their theological insights. Truthful drama, but not actual history."[25]

Perhaps the Bible never needed an Eden in the past for us to return to. The Bible is bookended with paradise, with the garden of Eden in Genesis and again in Revelation. When we walk downtown in the new Jerusalem, we will find the same river of life and tree of life we had left back in Genesis.

Then I saw a new heaven and a new earth; for the first heaven and the first earth had passed away, and the sea was no more. And I saw the holy city, the new Jerusalem, coming down out of heaven from God, prepared as a bride adorned for her husband. And I heard a loud voice from the throne saying,

> "See, the home of God is among mortals.
> He will dwell with them;
> they will be his peoples,
> and God himself will be with them;
> he will wipe every tear from their eyes.
> Death will be no more;
> mourning and crying and pain will be no more,
> for the first things have passed away."

And the one who was seated on the throne said, "See, I am making all things new." . . . Then the angel showed me the river of the water of life, bright as crystal, flowing from the throne of God and of the Lamb through the middle of the street of the city. On either side of the river is the tree of life with its

24. John F. Haught, "Science, Teilhard and Vatican II," *Lumen: A Journal of Catholic Studies* 2, no. 1 (2014): 4.
25. Owen Gingerich, *God's Planet* (Cambridge, MA: Harvard University Press, 2014), 91.

twelve kinds of fruit, producing its fruit each month; and the leaves of the tree are for the healing of the nations. (Rev. 21:1–5; 22:1–2)

The decisive theological point made by both the story of Eden in Genesis and the new Jerusalem in Revelation is this: the creation God intends is not the one in which we currently live. Whether we describe the evolutionary world in which we live as fallen from a pristine past or rising into an eternal future, the point is that what we experience today is out of sync with God's intention. We today are estranged, alienated, separated from God's judgment that creation is "very good" (Gen. 1:31).

The estranged state of the present creation is defined by its relation to God's promised new creation. Or, working within the proleptic model, the present creation is a stage in the arrival of the new creation. Russell puts it this way: "The eschatological future reaches back and is revealed in the event of the resurrection of Jesus. . . . Both creation and New Creation are part of a single divine act of creation *ex nihilo*."[26] The eschatological new creation incorporates and transforms the present creation. To say it another way, the new creation consummates while redeeming the now-evolving creation.

What Should We Conclude?

"Cosmic and biological evolution instruct us as never before that we live in a universe that is in great measure not yet created. . . . In an evolving cosmos, created being as such has *not yet* achieved the state of integrity," says Haught rightly.[27] For both the evolutionary biologist and the proleptic theologian, the future is open, anticipating newness. "The notion of an unfinished universe still coming into being . . . opens up the horizon of a new or unprecedented future. . . . In its depths, nature is promise."[28] Because nature is promise, the Christian hope for God's new creation can be rendered consonant with evolutionary theory.

Placing the *imago Dei* within the eschatological new creation means we creatures anticipate an end in two senses of the word: end as the *terminus*, or conclusion, of God's creative work within evolution, and end as evolution's goal, purpose, meaning, destiny, or *telos*. In Christian eschatology, "end"

---

26. Robert John Russell, *Time in Eternity* (Notre Dame, IN: University of Notre Dame Press, 2012), 15.
27. John Haught, *Deeper than Darwin* (Boulder, CO: Westview, 2003), 168 (emphasis original).
28. Haught, *Deeper than Darwin*, 170.

entails both conclusion and goal, both *terminus* and *telos*. Looking forward, we expect a transformation from old creation to new creation. We expect to see the divine image, the *imago Dei*, in its fullness. For creatures within the lengthy story of evolution, the *imago Dei* is the divine call forward, a call we hear and respond to now but that draws us toward transformation into a future reality.

The proleptic model of the *imago Dei* prepares us for a robust theistic evolution. When we turn to Darwin's theory of evolution, we find a scientific description of unredeemed biological and social processes that mark estrangement from God's end—both *terminus* and *telos*—for creation. Evolutionary processes may be God's way of creating today, but this divine creating will not be completed until all of nature is redeemed.

We began with one decisive assumption: the *imago Dei* derives not from Adam and Eve in the past but rather from the eschatological Christ in the future. This leads to the following conclusion: when we and the cosmos are redeemed, we will be fully created. Then God can finally say, "Behold, it is very good."

CONCLUSION TO PART I

Michael Burdett

The chapters in part 1 epitomize how rich and, at times, varied the conversation can be between theological scholars and evolutionary scientists at the intersection of the image of God, human personhood, and evolution. Each contribution represents a particular avenue or tradition of interpretation in the conversation, thus manifesting that there are many ways to make sense of the image of God in light of evolution that are both valid and supportable.

Van Huyssteen's essay opens us up to the whole issue of the relationship between evolution and the image of God by offering an important account of the evolutionary development of human personhood and suggests that we take a "bottom-up approach" to the image of God that takes seriously some of the latest developments in the evolutionary sciences. These developments include recognition of the complex and symbiotic relationship early hominids had with their environment so that "cooperation, empathy, compassion, the use of and engagement with materials, symbols and ritual, and the notion of a semiotic landscape" all provide key building blocks that "shaped and prepared our species to be physically, mentally, and spiritually 'ready' for faith." Van Huyssteen's major contribution is pointing out how the latest evolutionary science provides important information on the development of personhood and, hence, for our understanding of the developmental components that make up the image of God. Niche construction, hyperaltruism, and the development of the moral sense and imagination are all new and important areas for a changing conception of evolution in four dimensions that includes both genetic and cultural components. Some of the most exciting future work on evolution and the image of God will undoubtedly be in these areas.

Mark Harris has provided a comprehensive unpacking of the biblical material and the functional model, and he suggests the functional model is highly appealing relative to the other models for at least three reasons. First, it is most likely the view held by the biblical authors. As he says, there is near consensus among biblical scholars that the functional view is the exegetical crux of the Genesis *imago Dei* texts. But beyond historical and interpretive congruity, the functional model has contemporary worth for modern readers because, second, it is important for ecotheology and reappropriating just how important cultivation of creation is for the human as *imago Dei*. And, finally, the functional model's distance from specific structural components makes it less susceptible to evolutionary critique of these components (e.g., rationality and morality). Indeed, while the functional model seems to depend on physical similarity between God and humanity in the biblical text, as Harris points out, "The functional interpretation avoids the difficulties here simply by noting the evolution of human physicality *in general*—that the *imago Dei* is reflected in the appearance of *Homo sapiens* as an entire species."

Aku Visala argues that a modified structural version of the image of God can withstand evolutionary critiques. He argues for an emergent dualist approach to the soul that he claims not only provides sufficient explanation to evolutionary challenges but also synthesizes the findings of evolution with a theological and philosophical account of human development. In the first instance, he grants that the evolutionary sciences provide an important evolutionary explanation for how things such as morality, rationality, and altruism have come about and on which the human is built and depends. But the soul provides another kind of explanation altogether. While evolutionary explanations "explain why our perceptual, conceptual, and emotional systems work the way they do in terms of their selective advantages in our ancestral environments," souls "account for phenomena such as the existence of the person and self-consciousness, the unity of consciousness, the qualitative aspects of consciousness, intentionality, human dignity and value, and survival after death." Furthermore, Visala argues that the apparent loss of human uniqueness or distinctiveness since Darwin does not mean a complete collapse of the human into other proximate species, and he points out that even evolutionary scientists themselves are arguing for human distinctiveness.

Thomas Jay Oord represents the relational model of the image of God, highlighting how a "relational-love view" of the image of God best captures the meaning of the doctrine and makes the most sense of the relevant evolutionary sciences. While acknowledging the other models have an important perspective on the image of God, Oord contends the relational-love view incorporates the best elements of each. In this view, humans reflect God when they model the supreme divine virtue, love, in all their relationships. This presupposes basic structural qualities and certain acts and functions in the environment and is grounded in the ultimate image of Christ. Oord's most radical advancement is in arguing that humans aren't the only creatures that image God since other creatures exhibit similar relational capacities and loving dispositions to others.

Ted Peters's contribution further extends the unfinished and developmental component of the image of God in present humans. Peters claims that the image of God should be read not as something that has been complete in our past but as something that will only be finished in Christ at the end of human history. This dynamic, proleptic account of the image of God, Peters proposes, actively incorporates evolutionary developments into its model such that "through evolutionary history God is creating the world." Indeed, this model has no issue with giving an account of the potential friction between an original, Edenic human state and the evolutionary record, which shows predation, sin, and suffering all the way down. As Peters says, Eden is something for which we are bound and is made possible by the authentic human, Jesus, not necessarily something that we were ever part of in our past in this world.

Two items are worth noting to conclude this section. First, it is entirely possible that each of these models could be combined in interesting ways such that hybrid models could be constructed that rely on aspects from each one outlined here. For instance, it is entirely likely that one could hold to the relational, functional, and structural models of the image of God simultaneously. Gijsbert van den Brink claims as much when he writes:

> We are special because God has called us to be stewards of God's earthly creation, having endowed us with the capacity for responsible relationships with each other and with Godself, relationships which we need in order to take care of each other and of creation as a whole in a myriad of ways. Moreover, in order to live in these responsible relationships and to fulfil our tasks, God has given us some substantive character traits which are, if not unique in kind then at least unique in degree as compared to any other species in creation.[1]

So, when assessing the opportunities and challenges the evolutionary sciences make to the image of God, we ought to be aware that often beliefs regarding the image of God might draw on more than one of these approaches and that a combination of more than one model is warranted.

1. Gijsbert van den Brink, "Are We Still Special? Evolution and Human Dignity," *Neue Zeitschrift für systematische Theologie und Religionsphilosophie* 53, no. 3 (2011): 331.

Second, Harris's warning is important and instructive to all who study the *imago Dei* and evolution: "Quite simply, the *imago Dei* is a statement about God's grace to creation and not about human self-ability." Theology, it is often said, is knowing when to remain silent on a particular matter. This means that we ought to "major on the majors" and "minor on the minors," which is really the spirit of this volume. Therefore, we would do well to recognize that the main theological import of the image of God rests precisely on the acknowledgment that we are meant to focus not on the human person alone as the central subject of the text and teaching but rather on how God equips and graces this creature, the human being.

Further Reading

Deane-Drummond, Celia. *The Wisdom of the Liminal: Evolution and Other Animals in Human Becoming*. Grand Rapids: Eerdmans, 2014.

Grenz, Stanley. *The Social God and the Relational Self: A Trinitarian Theology of the Imago Dei*. Louisville: Westminster John Knox, 2001.

Jablonka, Eva, and Marion Lamb. *Evolution in Four Dimensions: Genetic, Epigenetic, Behavioral, and Symbolic Variation in the History of Life*. Cambridge, MA: MIT Press, 2005.

Middleton, J. Richard. *The Liberating Image: The* Imago Dei *in Genesis 1*. Grand Rapids: Brazos, 2005.

Moreland, J. P. *The Recalcitrant* Imago Dei: *Human Persons and the Failure of Naturalism*. London: SCM, 2009.

Moritz, Joshua M. "Evolution, the End of Human Uniqueness, and the Election of the *Imago Dei*." *Theology and Science* 9, no. 3 (2011): 307–39.

Rad, Gerhard von. *Genesis: A Commentary*. Translated by John H. Marks. Rev. ed. Louisville: Westminster John Knox, 1973 (London: SCM, 1961).

Shults, F. LeRon. *Reforming Theological Anthropology: After the Philosophical Turn to Relationality*. Grand Rapids: Eerdmans, 2003.

Smedt, Johan De, and Helen De Cruz. "The *Imago Dei* as a Work in Progress: A Perspective from Paleoanthropology." *Zygon* 49, no. 1 (March 2014): 135–56.

Tattersall, Ian. *Becoming Human: Evolution and Human Uniqueness*. New York: Harcourt Brace, 1998.

van Huyssteen, J. Wentzel. *Alone in the World? Human Uniqueness in Science and Theology*. Grand Rapids: Eerdmans, 2006.

PART 2

Original Sin and Evolution

BENNO VAN DEN TOREN, EDITOR

Challenges and Opportunities from Evolutionary Science

The doctrine of original sin is a recurrent and weighty issue in the debates that touch the interface between theological anthropology and scientific research in the evolution of the human species. For example, in his concluding reflection in the 2013 book *Four Views on the Historical Adam*, Philip G. Ryken offers as his second reason he believes the historical Adam to be of pivotal importance that "the historical Adam explains humanity's sinful nature."[1]

From its very beginning, evolutionary theory has presented challenges for the doctrine of original sin in some of its widely accepted forms. If the human is a latecomer to the long history of evolution, a human fall into sin cannot be blamed for the existence of death and decay, for these were continuous

1. Philip G. Ryken, "We Cannot Understand the World or Our Faith without a Real, Historical Adam," in *Four Views on the Historical Adam*, ed. Matthew Barrett and Ardel B. Caneday (Grand Rapids: Zondervan, 2013), 271. His first reason is that "the historical Adam gives confidence that the Bible is the word of God," and his third is that "the historical Adam accounts for the presence of evil in the world."

characteristics of evolution long before humans appeared on stage. For the same reason, it can also no longer function as an explanation for the existence of violence, predation, and aggression in the animal world, as certain readings of Genesis 3:17–19 in conjunction with Isaiah 11:6–8 suppose.[2]

A number of issues have been added or strengthened by recent advances in the research of human genetics, particularly through the research of genetic variations through the current human populations, comparisons with the genetics of related animal species, the modeling of how genetic material in populations changes through history, and the study of paleogenetics (i.e., the retrieval of genetic material of no longer existent hominin species).[3] This research significantly strengthens the more general evolutionary thesis that humans have prehuman ancestors that they have in common with other primates. This thesis is no longer based mainly on general physiological parallels, hypothetical relations between a limited number of bone fragments, and the general strength of the overall evolutionary theory. These earlier theories have largely been confirmed by detailed comparisons of very long and detailed sequences of human genomes with the genomes of nearer and further cousins in the evolutionary tree.

This recent genetic research into, and modeling of, human evolution also raises a number of new issues for the doctrine of original sin. Current models of the genetic development of the modern human suggest, first, that there was no first human couple at the headwaters of all currently existing humans but that the current human population came into being through a bottleneck of at least around ten thousand reproductive individuals. The traditional picture of a neatly distinguishable human population descending from a single couple is further complicated by the fact that paleogenetics suggests—many would say *proves*—a measure of interbreeding between our human ancestors and other *Homo* species. According to recent findings, Europeans share 1 to 4 percent of their DNA with Neanderthals, and certain groups of Asians share 5 percent with so-called Denisovans (a recently discovered species), while Africans share none of this foreign genetic material.[4] The genetic heritage amplifies earlier

2. Note, however, Stanley P. Rosenberg's argument in chap. 15 below that Augustine has been wrongly used by those who argue that decay and predation entered the world as one of the consequences of the fall, along with original sin.

3. See Dennis R. Venema, "Genesis and the Genome: Genomics Evidence for Human-Ape Common Ancestry and Ancestral Hominid Population Sizes," *Perspectives on Science and Christian Faith* 62, no. 3 (2010): 166–78; Dennis R. Venema and Scot McKnight, *Adam and the Genome: Reading Scripture after Genetic Science* (Grand Rapids: Brazos, 2017).

4. Cf. Dennis R. Venema, "Neanderthals, Denisovans, and Human Speciation," *Letters to the Duchess* (blog), BioLogos Forum, September 23, 2011, http://biologos.org/blogs/dennis-venema -letters-to-the-duchess/understanding-evolution-neanderthals-denisovans-and-human-speciation.

questions about whether and how humans have inherited strong dispositions to, for example, sexual promiscuity and aggression that in our ancestors were a prerequisite for survival but that the Scriptures would call sinful desires. We should, of course, remain careful not to draw quick conclusions. Even if a relationship can be established between certain genes and a disposition to certain behavior, the precise link between these two realities is so far little understood and cannot be established in our extinct ancestors.

According to the authors in the following essays, none of these issues precludes holding to the doctrine of original sin even in a robust form. Yet the authors also agree that these issues are important and need careful attention. In what follows it will become clear that newer developments in evolutionary theory not only complicate certain traditional understandings of original sin but also provide new opportunities for constructive dialogue. They do so particularly by confirming a common genetic lineage of the modern *Homo sapiens* over against older polygenetic theories—which assumed the existence of multiple unrelated ancestors of different human races—and by blurring the nature-and-culture dichotomy that has characterized recent evolutionary anthropology.[5]

The Doctrine and Different Theological Models

One of the main analytical tools used in this volume to create space for a constructive and critical interaction at the interface between the current scientific picture of human evolution and the Christian faith is the distinction between doctrine and theological theory. The relevance of this distinction becomes clear in the following chapters. Gijsbert van den Brink sets out to show that what he calls the "network" of particular doctrines that cluster around the doctrine of original sin encompasses a range of doctrines. All authors in this volume would agree on a core of these doctrines, particularly concerning the universality, pervasiveness, and inherited nature of the human disposition to sinning and the unavoidability that humans therefore all fall into sin. There is disagreement with regard to other elements of this doctrinal network, particularly concerning whether the doctrine implies that sin originated with a first human or couple (as particularly contested by Chris Hays) and possibly also with regard to whether the inheritance of *guilt* is an essential or even acceptable part of this doctrinal cluster (though the decisive questions here are theological and relatively unrelated to scientific theories

5. On these points, see chaps. 9 and 12 below, by Andrew Pinsent and Benno van den Toren, respectively.

concerning evolution). All authors do, however, believe and argue that their understanding of the doctrine does justice to the central content of the historical doctrine and to the Scriptures while allowing for a critical dialogue with, and accommodation of, crucial scientific insights. The authors do so by drawing on different theological theories that help them understand the unity of the human race in sin and (if they consider this to be an essential part of the doctrine) the crucial difference that the first sin brought into the world. As we will see, these models are not necessarily or entirely mutually exclusive.

Andrew Pinsent draws on the classical Augustinian model and its later development by Thomas Aquinas, which understands the unity of the human race in a "realistic" sense. The unity of the human race in sin is based on a real and ontological unity with its ancestors. Interestingly, according to Pinsent, this inherited "disposition to acquire a disposition to sin" is characterized not by something that can be positively detected in human nature but rather by an absence. The disposition is the consequence of the absence of the original relationship with God, in which humans were upheld by God's special graceful provision and communion through which they could appropriately guide their dispositions, which would otherwise lead them into and bind them to sin. This means that the presence of problematic inherited dispositions that might even have a prehuman origin does not preclude the goodness of the original human because these dispositions were originally properly controlled and directed when humankind lived (even though for possibly a short period that can probably never be detected by evolutionary science) in perfect unity with its Creator.

Jack Collins draws on the federal understanding of original sin that has been developed in the Reformed tradition. According to this model, the unity of the human race in sin depends not on a metaphysical unity at the ontological level but rather on the unity of humanity as included in the same covenant with Adam. Consequently, according to Collins, Adam and Eve might well have been the equivalent of a king and queen of the first community of humans as long as they were appointed by God to be their covenant head and as long as the community expressed a sufficient degree of unity that they could sensibly exercise this headship role.

Irenaeus is often used as the spokesperson for a theodicy that does not require a perfect and sinless paradise because humankind was created in view of a gradual development to maturity and holiness. Andy McCoy criticizes this use of Irenaeus because Irenaeus maintained that Adam and Eve were created sinless, though immature. The distinction between sinlessness and lack of maturity does, however, allow McCoy to accept a gradual evolutionary development of humankind. On this account, we should not project the perfection of the heavenly Jerusalem back into paradise. Jesus came to save humans from the sinful predicament in which humanity has found itself since Adam's fall, but he not only saves humans from sin. He also recapitulates all humanity under himself by bringing humanity to its originally intended maturity and thus completes the maturation process that was aborted by Adam's sin.

Whereas McCoy focuses particularly on original sin as the *first* sin, Benno van den Toren draws attention again to original sin as the *unity* of the human race in the sinfulness inherited from their ancestors. He argues that modern evolutionary theory deepens the theological theory that saw the unity of the human race in sin as rooted particularly in cultural transmission. Pelagian and modern varieties of this theory risk making human sinfulness a mere fact of imitation rather than enslavement. Recent evolutionary theory suggests, however, that human nature is always profoundly cultured and that we cannot but imbibe and inhabit the cultural patterns of our parents and educators—thus giving the idea of the cultural inheritance of sin new depth and relevance.

Finally, Christopher Hays explains why he believes that Scripture gives the foundation for a strong doctrine of original sin as the sin we inherit but does not require us to embrace the notion of a first sin that subsequently explains the later sinfulness of humankind. His biblical and hermeneutical considerations lead him to consider as theologically irrelevant the question of how to place a historic fall on the evolutionary time line. He rather focuses on ways in which evolutionary theory helps us flesh out our understanding of why every human is inherently disposed and bound to behave destructively and sinfully. This provides a counterpoint both to the hermeneutical considerations of Collins and to the analysis of van den Brink.

Biblical, Historical, Systematic, and Contextual Theology

The authors come at the central question from various angles, providing in part 2 a wide-ranging discussion of the issues at stake. The biblical material and hermeneutical questions are most elaborately discussed by Collins and Hays, though they arrive at different conclusions—with Hays arguing for a nonhistorical, symbolic reading of the Genesis story of the fall and Collins arguing for a fundamentally historical account that nevertheless uses "pictorial description, anachronism, and symbolism." Hermeneutical questions further receive elaborate attention in van den Brink's critical analysis of Denis Lamoureux's symbolic reading of Genesis 3.

The history of the doctrine receives most attention in the contributions of Pinsent (on Augustine) and McCoy (on Irenaeus). Systematic questions receive most elaborate attention in van den Brink's overview of the different doctrines that make up the network of the doctrine of original sin and in van den Toren's analysis of how the doctrine ties in with broader Christian doctrines concerning the goodness of creation, the goodness of God, and the enslaving character of sin.

Given the nature of this volume, all the authors engage elaborately with contextual issues. Contextual questions relating to the doctrine of original sin could cover debates with other religious traditions such as Islam and Hinduism, modern optimism and pessimism, psychology, modern free-market economics, art, and literature (explorations initiated by Pinsent), but in this volume they focus on the relationship with science. Given the range of angles essential to theological reflection in the contemporary world, a conjoint reading of these chapters will provide a broad introduction to the doctrine of original sin.

8

Questions, Challenges, and Concerns for Original Sin

GIJSBERT VAN DEN BRINK

A theistic believer who seriously studies the ramifications of evolutionary theory may go through some bewildering experiences. If evolutionary theory explains the way in which God orchestrated the rise and development not only of animal life but also of the human race, what happens to old, venerated, doctrinal notions of an original human couple (Adam and Eve) with whom it all began, their sudden fall into sin, and the subsequent sinfulness of their entire offspring? Shouldn't these notions (just like the notion of an initially pain-free creation) be dismissed as overly romantic and out of touch with empirical reality? Or is it possible to reinterpret them within an evolutionary context so that we can still maintain what they were intended to convey about our human condition?

In this chapter I explore these questions by focusing on the doctrine of original sin—which traditionally binds together in an intricate way the three notions mentioned above—and asking whether evolutionary theory requires the abandonment of this doctrine. Precisely which problems, challenges, and concerns does evolutionary theory raise for it? First, I briefly sketch the

An earlier (Dutch) version of this chapter appeared in Gijsbert van den Brink, *En de aarde brachtmensen voort: Christelijk geloof en evolutie* (Utrecht: Boekencentrum, 2017), 245–58.

contours of the doctrine of original sin as developed in the history of Christian thought. Second, I tease out the main questions that play a role here by surveying a recent paper by Denis Lamoureux in which he argues that evolution requires the radical abandonment of the doctrine of original sin. Third, I suggest that a nuanced examination of the issues may point to the possibility of a *recontextualization* of original sin within an evolutionary framework. If that is a fruitful avenue—a question that is further explored in subsequent essays in this volume—perhaps we don't have to choose between evolution and original sin.[1]

What Is Original Sin?

Strictly speaking, original sin is the sin that *Adam and Eve* committed in the garden of Eden. This can still be seen, for example, in the Scots Confession (1560), which starts its third article as follows: "By this transgression [viz. of Adam and Eve in paradise], generally known as original sin, the image of God was utterly defaced in man."[2] Accordingly, in medieval Scholasticism a distinction was made between the originating (or causing) original sin of Adam and Eve (*peccatum originale originans*) and the originated (or caused) original sin in later humans (*peccatum originale originatum*).[3] Let us try to get an even more refined understanding of the doctrine of original sin by carefully distinguishing the various layers usually associated with it in classical forms of Christian theology—leaving aside for a moment whether each one of them is a proper part of the doctrine, a constitutive presupposition, a necessary implication, or just a coincidental extension of it. We can then distinguish a number of closely connected assumptions (or propositional claims) that together can be considered as forming the "network" of original sin:

1. Cf. Denis R. Alexander's widely acclaimed book *Creation or Evolution: Do We Have to Choose?*, 2nd ed. (Oxford: Monarch, 2014). Alexander does not pursue the issue of original sin in this book, but the question that serves as the subtitle of his book can be applied to this topic.

2. Quoted from the Office of the General Assembly—Presbyterian Church (USA), *The Book of Confessions* (Louisville: Westminster John Knox, 2007), 11. Note that Adam's later sins, as distinct from his (and Eve's) first one, did not have the same effects as this original transgression; they were just actual sins like those of anyone else.

3. Cf., e.g., James T. Bretzke, *Consecrated Phrases: A Latin Theological Dictionary; Latin Expressions Commonly Found in Theological Writings*, 3rd ed. (Collegeville, MN: Liturgical Press, 2013), 175. The *peccatum originale originans* is more generally identified as "the fall" (*lapsus*) into sin—which may be the reason why "original sin" came to be used mainly in the sense of *peccatum originale originatum*.

1. All humans are sinful (i.e., they sometimes commit acts that go against God's will).
2. All humans have a tendency or inclination toward sinning from the beginning of their lives.
3. The tendency toward sinning is not restricted to particular domains of human life (e.g., the body or our emotions and desires) but affects every human faculty.
4. The tendency toward sinning is the well from which all sorts of actual sins spring in everyone's life.
5. The tendency toward sinning is not part of our original makeup but a result of the first sin that took place at the dawn of human history. So it is, basically, a corruption.
6. This corruption is an effect of the first sin that is passed on to all later generations through sexual reproduction.
7. In connection with this corruption the guilt of the first sin is also passed on (or imputed) to all later generations; therefore, all humans deserve God's judgment and condemnation even when they have not yet committed actual sins (e.g., infants).[4]

To phrase all this in one sentence: original sin is humans' universal, radical, total, effective, acquired, hereditary, and inculpating inclination toward sinning.

By unraveling the various threads that compose the network of original sin in this way, we gradually move from its more plausible and generally accessible aspects to its more counterintuitive and contested assumptions. Clearly both the notion of original guilt and the supposed sexual transmission of original sin belong to the most disputed parts of the doctrine in contemporary theology. Obviously, more could and should be said in order to gain greater clarity about the doctrine, especially on the biblical backgrounds of the various assumptions distinguished here and the historical trajectories that led to their explicit formulation in various parts of the church. This preliminary orientation, however, will suffice to set the context of Denis Lamoureux's recent argument, to which I turn now.

---

4. For a similar account, distinguishing no less than ten aspects that original sin features, see T. A. Noble, "Original Sin and the Fall: Definitions and a Proposal," in *Darwin, Creation and the Fall*, ed. R. J. Berry and T. A. Noble (Nottingham: UK: Inter-Varsity, 2009), 101–12. Unlike mine, Noble's list also includes aspects that are characteristic of contemporary reinterpretations of the doctrine, such as the contagiousness of sin and its corporate character.

Original Sin and Concordism

Those who want to maintain the compatibility of original sin and evolution have a hard time. On the one hand, many conservative theologians firmly reject this compatibility thesis, upholding original sin at the expense of evolutionary theory.[5] On the other hand, those known as theistic evolutionists (or evolutionary creationists) tend to do exactly the opposite: they jettison original sin because they argue evolutionary theory does not leave any conceptual space for it. In this section, I critically address a recent specimen of this latter strategy in order to tease out the various problems that are involved and to question the idea that we have to choose here between religion (original sin) and science (evolutionary theory). Instead, I tentatively suggest in the next section that the doctrine of original sin can be recontextualized in such a way that it helps us make sense of our evolutionary history.

I take as my starting point a recent paper by Denis Lamoureux—a biologist and theologian who is well known from some excellent and thought-provoking books on Christian faith and evolution.[6] Lamoureux's position is exemplary for what is perhaps the most common position on this issue, and his argument is clearly stated. Lamoureux rightly acknowledges that "the doctrine of original sin has been a foundational belief of the Christian faith throughout most of Church history."[7] He develops the doctrine along the lines set out in the previous section, especially focusing on the distinction between the "originating sin" of our first ancestors and the "originated sin" that operates in each of their descendants. He then goes on to argue that both of these depend on the historicity of biblical Adam (and presumably Eve): "If Adam did not exist, then he could never have committed the first sin. And if there was no Adam, then all of humanity did not descend from him, and his sin could never have been passed on to every human being" (35). Lamoureux recognizes, however, that belief in the historicity of Adam is deeply entrenched in both the Bible and the Christian tradition. Paul, for

---

5. See, e.g., the various contributions in Hans Madueme and Michael Reeves, eds., *Adam, the Fall, and Original Sin: Theological, Biblical, and Scientific Perspectives* (Grand Rapids: Baker Academic, 2014); for an excellent review, which is as sympathetic to the authors' overall intention as it is critical of some of their arguments, see Stephen N. Williams, "*Adam, the Fall, and Original Sin*: A Review Essay," *Themelios* 40 (2015): 203–17.

6. Cf. Denis O. Lamoureux, *Evolutionary Creation: A Christian Approach to Evolution* (Eugene, OR: Wipf & Stock, 2008); its slimmer, popularizing sequel, Denis O. Lamoureux, *I Love Jesus & I Accept Evolution* (Eugene, OR: Wipf & Stock, 2009); Lamoureux, *Evolution: Scripture and Nature Say Yes!* (Grand Rapids: Zondervan, 2016).

7. Denis O. Lamoureux, "Beyond Original Sin: Is a Theological Paradigm Shift Inevitable?," *Perspectives on Science and Christian Faith* 67 (2015): 35; subsequent page references in the body of the text pertain to this article.

one, thought of Adam as a historical person, as is clear from his phrase "from the time of Adam to the time of Moses" (Rom. 5:14 NIV). In Paul's view, sin entered the world along with death as God's condemnation for Adam's disobedience (36). Both Adam's sin and its divine punishment (i.e., death) were transmitted to his offspring. What is more, not only humans had to die as a result of Adam's sin but also all other species. Lamoureux infers from Romans 8:20–22 that for Paul "it is clear that decay, suffering, and death entered the world with Adam in Genesis 3" (37). Thus, Paul believed in a "cosmic Fall" as a result of Adam's originating sin.[8] Regarding the Christian tradition, Lamoureux rightly points out that the doctrine of original sin did not start from scratch with Augustine since, for example, Irenaeus already "believed that humans became sinful and mortal because Adam sinned" (37).[9] Though Augustine was the first one to formulate the doctrine, he synthesized intuitions that had been part of Christian thinking all along.[10] And he in turn profoundly influenced many subsequent creedal and doctrinal affirmations on original sin in both the Catholic and the Protestant parts of the Western church (37–38).

Lamoureux's succinct rendering of the biblical backgrounds and historical trajectories of the doctrine is remarkable for its simplicity and candor. Often those who reject original sin try to drive a wedge between Paul and the author(s) of Genesis 3, suggesting that Paul imposed an interpretive framework of his own on a Genesis account that does not refer to original sin at all. Or, alternatively, they drive a wedge between Augustine and Paul, arguing that Augustine misled the entire Western tradition by reading Paul from the perspective of his own pessimistic (or Greek or neo-Platonic or Manichaean) anthropology.[11] Lamoureux does not take any of these tacks—and rightly

---

8. On this notion of a cosmic fall, see, e.g., John J. Bimson, "Reconsidering a Cosmic Fall," *Science & Christian Belief* 18, no. 1 (2006): 63–81.

9. For substantiation of this point, Lamoureux might have pointed to, e.g., A. N. S. Lane, "Irenaeus on the Fall and Original Sin," in Berry and Noble, *Darwin, Creation and the Fall*, 130–42.

10. For a thoroughgoing account of its trajectories in the Eastern part of the early church, see Manfred Hauke, *Heilsverlust in Adam: Stationen griechischer Erbsündenlehre; Irenäus—Origenes—Kappadozier* (Paderborn, Germany: Bonifatius, 1993).

11. For the first strategy, cf. Patricia Williams, *Doing without Adam and Eve: Sociobiology and Original Sin* (Minneapolis: Fortress, 2001), 42; for the second strategy—which became common since John Hick's *Evil and the God of Love*, 3rd ed. (New York: Palgrave Macmillan, 2010), introduced Hick's famous stereotypical distinction between Augustinian and Irenaean types of theodicy—see, e.g., Elaine Pagels, *Adam, Eve, and the Serpent* (New York: Random House, 1988), 98–126; John R. Schneider, "Recent Genetic Science and Christian Theology on Human Origins: An 'Aesthetic Supralapsarianism,'" *Perspectives on Science and Christian Faith* 62 (2010): 202–3.

so, to my mind.[12] As a result, he cannot downplay the biblical and historical significance of the doctrine of original sin. In his view, original sin is not a foreign intruder in the Bible or in the Christian tradition but is deeply embedded in its formative embodiments. Therefore, he rightly points out that "everyone should feel the weight of challenging this historical doctrine" (38). Yet challenging this doctrine is exactly what he does.

Here is Lamoureux's main line of argument: Just as Paul's notion of original sin was based on a "concordist" reading of Genesis 3, the later tradition read both Genesis and Paul in a concordist way. That is to say, "They read Genesis 3 and Romans 5 as accounts referring to actual historical and scientific events. In particular, they accepted the historicity of Adam as the very first human and believed that every man and woman had descended from him" (38). Such a reading of the Bible, however, is theologically incorrect. In order to substantiate this claim, Lamoureux points to scriptural passages that feature the way in which our physical world is structured. As virtually all interpreters agree, the three-tier "worldpicture" that we find in the Bible—with (1) the earth, (2) heaven and the waters above the earth (held in place by the firmament), and (3) the waters below the earth (cf. Gen. 1:6–7; Exod. 20:4)—was part of ancient Near Eastern cosmology. This picture is not only characteristic of the Old Testament; it is clear from passages such as Philippians 2:9–11 that Paul as well believed in a universe consisting of three tiers. We now know, however, that this worldpicture is wrong (and hardly anyone will be found to contest this fact). Lamoureux draws the following conclusion from these observations: "In the light of this biblical evidence, it is obvious that concordism fails. The world is not made up of three tiers. Therefore, scripture does not offer us an account of actual historical and scientific events in the creation of the universe" (39).[13]

In this connection, Lamoureux appeals to the concept of *accommodation* (which he could have traced back to John Calvin and even to some of the early church fathers): when inspiring the biblical writers, the Holy Spirit "descended to their level" and took care that they made use of the "science-of-the-day" (Lamoureux's phrasing), which could be understood by their first readers (39).[14]

12. Cf. Gijsbert van den Brink, "Should We Drop the Fall? On Taking Evil Seriously," in *Strangers and Pilgrims on Earth: Essays in Honour of Abraham van de Beek*, ed. E. van der Borght and P. van Geest (Leiden: Brill, 2012), 761–77, esp. 769–77. Though both of them definitely used their own hermeneutical lenses, it can be argued that Augustine was a careful reader of Paul, just as Paul was a careful reader of Genesis.

13. For Lamoureux's hermeneutics, see also his article "Lessons from the Heavens: On Scripture, Science and Inerrancy," *Perspectives in Christian Faith and Science* 60 (2008): 4–15.

14. Calvin especially used this hermeneutical strategy when dealing with the ascription of emotions and feelings to God by the biblical writers, but also in other contexts. Cf. Arnold

Clearly, Lamoureux argues, the primary purpose of the Bible is not to inform us about the physical structure of the universe or about other "scientific" facts but to reveal "life-changing messages of faith" (39). He then contends that this should be kept in mind not only when we come across astronomical or geological aspects of ancient science but also when we find traces of ancient *biology*.[15] In this connection, a direct (*de novo*) creation of the human species by means of a special divine act was part and parcel of ancient Near Eastern biology. As in Genesis 1:27, the Godhead is often portrayed as a *craftsman* in this connection, using earth to mold the first humans.

This picture is clearly at odds with contemporary science. Lamoureux points to two facts in this connection: first, according to fossil discoveries and the science of genetics (each of which reinforces the other), "humans were not created de novo, but evolved from a population of about 10,000 pre-humans" (40); and, second, geology disproves the notion of a cosmic fall. If Adam were responsible for death and decay entering the world, human bones would have been found at the bottom of the earth's fossil archive—whereas in fact they appear at its top, suggesting that death and decay were around all along. Lamoureux thus concludes: "These are facts of science. All the lines of biblical and scientific evidence point to only one conclusion: *Adam never existed*" (40, emphasis original). If we want to escape from this conclusion and continue to uphold a historical Adam, we should be consistent and also accept the three-tier universe presupposed in Scripture.

The final step of Lamoureux's argument follows logically: since Adam is the hinge on which the door of original sin turns, it is clear that if Adam never existed, talk about original sin vanishes into thin air. "No one today believes in a firmament, a heavenly sea, a three-tier universe, or a geocentric world. Nor should we . . . believe in the historicity of Adam, and as a consequence, the doctrine of historical sin" (46). If the doctrine of original sin is wrong, however, how did we then become sinners? Drawing on modern science, Lamoureux believes that "the manifestation of the image of God . . . occurred roughly 50,000 years ago with the emergence of behaviorally modern humans" (43). These first humans (a group of about 10,000 individuals) were equipped with moral awareness and were therefore accountable before God. Although, like other primates, they often acted out of empathy and did good things, at the same time they also started to sin, feeding their evolutionary self-preserving and selfish inclinations. In the end, sinfulness became "humanity's greatest problem" (43).

Huijgen, *Divine Accommodation in John Calvin: Analysis and Assessment* (Göttingen: Vandenhoeck & Ruprecht, 2011).

15. Obviously, the use of words such as "science" and "biology" here is highly anachronistic, but I take it that the reader grasps their meaning and function.

Lamoureux emphasizes that in order to move from the doctrine of original sin to this scientifically warranted view of how sin entered the world, a
paradigm shift in the Kuhnian sense may be needed.[16] Such a shift can only
take place through a "theological crisis" (47) in which the doctrine of original
sin, along with the concordist reading of the Bible in which it is embedded,
will finally be overthrown. That is an enormous revolution since "normal
theology" has been deeply influenced by "creedal statements that authorize
the historicity of Adam and the doctrine of original sin" (46). Still, pointing to
some recent evangelical publications, Lamoureux ventures that evangelicalism
may already be in the initial stages of this theological crisis, which will lead
evangelicals to view things "in a radically different way" (46).[17] Apparently,
the promised land is just on the horizon.

Rejecting or Recontextualizing Original Sin?

In what follows, I suggest that, contrary to Lamoureux's suggestions, we
do not have to choose between evolution and original sin. To be sure, the
recent scientific developments to which Lamoureux rightly points force us
to *recontextualize* the doctrine within a new, evolutionary setting. But that
is something other than rejecting the doctrine out of hand. What is needed
is not so much a theological paradigm shift as some adjustments to classical
versions of the doctrine. Though these adjustments have their impact and do
not leave everything as it was, they affect later embellishments of the doctrine
rather than its biblical heart.

First, let us briefly revisit the seven aspects of the doctrine of original sin
distinguished above. It seems to me that aspects (1)–(4) remain virtually unaffected if we presuppose an evolutionary context in which humans emerged.
For example, that all humans are sinful (1) continues to be an assumption
that can almost be empirically verified.[18] Regarding (2), (3), and (4)—the
radicality, totality, and effectiveness of our inclination toward sinning—one

16. Cf. Thomas S. Kuhn's famous study *The Structure of Scientific Revolutions*, 2nd ed.
(Chicago: University of Chicago Press, 1970).

17. In particular, Lamoureux points to Peter Enns, *Inspiration and Incarnation* (Grand Rapids: Baker Academic, 2005); Christopher M. Hays and Christopher B. Ansberry, eds., *Evangelical
Faith and the Challenge of Historical Criticism* (Grand Rapids: Baker Academic, 2013). He
apparently overlooks Enns's more recent and to-the-point *The Evolution of Adam: What the
Bible Does and Doesn't Say about Human Origins* (Grand Rapids: Brazos, 2012).

18. Cf. Reinhold Niebuhr's favorite quip, "The doctrine of original sin is the only empirically
verifiable doctrine of the Christian faith," in *Man's Nature and His Communities* (New York:
Charles Scribner's Sons, 1965), 24. Niebuhr had found this dictum in an issue of the *London
Times Literary Supplement*, but it figured already in G. K. Chesterton's *Orthodoxy* (New York:

can discuss their credentials from both a biblical and a scientific perspective; it is not immediately clear, however, in what way evolution might make a difference to their truthfulness. Thus, it seems to me that at least a number of important aspects of what has traditionally been understood by original sin can be retained within a worldpicture that is largely determined by standard accounts of evolutionary theory.

Next, assumptions (6) and (7) are highly debatable, but not so much because of evolutionary theory. The identification of sexual intercourse as the vessel through which original sin is passed on (6) cannot be found in the Bible. If Augustine was original and innovative anywhere with regard to the doctrine of original sin, it was here. To his credit, it might be argued that it is hard to avoid the impression that sexual intercourse plays a role in the transmission of our sinful inclinations since that is the way in which all our typically human character traits are passed on. Augustine's association of original sin with concupiscence (the lust that typically accompanies sexual intercourse), however, was in fact coincidental and presumably inspired by the negative attitude toward the body that he inherited from the Platonizing philosophical tradition in which he stood. In any case, it is very well possible to consider (6) as an add-on to the actual doctrine of original sin rather than a constitutive part of it. In Protestant expositions of original sin, (6) is usually downplayed (if addressed at all).

Let us, however, for the sake of argument assume that (6) is part and parcel of what the doctrine of original sin conveys. In that case it could be argued that, far from detracting from it, evolutionary theory actually *reinforces* (6). Evolutionary theory informs us about the background of our inborn aggressions, sexual drifts, and mechanisms of self-defense in the struggle for life that led to the emergence of the human species.[19] Thus, that we inherited from our ancestors the inclination toward types of behavior that the tradition considered sinful has become much more plausible in the light of evolutionary theory.[20] The critical question here is whether such types of behavior, and even the inclination toward them, should indeed be deemed sinful if we inherited them. How we answer this question, however, is again largely independent from the data of evolutionary theory. Rather, one's theory of moral accountability is decisive here. Can we be held accountable for our aggressive behavior? Most people would say we can. Can we be held accountable

Dodd, Mead, 1908; repr., Milwaukee: Cavalier, 2015), chap. 2: "Certain new theologians dispute original sin, which is the only part of Christian theology which can really be proved."

19. Cf. Keith Ward, *Religion and Human Nature* (Oxford: Oxford University Press, 1998), 163.

20. Cf. Daryl P. Domning, *Original Selfishness: Original Sin and Evil in the Light of Evolution* (Burlington, VT: Ashgate, 2006).

for our drifts, aggressions, and other inclinations toward self-assertion? Here opinions differ. It seems reasonable to think that mature humans can at least be held accountable for *giving in* to aggressions that harm others without good reason and for cherishing instead of constraining biological drifts that issue in harmful behavior. In line with important strands in the Bible (e.g., Rom. 7), the doctrine of original sin holds us accountable not only for our behavior but also for our underlying desires. However one may assess this, the arguments that play a role here seem independent from evolutionary theory.

The same is true when it comes to (7). The notion of original *guilt* that is captured by (7) is presumably the most widely contested part of original sin. Even those who want to retain the doctrine's other aspects usually reject original guilt.[21] The reason for this rejection is once again unrelated to evolutionary theory but is instead the sheer counterintuitiveness of being held responsible for the sin of someone else. Others (re)interpret original guilt in terms of us humans being guilty for the fact that our will is depraved so that we direct our desires to the wrong goals. Since this is arguably the case from the very inception of our lives, we can rightly be termed "born sinners."[22] The fact that in our infant (let alone fetal) life we haven't performed any actual sins is irrelevant here since it is this spiritual state of the will that makes us guilty—a state or disposition or *habitus* being "activity constantly renewed."[23] Indeed, if the concept of guilt can be seen as extending in this way not only to external actions but also to inward tendencies and states of will, maintaining a notion of original guilt is perhaps not entirely outrageous. But, once again, whether one endorses such a position or not is disconnected from one's take on evolutionary theory. Therefore, evolutionary theory does not impinge on (7).

It seems, then, that evolutionary theory only causes problems with regard to assumption (5). Although the exact number of individuals constituting the first human population (only around ten thousand?) and the exact time when they appeared (fifty thousand years ago?) can be debated, I believe Lamoureux is right to infer from the data of evolutionary science that humans emerged from prehuman ancestors in times immemorial as a group rather than as a couple. Especially after the recent (and ongoing) genomic discoveries, it seems

21. A recent example here is Oliver Crisp, "On Original Sin," *International Journal of Systematic Theology* 17 (2015): 252–66; Crisp defends a "moderate Reformed doctrine of original sin" that does not include the notion of original guilt.

22. Cf. Henri Blocher, *Original Sin: Illuminating the Riddle* (Grand Rapids: Eerdmans, 1999), 128–29. Blocher rejects any doctrine of "alien guilt transferred" as being unscriptural and argues that it is the "anti-God tendency" of our own will that makes us guilty from the very beginning of our lives.

23. Blocher, *Original Sin*, 128. These activities need not be actual ones but can also be volitional, or acts of the will.

no longer reasonable to avoid or scale down this conclusion.[24] This is simply what the book of nature at this moment shows us. Does that mean that Adam never existed? That depends. We might just as well argue that not just one but several thousand Adams existed. For why could the sinister act of bringing sin into the world not be performed by a group of humans rather than a single couple? Although we have no empirical access to what may have happened to this primal group of humans, it seems a logical necessity inferred from our current experience of sin that the first sin must have been committed at *some* point in the past.

It is important that we try to envisage how this might have come about since we cannot do without narratives. Karl Rahner, one of the greatest Roman Catholic theologians from the twentieth century, suggested that the first population of humans was a biological and historical unity, sharing the same biotope and also a common divine destination. Having received—either by divine intervention or (more plausibly perhaps) through "emergence" or in some other way—a (self)consciousness, the scope and depth of which was incredibly enlarged in comparison to that of the higher primates, for the first time in history beings had come about that were in conscious knowledge of what they did. At that stage, moral accountability entered the picture.

Given such a scenario, the classical notion of a "state of integrity" characterized by "original holiness" need not be dismissed out of hand but can be recontextualized as the state in which moral consciousness had emerged. When revealing himself to these first humans or to their leaders (and why not think of these as a couple?), God appealed to this newly arisen consciousness, calling the first humans to find their deepest fulfillment in a life of obedience to his perfect will. At that point the originating sin took place. As Keith Ward imagines:

> The first human beings had a responsible choice between their lustful, aggressive dispositions and the more altruistic, co-operative dispositions that would have led them to grow in the knowledge and love of God. . . . From a religious viewpoint, the deepest purpose of human existence is the free development of a relationship of joyful obedience to the will of God. . . . It is that purpose which was rejected when the fateful choice was made of a path of autonomy, of rational self-will, which placed the descendants of those first human beings in bondage to self and its consequent conflict and suffering.[25]

24. On the genetic evidence, see Alexander, *Creation or Evolution*, 67–111.
25. Keith Ward, *God, Faith and the New Millennium* (Oxford: Oneworld, 1998), 133. For a similar account, see James K. A. Smith, "What Stands on the Fall? A Philosophical Exploration," in *Evolution and the Fall*, ed. William T. Cavanaugh and James K. A. Smith (Grand Rapids: Eerdmans, 2017), 62. Smith rightly argues that the fall should be envisaged as a gradual process rather than a "split-second Fall as the result of a single decision" (63).

It seems reasonable to assume that *multiple* groups of cognitively modern "first human beings" were around more or less simultaneously. Therefore, we have to reflect on the ways in which sin may subsequently have spread throughout these groups.[26]

Note that Ward does not suggest that after the first human sin a "cosmic fall" took place that brought suffering and death in the world for the first time. Decay and death had been part of the natural world all along; the situation was aggravated, however, since humans now had to face death as well and also would threaten the well-being of the natural world because they had chosen the path of autonomy instead of humble recognition of the interconnectedness of all forms of life.

The theory of a cosmic fall is not to be found in any greater detail in the Bible. For example, in Romans 8:20–22—Lamoureux's prooftext—it is remarkable that the human fall into sin is not even mentioned as a critical factor. As a result, this text on "the whole creation [that] has been groaning in labor pains until now" is open to an evolutionary interpretation.[27] John Bimson has pointed out that the theory of a dramatic cosmic fall as a result of Adam's sin can only be traced back to the second century AD and not to the Bible.[28] Thus, when Lamoureux contends that according to Paul "decay, suffering, and death entered the world with Adam in Genesis 3" (37), he seems to be jumping to conclusions, ignoring important strands of contemporary scholarship on this issue. Even if Lamoureux were right, however, in suggesting that the theory of the cosmic fall is a biblical doctrine, this would make no difference for our assessment of the doctrine of original sin since both are logically independent from the other. The idea of a cosmic fall is not part of the nexus of assumptions that constitute the doctrine of original sin.

Conclusion and Afterthought

In this chapter I have scrutinized the problems raised for original sin by evolutionary theory and suggested that the two may be mutually compatible after

26. For more on the ways in which sin may subsequently have spread throughout the human population, see chap. 12 below by Benno van den Toren.

27. Cf. Christopher Southgate, *The Groaning of Creation: God, Evolution, and the Problem of Evil* (Louisville: Westminster John Knox, 2008), 92–96. One important argument in favor of a "fall-free" reading of this text is that the metaphor of giving birth is employed, a metaphor that suggests that the labor pains have been right there from the beginning of life.

28. John J. Bimson, "Doctrines of the Fall and Sin after Darwin," in *Theology after Darwin*, ed. Michael S. Northcott and R. J. Berry (Milton Keynes, UK: Paternoster, 2009), 120; cf. Bimson, "Cosmic Fall."

all. From the seven assumptions that constitute the doctrine of original sin, only one—the notion that (original) sin goes back to the transgression of a first human couple—cannot be sustained in the light of evolutionary theory. But even here there seems no need for panic since a hermeneutically sensitive reading of this assumption makes clear that it is open to recontextualization within an evolutionary narrative of human origins. We will leave it to later chapters in this volume to investigate more closely what type of solutions (if any) are available here.

Recontextualizing the doctrine of original sin in the way suggested above instead of rejecting it has two advantages. First, we need not sever the link between the doctrine and what happened in human history. It seems to me that this link is vital from a Christian theological point of view (as is clear from the cross and resurrection of Jesus Christ) and that therefore we should not follow Lamoureux in his Bultmann-like separation of theology from history, reducing, as it seems, the biblical account to timeless and ahistorical "life-changing messages of faith" (39) or "inerrant spiritual truths" (40). Second, if we can recontextualize the doctrine of original sin rather than replace it by a new paradigm that is incommensurable with it (47), we may avoid the battle over paradigm change and the concomitant theological crisis that Lamoureux foresees. Paradigm changes in the sciences usually take place only by virtue of the death of all adherents of the older paradigm, and paradigms in theology are usually even more resilient. But if what is needed is no more (or less) than a recontextualization of some parts of the doctrinal tradition within an evolutionary framework, it is much less costly for Christians to take contemporary evolutionary science with proper seriousness.

9

Augustine, Original Sin, and the Naked Ape

Andrew Pinsent

The Shame of the Naked Ape

Augustine of Hippo (354–430) is so closely associated with the doctrine of original sin that he is incorrectly thought by some to have invented it. His diagnosis of human nature is undeniably bleak, framed by the chaos of the accelerating disintegration of the Roman Empire. According to Augustine, most of humanity is a condemned mass (*massa damnata*), suffering from the miserable effects of sin in this life and facing eternal damnation after death. This condemnation is due not merely to particular sins but also to a stain called "original sin" inherited from the first man, Adam.[1] On this account, even infants who die without the grace of baptism will be condemned to hell, albeit the mildest form of hell.[2] Only by the unmerited grace of God, made possible through Jesus Christ, is there any hope of salvation.

---

1. Augustine, *The City of God* 21.12: "Hence, the whole mass of the human race is condemned. For he who first gave admission to sin has been punished together with all those who were in Him as in a root, so that no one may escape this just and deserved punishment unless redeemed by mercy and undeserved grace." Translation from Augustine, *The City of God against the Pagans*, trans. R. W. Dyson (New York: Cambridge University Press, 1998).

2. *Enchiridion* 93: "Surely, the lightest of all punishments will be laid on those who have added no further sin to that originally contracted." Translation from Augustine, *Confessions and Enchiridion*, trans. Albert Cook Outler, Library of Christian Classics 7 (London: SCM, 1955).

Augustine's thought was extremely influential on the medieval period and especially the attempts of the thirteenth century onward to clarify and unify all the teachings of Christianity in a systematic and complete manner.[3] On original sin, Thomas Aquinas collated and refined Augustine's arguments, especially in Aquinas's work *On Evil*, although he carefully reinterpreted Augustine's account of the fate of unbaptized innocents. Aquinas argued that they not only suffered no pain but also had no sense of unfulfilled desire and might even enjoy a natural happiness.[4]

As regards human life lived between birth and death in the current dispensation, the most important practical effects attributed to original sin by Augustine, as filtered through Aquinas, can be stated roughly as follows:[5]

1. We desire some things that are bad ("concupiscence"), even when we know that they are bad for us, others, our society, and our relationship with God. As two of many examples, the existence of vast enterprises of dieting (illustrating the ubiquity of gluttony) and pornography testify to concupiscence, and new virtual worlds online have quickly become filled with the detritus of disordered imagination and reason.[6] Moreover, concupiscence is apparent even in the very young, who often claim to love their parents but are also often willfully disobedient, even when obedience would be easy.

2. We are dissatisfied with the inadequacies and decay of our biological condition, and unlike nonhuman animals we reflect intellectually on disease, aging, and death. This reflection augments our sense of suffering,

3. It is much easier to study the later syntheses of the Augustinian tradition than Augustine himself because his views are scattered across a vast corpus and also because much of the pertinent material is not systematic but written in response to contemporaneous pastoral needs. As an example, in *On the Grace of Christ, and on Original Sin*, he points out that Pelagius and his follower Caelestius concede baptism for infants, in apparent agreement with Catholic practice, but this concession is deceptive since they actually believe that infants have no original sin to be remitted in baptism (1.35–36). On this and similar occasions, Augustine's concern is not so much to present a single, systematic thesis but to respond to subtle adversaries who were seeking to disguise their innovations and mislead the unwary. One point, however, is clear even from a cursory reading. The content, quantity, and sheer effort of such writing, involving complex and probably wearisome analyses, show that Augustine considered the doctrine of original sin to be absolutely essential to Christianity.

4. Thomas Aquinas, *De malo* 5.1–3. For a modern translation, see Thomas Aquinas, *On Evil*, ed. Brian Davies, trans. Richard Regan (New York: Oxford University Press, 2003).

5. In this list, I have adapted the traditional terms to modern situations. I have also used the first-person plural "we" because these problems are so widespread, even though they are not always suffered to the same degree by every person.

6. See, e.g., Jamie Bartlett, *The Dark Net: Inside the Digital Underworld* (Portsmouth, NH: William Heinemann, 2014).

motivates regret or mourning, and leads to various compensatory actions. Humans commonly wear some kind of makeup, for example, and
burial of our dead is one of the distinctive marks of our species in the
archaeological record.

3. We are restless and dissatisfied in mental and spiritual senses. We want
   happiness, but we do not know precisely what happiness means or where
   to find it. No matter what we do and what we find, we have a vague
   sense that our homeland is elsewhere and involves some transformation
   of our present state. Advertisers exploit this desire. Everyday products
   are frequently saturated with soft-focus versions of religious terms of
   transcendence, such as biscuits that offer the buyer "snacking nirvana,"
   yogurts with names like "bliss," and cheese called "heaven."

An awareness of these disordered desires and dissatisfactions has many
consequences, one of the most significant being our relations with other
people. Self-disclosure becomes uncomfortable, like holding up a mirror and
being ashamed at what we see. This shame at self-revelation is manifested in
a divided heart toward others and a desire to shield ourselves from others,
as a result of which,

4. We wear clothes. Almost all humans with a mature awareness of themselves, across an extraordinary diversity of cultures, wear clothes most
   of the time in company and even in private. This instinct is so strong
   that we even clothe the dead in their coffins. In most situations, naked-
   ness is disgraceful, a word that resonates with theological overtones
   since it suggests an inchoate awareness that the so-called naked ape is
   disgraced or "stripped of grace." Clothing has a vast range of useful,
   good, and even holy functions, from the astronaut's suit to the sacred
   vestments of Aaron in the Old Testament (Exod. 28). Nevertheless, the
   most basic desire to clothe ourselves is consistent with the fact that we
   need something put over us, something that is not part of our nature
   itself and yet that our nature needs for its honor.[7]

5. We have disordered sexual desires. This is not the same as having sexual
   desires per se and does not mean that the disorder consists merely of a
   desire for someone in an inappropriate way. The deeper problem seems
   to be a conflict between the desire for intimacy and a sense of shame, a
   conflict that is accentuated in intimate relations and especially sexual

7. Additional symptoms might include the disposition to present oneself in a misleadingly
optimistic and positive light on social media.

relations. Contrary to popular belief, this dissonance existed and was recorded long before Christianity. For example, the lists of philosophical problems in the Aristotelian corpus include the question of why those who desire to submit to intercourse feel great shame about confessing it and why the young, when they first begin to have intercourse, feel loathing afterward for their partners.[8] Christianity has taught that just as humans need clothes, sexual union needs the gift of grace that is called sacramental marriage.[9]

Commentators on the human condition may disagree about this or that item in the list above. Nevertheless, all known cultures, histories, and records testify to human disorders and dissatisfactions. For example, the second-oldest extant work of ancient Greece, *The Odyssey*, is a story of one man's exile from his true homeland and his long struggle to return. It is plausible that this story resonates with us, just as it did with the ancient Greeks, because we also have a sense of exile from our proper home, consistent with the notion that we are not what we should be.

G. K. Chesterton helpfully sums up the widespread perception of these problems: "The ancient masters of religion . . . began with the fact of sin—a fact as practical as potatoes. Whether or no man could be washed in miraculous waters, there was no doubt at any rate that he wanted washing. But certain religious leaders . . . have begun in our day not to deny the highly disputable water, but to deny the indisputable dirt. Certain new theologians dispute original sin, which is the only part of Christian theology which can really be proved."[10] When Chesterton claims in this passage that original sin is the "only part of Christian theology which can really be proved," he means that the disorder that is, properly speaking, the effect or symptom of original sin can be perceived without special revelation.

Corroboration comes from some unlikely sources. Many of the most effective rivals of Christianity do not deny that humans suffer from some kind of moral distortion and alienation. For example, Karl Marx argued, "This

8. Aristotle, *Problems* 4.10.27. For an English translation, see *The Complete Works of Aristotle*, ed. Jonathan Barnes (Princeton: Princeton University Press, 1984), 2:1353, 1356. Note that the debate over whether Aristotle was the actual author of this work is irrelevant to the main point—namely, that these problems were recognized long before Christianity.

9. Christianity has always taught that marriage is the only moral context for intercourse. In a sacramental marriage, the grace of God, charity, and the security of a mutual commitment till death help overcome the disorder of a tension between desire and shame, making the union of husband and wife holy and supernaturally fruitful.

10. G. K. Chesterton, *Orthodoxy* (New York: Dodd, Mead, 1908; repr., Milwaukee: Cavalier, 2015), 16.

primitive accumulation [of wealth] plays in Political Economy about the same part as original sin in theology."[11] In other words, in seeking to supplant Christianity, Marxism does not abolish the Christian account of original sin, which is plausible precisely because it acknowledges an alienation that is almost universally recognized. Instead, Marxism transmutes this account into a materialistic alternative with some of the same features. It is also plausible that at least some of the impact of the modern environmental movement derives from a similar sense that humans are flawed, have damaged the earth as a result, and need to repent and make sacrifices to atone for their guilt. All these reflections can be summed in one sentence: *we are not what we should be.*

The Underlying Problem

If we are not what we should be, what is our defect and where does it come from? Are we conceived damaged and vicious, with a bent toward evil? Are we like the destructive little monsters called "gremlins" in the film of the same name produced by Steven Spielberg?[12]

The Augustinian tradition filtered through Aquinas is far more subtle than this representation. A hint of this subtlety can be seen in Aquinas's treatment of the fate of the unbaptized innocents, noted previously, who die with original sin alone. This state of "pure nature" is a state without sin and without any actual disposition to sin. On this account, these innocents are *not* gremlins, even though those who survive infancy in this world will usually and quickly start to show some gremlin-like behavior. According to Aquinas, if they do not survive infancy and die in this state of innocence, without any actual sin, they suffer no pain or any sense of loss in eternity.[13]

But the difficult question remains: What is this state of pure nature like, and in what way is it defective compared to the state of grace? One way to approach this question is to compare the characteristic ways in which exemplary humans related to God before and after the coming of Jesus Christ. Prior to any special gifts of Christian revelation, Aristotle and other pre-Christian Greek philosophers referred to God and even offered proofs for the existence of God. Nevertheless, Aristotle argued that humans cannot be friends with gods, for human and divine beings are disproportionately different.[14] Even though

11. See, e.g., Karl Marx, "The Secret of Primitive Accumulation," chap. 26 in *Capital*, vol. 1, *Economic Manuscripts*, trans. Samuel Moore and Edward Aveling, first published in German in 1867, https://www.marxists.org/archive/marx/works/1867-c1/ch26.htm.

12. Joe Dante, *Gremlins* (Burbank, CA: Warner Brothers, 1984), DVD.

13. Thomas Aquinas, *De malo* 5.

14. Aristotle, *Nicomachean Ethics* 10.8.1159a3–9.

Aristotle referred to God (in the singular) as perfect, living, and eternal, he never addressed God as "you." By contrast, several centuries later, Augustine addressed God as follows:

> Late have I loved you, O Beauty so ancient and so new; late have I loved you! For behold you were within me, and I outside; and I sought you outside and in my ugliness fell upon those lovely things that you have made. You were with me and I was not with you. I was kept from you by those things, yet had they not been in you, they would not have been at all. You called and cried to me and broke open my deafness: and you sent forth your beams and shone upon me and chased away my blindness: you breathed fragrance upon me, and I drew in my breath and do now pant for you: I tasted you, and now hunger and thirst for you: you touched me, and I have burned for your peace.[15]

The interplay of "I" and "you" in this text is in stark contrast to the work of the pre-Christian Greek philosophers. Whatever else is meant by the state of grace, there is at least one profound change in grammar. The state of nature is one in which God is generally described in remote, third-person terms. The state of grace is one in which God is described both in third-person terms and in surprisingly intimate and even passionate second-person terms.

As I have argued in detail elsewhere, the key to understanding what is missing in the absence of grace is precisely the ability to relate to God as "I" to "you."[16] Recent scientific studies have given a name to this condition in the case of human relationships. A comparative inability to relate to other human persons as "I" to "you" is a range of conditions to which modern psychology has applied the name *autistic spectrum disorder* (ASD). Those with autism do not seem to have any difficulty in recognizing persons as distinct kinds of beings in the world, but they have a varying and comparative inability to align psychologically with other persons, relating to them as "I" to "you." For this reason, those with ASD are sometimes described as not seeing persons, and they often have a special difficulty with learning the correct use of second-person grammatical forms.

Just as blindness has sometimes been used as a metaphor for a certain kind of spiritual state without implying that physical blindness is spiritually

---

15. Augustine, *Confessions* 10.27.38. The text cited here is the one used in the contemporary liturgy of the hours of the Catholic Church, *The Divine Office: The Liturgy of the Hours according to the Roman Rite* (London: Collins, 1974), 225; the translation is a modified version of Augustine, *Confessions of St. Augustine, Books I–X*, trans. Francis J. Sheed (New York: Sheed & Ward, 1942).

16. For a full account of the argument, see Andrew Pinsent, *The Second-Person Perspective in Aquinas's Ethics: Virtues and Gifts* (New York: Routledge, 2012).

defective, so also ASD can be used as a metaphor for the human condition—or, more specifically, for the state of pure nature in the absence of grace. One might describe all of us who are born without grace as being born into a state without second-person relatedness to God. In this condition, one can know or discover that there is God, but one cannot relate to God as "I" to "you" in a manner that expresses a union of the soul with God in the style of Augustine's famous prayer. This claim is consonant with the peculiarity of the first question that God asks of the man and woman after the account of the fall in Genesis: "Where are you?" (Gen. 3:9). God cannot lose anything in space, but if we lack the grace to respond to God, then there is a sense in which God can lose us—insofar as there is no longer any "I" capable of relating to God as "you."

This raises the question of whether the lack of second-person relatedness implies that human nature is defective. The answer is both no and yes. On the one hand, the answer is no since God and humans are disproportionately different and since God is uncreated, whereas humans are created. There is nothing in human nature, or any created nature, to suggest that a relationship to God as "I" to "you" culminating in friendship would be possible without a special divine action—namely, grace—to enable us to participate in God's life as children of God. This participation is precisely what is indicated in Scripture by the special use of the word $z\bar{o}\bar{e}$ (as, e.g., in John 3:15; 5:40) for the divinely communicated divine life of grace made possible through Jesus Christ. Since this life of grace is a free gift, added to created human nature and not part of that nature, the absence of grace cannot be regarded as a defect of nature.

On the other hand, human nature is defective insofar as revelation implies that humans were created for this gift of grace, were meant to have this gift, and were never meant to be without this gift. Parents often find autism in their children an especially challenging condition precisely because the children are not responsive to them. From a parent's perspective, the state is certainly defective even if the child is otherwise quiet and well behaved. If we are nearly all born into a state of spiritual autism to God because we lack a gift for which we were created, then that state is certainly "defective" from God's perspective. As in the case of a parent faced with an unresponsive child, it is plausible that God will do anything that can possibly be done without overriding our free will in order to bring us out of this state.[17]

This state is defective in a secondary sense as well—namely, its instability. If our remarkable minds and hearts were created to know and to love God

17. For an influential and insightful account of a parent faced with this situation, see Clara Claiborne Park, *The Siege: The First Eight Years of an Autistic Child; With an Epilogue, Fifteen Years Later* (Boston: Little, Brown, 1982).

and all other things in union with God, then the lack of a gift for relating to God as "I" to "you" will leave its mark in terms of a tendency to seek substitutes, including substitutes that are hostile to God. Hence "sin" is sometimes described in Scripture not just as a name denoting evil deeds but also as something like a personal agent.[18] On this account, it is not so much that a person begins with a disposition to sin but that a person begins with a disposition to acquire a disposition to sin and will in practice quickly fall into actual sin by choosing flawed substitutes for God. Thomas Aquinas compares this situation to that of a barrel of wine without its hoops. All the wood is present and complete, but what keeps the barrel together and enables it to fulfill its true function is missing. Under these circumstances, the barrel will tend to burst, just as human nature without grace is in a state of unstable equilibrium and will tend quickly to fall into disorder.[19] Each generation that is born with a human nature deprived of that gift of grace will face this problem.

Spurious Tensions with Science

Disordered desires and dissatisfactions may testify to a problem with humans, and divine revelation may testify to a disruption of human relations with God. Given the limitation of scientific methods to empirical measurement rather than moral judgment, however, it is hard to see how science has much to say about these matters. But Augustine's doctrine of original sin not only is about the present state of humans but also includes an explanation of the origin of this problem. If there is a tension between faith and science on this matter, it is surely in regard to this explanation.

According to Genesis 3, the first woman, Eve, ate the fruit of the tree forbidden by God and gave some of the fruit to her husband to eat, who accepted the offer. They both then hid from God and were expelled from the garden of Eden. A story from ancient Greece has some similar elements. Hesiod's Works and Days (ca. 700 BC) describes how Zeus created Pandora (the "all gifted"), a beautiful but risky helpmate for man, who opened a dangerous jar and released all the evils of the world.

Whatever the details, the Christian tradition, as well as its various parallel accounts, describes the fall of humanity in terms of a particular event—specifically,

18. Susan Eastman, "The Shadow Side of Second-Person Engagement: Sin in Paul's Letter to the Romans," European Journal for Philosophy of Religion 5, no. 4 (2013): 125–44.

19. On the basis of this approach, Thomas Aquinas diverges from the way that original sin is often conceived—that is, in terms of a damaged or even changed human nature. See, e.g., Peter King, "Damaged Goods: Human Nature and Original Sin," Faith and Philosophy 24, no. 3 (July 2007): 247–67. The image of a barrel of wine without hoops comes from Thomas Aquinas, On Evil 4.2 and 7.

the consequence of a single, freely chosen action. This claim immediately raises a question: On the basis of the slow evolution of life on earth and the long prehistory of humans, what evidence is there for a singular event producing the problems that we experience today? There is certainly no direct evidence of a prefallen state in which humans were morally and physically perfect. Throughout much of the vast sweep of archaeological time for which we have any kind of record, evidence of human flaws is lamentably easy to find. For example, a prehistoric skull from about 430,000 years ago shows puncture wounds that suggest murder.[20]

Before tackling this challenge directly from the standpoint of the Augustinian tradition, it is worth dismissing briefly a few spurious points of tension. Augustine made extensive use of Genesis in his account of original sin, but he also had no problem in recognizing that Genesis uses symbolic language. He pointed out, for example, that the days of creation in Genesis cannot be read in a literalistic fashion since the sun and moon are created on the fourth day. He also warned fellow Christians of the need for caution in interpreting Genesis, lest the pagans ridicule the faith.[21] Developing a line of thought that dates back at least to the second century, Augustine describes creation in terms of an unfolding from seminal forms, a process denoted by the Latin word *evolvere*, from which we derive the word "evolution." Augustine also recognized the relativity of time to creation.[22] These insights, foreshadowing both evolution and relativity, are remarkable achievements for a man living at the beginning of the fifth century. In modern terms, we might describe Augustine's treatment of Genesis as a *revealed symbolic history*. Hence disputes about the age of the earth or the modes of secondary causation by which God brought about the life that now exists on earth do not have a direct bearing on the core principles of an Augustinian reading of human origins or of original sin.

The key issue is this: Augustine clearly thought of the fall as an *event*, even if expressed using symbolic language. For Augustine, it was a primeval disaster at the beginning of the human race, the effects of which have henceforth been propagated by physical descent to every human alive. Moreover, this Augustinian interpretation is not simply the opinion of one theologian, no matter how eminent, but remains the official teaching of the Catholic Church

20. Nohemi Sala et al., "Lethal Interpersonal Violence in the Middle Pleistocene," *PLOS ONE* 10, no. 5 (May 2015): e0126589, doi:10.1371/journal.pone.0126589.

21. Augustine, *The Literal Meaning of Genesis (De Genesi ad Litteram)* 1.19.

22. On time as part of creation, see Augustine, *Confessions* 11.13; on the gradual unfolding of creation from potentials or seed-like forms created by God, there are various passages in *Literal Meaning of Genesis*, such as 5.20.41 and 5.23.44–46.

today, a teaching that is also held in common by many Protestant communities. This teaching most recently was articulated formally in the *Catechism of the Catholic Church*, promulgated by Pope John Paul II in 1991: "The account of the fall in Genesis 3 uses figurative language, but affirms a primeval event, a deed that took place at the beginning of the history of man. Revelation gives us the certainty of faith that the whole of human history is marked by the original fault freely committed by our first parents."[23] Original sin is therefore the name given not simply to current human flaws but to the event that gave rise to these flaws at "the beginning of the history of man," expressed in Genesis 3 using figurative language. Moreover, "our first parents" refers to common ancestors of all those alive today. For this reason, the Catholic Church has tended to oppose the theory of polygenism, which posits multiple origins of humans, principally because of the difficulty of reconciling this theory with common human descent.[24]

The question might be raised about whether the doctrine of original sin requires the need for a singular fall by persons from whom all humans are descended. Many people who self-identify as Christian have denied the physical transmission of original sin, including the Pelagians against whom Augustine contended in his own lifetime. Early Protestants often took a harsher view of human nature than Augustine did, yet today many deny the importance of physical descent. Why, then, did Augustine and his tradition regard physical descent as central to the doctrine?

A full examination of these arguments is beyond the scope of this chapter, the focus of which is on the Augustinian interpretation in the light of contemporary science.[25] In outline, however, defenders of physical descent cite especially Romans 5:12, where Adam is described as transmitting death with sin. But in addition, physical descent is coherent with a whole package of interrelated ideas and practices, including the universality of human corruption across different cultures, a parallel emphasis on physical descent in salvation history (notably the chosen people of the Old Testament), and the importance placed on baptism, including of infants, from an early stage in the history of the church.

23. *Catechism of the Catholic Church: Revised in Accordance with the Official Latin Text Promulgated by Pope John Paul II*, 2nd ed. (Vatican: Libreria Editrice Vaticana, 2000), n390.

24. Pope Pius XII, "Humani Generis: Concerning Some False Opinions Threatening to Undermine the Foundations of Catholic Doctrine (Encyclical)," *Libreria Editrice Vaticana*, August 12, 1950, §37, http://w2.vatican.va/content/pius-xii/en/encyclicals/documents/hf_p-xii _enc_12081950_humani-generis.html.

25. A survey of the arguments for the Augustinian account can be found in Stéphane Harent, "Original Sin," *Catholic Encyclopedia* (New York: Appleton, 1911), http://www.newadvent .org/cathen/11312a.htm.

Science and the Augustinian Tradition Today

We turn finally to how the Augustinian interpretation compares to the fragmentary accounts of human origins that are slowly being pieced together by contemporary science. As noted previously, the issue is not the long time-scale of prehistory or the need to interpret Genesis as a revealed symbolic history. The crucial issue is how to make sense of a singular fall, the effects of which have been propagated by direct descent to all humans since. Given that a prefallen state, if such a state ever existed, could have been extremely brief, direct knowledge of such a state is extremely unlikely even in principle, and scientific findings have no bearing on this issue. Nevertheless, there are three issues, I think, on which the Augustinian claims need to be evaluated by human reason and science in the light of what is gradually emerging from the study of human nature and its origins.

The first issue is what, precisely, is propagated. Is original sin the moral equivalent of a genetic disease, a poisonous defect passed down through all human generations? According to the Augustinian tradition interpreted above, original sin is not really any positive thing at all. Original sin consists principally in the absence of a supernatural gift of grace, a sharing in God's divine life by which humans were meant to be born in communion with God, capable of second-person relatedness and friendship with God. In the example of the barrel of wine, the absence of the hoops around the barrel does not mean that there is anything deficient about the wood of the barrel. Similarly, the absence of divine gifts does not mean that human nature itself is damaged, except perhaps indirectly insofar as nature is thereby susceptible to moral instability and all the vagaries of biological life (including, indeed, ordinary genetic damage). What has been propagated to us by our remote ancestors is no more and no less than human nature. Since there is nothing that is naturally missing or supernaturally added to fallen human nature, the propagation of original sin is only manifested by its moral effects. Hence the methods of science cannot be used to ascertain the propagation of original sin, though they cannot be used to deny this propagation either.

The second issue is whether propagation could have started, even in principle, as a result of a single action by remote human ancestors, our "first parents." For this process to be possible, the key question seems to be this: Can everyone on earth today call at least one man "Father" and at least one woman "Mother"? Are we all ultimately one family? At the time of writing, the surprising answer is yes, many times over. The relative genetic homogeneity of contemporary humans, together with other findings, suggests that modern humans are descended from a relatively small group of ancestors. Moreover, subject to all the reservations typical of complex and subtle empirical measurements, a worldwide analysis of mitochondrial DNA has indicated that mitochondrial lineages all coalesced in a matrilinear common ancestor, a "mitochondrial Eve" from Africa between 140,000 and 290,000 years ago. There is an analogous patrilinear "Y-chromosomal Adam" from between 200,000 and 300,000 years ago.[26] These findings are subject to very wide uncertainties, and it would be a mistake to infer from genetics that Y-chromosomal Adam was contemporaneous with mitochondrial Eve or that there were not other genetic "Adams" and "Eves" in human prehistory. It would also be a mistake to conclude from genetics that the various Y-chromosomal Adams or mitochondrial Eves completely lacked other company during their lives. Nevertheless, the notion of the universal propagation of some condition from singular ancestors, a state that is really the absence of a divine gift, is not excluded by our present understanding of science, even if science cannot determine anything about such a condition.

The third issue is that of gradualism—and particularly the apparent dissonance between a singular event and what normally takes place in a biological world shaped by evolution. Evolution, as it is commonly considered, tends to be thought of as a gradual process; and for certain kinds of changes, such as skin color, a continuum often exists even in contemporaneous populations. This raises the question: If all the capacities of contemporary humans emerged slowly and gradually, how can this narrative be reconciled with any interpretation of the story of the fall from grace due to a singular action by humans who enjoyed the gift of grace as part of their creation by God as a singular act?

There is no easy answer, but it should be recalled that smooth continuity is not necessarily the whole story of natural processes, even without special divine intervention. For example, relatively simple physical systems can exhibit discontinuous and qualitative changes, switching dramatically from one state into another with a small change of input conditions. Examples include water turning from a liquid state to a gas with a small increase in temperature and carbon turning into diamond under high pressures and temperatures. Evolutionary records also witness (albeit at a crude resolution) to quite sudden

---

26. Rebecca L. Cann, Mark Stoneking, and Allan C. Wilson, "Mitochondrial DNA and Human Evolution," *Nature* 325 (1987): 31–36, doi:10.1038/3225031a0. The estimated dates for "Y-chromosomal Adam" have been subject to widely divergent revisions, but a recent study estimates 254,000 (95% confidence interval 192,000–307,000) years ago; cf. Monika Karmin et al., "A Recent Bottleneck of Y Chromosome Diversity Coincides with a Global Change in Culture," *Genome Research* 25, no. 4 (April 2015): 459–66, doi:10.1101/gr.186684.114.

appearances and disappearances of species.[27] Moreover, without denying a rich diversity of precursors in nonhuman animals, a great deal of what is distinct about human capacities is hard to express in terms of degree, even if the cultural expression of these capacities only emerged slowly. Given that even many simple mechanical and biological systems exhibit discontinuities in response to small changes, it does not seem necessary to deny an all-at-once appearance of certain human abilities, even on naturalistic grounds.

Given an all-at-once appearance of human capacities for abstract thought and moral decisions, the speculative reconstruction of the course of events can be taken a little further. Like seeding a cloud to produce rain, once such capacities are catalyzed or triggered, the effects of this transformation could and probably would spread quickly, not least because of the immense advantages they would convey. Starting with very small numbers, those with these new capacities would outstrip other populations, giving rise to the relative genetic uniformity that is seen today.

What is needed to complete the basic outline of the Augustinian account is simply the following: Humans, when they awoke to the capacity for abstract thought and moral decisions (however this happened), received also the gift of grace and various other divine gifts to know and to love God, as stewards of creation. Yet they freely chose to reject the love of God and so lost these gifts, their nature being stripped bare of grace. Their descendants, who inherit human nature without these gifts, suffer the effects, most evidently in a bent toward what is broadly acknowledged as evil. Whether or not one chooses to accept this account on moral, philosophical, or theological grounds, what can at least be said is that we are not compelled to reject it on scientific grounds.[28]

27. Stephen Jay Gould and Niles Eldredge, "Punctuated Equilibria: An Alternative to Phyletic Gradualism," in *Models in Paleobiology*, ed. Thomas J. M. Schopf (San Francisco: Freeman Cooper, 1972), 82–115.

28. I am grateful to the reviewers of the first draft of this chapter. This publication was made possible through the support of a grant from the John Templeton Foundation. The opinions expressed in this publication are those of the author and do not necessarily reflect the views of the Foundation.

10

Adam as Federal Head of Humankind

C. John Collins

In this brief essay I cannot say everything I deem worth saying on the subject of human origins, or of Genesis, or of theology, or of anything else. Instead, I aim to show why I think that a federal understanding of how sin came into the world makes good sense of the Bible and also rings true to our own experience. There may at times be tensions between this and certain kinds of scientific theories about the human story, no doubt; but these tensions can stimulate creativity—if we let them!

When it comes to the story of how humankind came about, geneticists tell us that the evidence points decisively to some kind of "ancestry" for humans—that is, we are descended from animals that are now extinct, and if you go back far enough (five–six million years), we have ancestors in common with the chimpanzees (who are considered to be our nearest kin).

Since the mid-1990s, a further twist has been added: by current genetic thinking, the initial human population numbered in the thousands—an estimate of ten thousand is quite common nowadays. Now, I have no way of assessing whether the "current genetic thinking" has made mistakes; no one can tell how long the current trend of thinking will last and what in it will be revised.

I know biologists who think very carefully about these matters, and they tell me that the evidence for common ancestry is secure, while the estimates for the initial human population may well change (but probably won't go down to two). My task is not to speculate on those matters but is the humbler one of assessing whether this is absolutely incompatible with "mere Christianity."

My own theological convictions are "traditionally Reformed," but I am here to be broadly "traditionally Christian." So I'll begin with an observation from C. S. Lewis (famous for popularizing "mere Christianity"): "Christianity, going on from [the Hebrew Bible], makes world history in its entirety a single, transcendentally significant, story with a well-defined plot pivoted on Creation, Fall, Redemption, and Judgement."[1] I'll save for another venue the demonstration that this is a fair summary of such early Christian thinkers as Irenaeus (late second century) and Athanasius (early fourth century). We can see that this narrative underlies the Nicene Creed, if we allow that the fall is included in the phrase "for our salvation" (otherwise what do we need saving from?). I also think that this accurately expounds what we have in the Bible, but I will have to save that discussion for elsewhere as well. At least I can mention, however, that several New Testament passages seem to allude to early creeds (such as 1 Cor. 15:3–8; 1 Tim. 3:16), and this overall narrative makes sense of them.[2] Christians certainly affirm that Jesus died for sins and rose from the dead as actual events, but these events are not alone—they are epoch-making steps in the larger story (as Paul has it in Rom. 1:1–6).

We can take agreement on this basic story, or a telling that does the same job, as a criterion for common Christianity. What supports that story is in; what counteracts that story is out. Further, this way of describing things enables us to see whether scientific theories really are at odds with the faith by asking whether they would have us change the story.

But there's another advantage to this story orientation: in the past several decades students of worldview have come increasingly to appreciate that a community inculcates its worldview into its members by means of its Big Story, which answers the key questions:

- Where did we come from?
- What has gone wrong?

1. C. S. Lewis, *The Discarded Image: An Introduction to Medieval and Renaissance Literature* (Cambridge: Cambridge University Press, 1964), 174.
2. See further Philip Schaff and David Schaff, *The Creeds of Christendom* (New York: Harper & Row, 1931), 2:3–8.

- What has been done about it (by gods, nature, humanity, or some combination)?
- Where are we now in the whole process?
- Where is the whole thing headed?

This story helps the members take their places in the world and calls them to indwell the story and to participate in its outworking. The biblical story, as Christians have traditionally understood it, is therefore a Big Story; and it is not simply a local one, dealing with a limited group of people, but it tells the Big Story of the whole world.

Now we can focus on whether any view of the origin of humankind—and particularly of our sin—holds a critical place in the Big Story.

Which Texts, and How Should We Read Them?

If I am to call this Big Story that Christians have told the biblical story, I should show how particular Bible passages support that telling. There are at least two aspects of this: what a Bible passage actually says and what it either takes for granted or implies (such as what I have called the Big Story).

We also face issues of "hermeneutics"—that is to say, how we know that we have a good reading of a biblical text. The simplest answer is that we have to use our best judgment, which means that we have to think clearly and openly acknowledge our own preferences and predispositions, even being willing to criticize them. It also means we have to learn how best to read the ancient writings in the way that their ancient audiences would have read them—after all, Moses and Paul have been dead for a long time, and neither of them wrote in English. One aspect of the biblical way of telling stories is that they rely more on showing than on telling—that is, they often don't give an explicit evaluation of someone's action but expect the reader to figure it out.

Further, there is the question of how the traditional triad of *reason, authority*, and *experience* (or the Wesleyan version, Scripture, tradition, reason, and experience) relate to one another and even what things fit into those categories. All Christians *say* they give primacy to the Bible, but they don't always agree on what that looks like. We'll do a reasonable job so long as we aim to keep the Bible supreme and own up to the simple fact that our interpretation of it comes from a complex interaction of all these factors.

Finally, to say what it is we look for in reading the Bible, I'll take the moderate approach of Lesslie Newbigin as a place to start: "I believe and trust that the Bible is the true rendering of the story of God's acts in creation and redemption and therefore the true rendering of the character of God."[3] So we consider the writers to be divinely authorized tellers and interpreters of the story. That means we really care less about what they knew or felt and more about what story they told. It also means that we allow them the same freedoms we do other storytellers, such as selectivity (they don't have to say everything), idealization, humorous characterizations, even some combining of several events into one, and some hyperbole, if need be—and we don't count that as telling an untruth. We must learn to cooperate with all these and other techniques so that we can indwell the story.

The standard biblical texts dealing with Adam and Eve and their place in Christian theology are usually taken to be Genesis 1–11 and Romans 5:12–21 (cf. also 1 Cor. 15:20–28, 42–49). I will add a couple more: an incident in the Gospels showing how Jesus thought about the subject, and the picture that Revelation gives us of the consummation.[4]

Genesis 1–11

Most peoples, ancient and modern alike, have a story of where the world came from, in order to explain why things today are the way that they are. The book of Genesis was intended for ancient Israel; Jews have traditionally understood it to come from Moses, to have been addressed to the people of Israel as they prepared to take the promised land. Many people think that the book received its final form a bit later—say in the time of David and Solomon[5]—but that won't change what we do with the book here.

I agree with those who take the purpose of Genesis to be, first, to oppose the origin stories of other ancient peoples by telling of one true God who made heaven and earth and who dignified humankind with a special nobility, the task of ruling the world wisely and well. Further, the book identifies the people of Israel, who followed Moses out of Egypt, as the heirs of God's promises to Abraham. We find in Genesis 12 that God called Abraham so that his family would be the vehicle of God's "blessing" to "all the families of

---

3. Lesslie Newbigin, *Proper Confidence: Faith, Doubt, and Certainty in Christian Discipleship* (Grand Rapids: Eerdmans, 1995), 98–99.

4. There are other texts, in the Old Testament, New Testament, and Deuterocanonicals, which I have discussed at more length elsewhere. See C. John Collins, *Did Adam and Eve Really Exist? Who They Were and Why You Should Care* (Wheaton: Crossway, 2011).

5. For a fair treatment, see Gordon Wenham, *Story as Torah: Reading Old Testament Narrative Ethically* (Grand Rapids: Baker Academic, 2000), 41–42: "The Mosaic era certainly accounts for many of the key features in Genesis." While "critical orthodoxy" prefers a date in the fifth-century postexilic era, Wenham shows some of the problems with that view: "None of these observations are problems for a date in the united monarchy period."

the earth"—and since Genesis 10 recounts the various "families" or "clans" of the earth, this means "to all non-Israelite peoples everywhere." So the purpose of Genesis 1–11 is to set the stage for Genesis 12–50; it does this by clarifying that the God who has called Abraham is in fact the one true God, for whom all humankind yearns.

In Genesis 1:28, God "blessed" humans and encouraged them to "be fruitful and multiply." This gets repeated for Noah (Gen. 9:1) and then for Abram and his sons (see Gen. 22:17–18; 26:3–4; 28:3; 48:3–4). Thus scholars often see Noah and Abram as new starts on humankind, taking the "disobedience" of Genesis 3 to mark a disastrous disruption of humankind's relationship to God, to one another, and to the world. Hence the purpose of the fresh start in Abram is stated clearly: that in Abram (Gen. 12:3; or "by [Abram's] offspring" in 22:18) "all the families of the earth shall be blessed." It comes as no surprise, then, to find an interest in the origin of the whole show; we might suspect that the stories in Genesis are told specifically to establish the continuity between the Israelite audience and their ancestors in these stories, and there might even be anachronisms (describing the older times in terms of what the writer and his audience are familiar with) with this end in view.[6]

But this leads us to important questions about Genesis 1–11—namely, whether we are to call it "historical" and whether we are to read it "literally." Two types of readers insist that, if Genesis is historical, we must read it literally—by which they mean that we must treat it as if it were an effort at "scientific" description. First, we have the young-earth creationists: they are sure that we are to call all of Genesis "history" and that therefore we must read it as "straight" description.[7] Second, we have those who think that Genesis intends to be an ancient scientific description but that we ought not believe it has any bearing on history.[8]

Neither of these approaches does justice to the kind of literature we have in Genesis—a kind that has been recognized by Jewish and Christian believers from the earliest stages. A simple statement about Genesis comes from Oxford scholar John Colet (1467–1519): "Moses arranged his details

6. N. T. Wright, for example, is correct to see a parallel between the calling of Israel and the calling of Adam, although he does not see the device of anachronism as the explanation. See his *Surprised by Scripture: Engaging Contemporary Issues* (New York: HarperCollins, 2014), 26–40.

7. See, e.g., Douglas Kelly, *Creation and Change: Genesis 1.1–2.4 in the Light of Changing Scientific Paradigms* (Ross-shire, UK: Christian Focus, 1997), 41–42, 51: "The text of Genesis is clearly meant to be taken in a literal, historical sense."

8. See, e.g., Denis Lamoureux, *Evolutionary Creation: A Christian Approach to Evolution* (Eugene, OR: Wipf & Stock, 2008), 150: "Therefore, since the heavens are not structured in this way [i.e., according to a literalistic reading of Gen. 1], Gen 1 cannot be a historical account of the actual events that created the heavens."

in such a way as to give the people a clearer notion, and he does this *after the manner of a popular poet*, in order that he may the more adapt himself to the spirit of simple rusticity."[9] That is, we should recognize that we do not have even an attempt at a scientific account, and we must allow for things such as pictorial description, anachronism, and symbolism. Indeed, I mentioned that one goal of the storytelling in Genesis is to provide an alternative story to that told in other cultures of the ancient Near East (especially in Mesopotamia).[10] The Mesopotamian stories include divine action, symbolism, and imaginative elements, and the purpose of the stories is to lay the foundation for a worldview without being taken in a literalistic fashion. At the same time, these stories refer to what their tellers took to be actual events. Thus Genesis aims to tell the story of beginnings the right way to counter the other stories; it offers the divinely authorized way for us to picture the events (which, as I discuss below, leaves us some leeway in scientific theorizing).

However, many who study Genesis doubt that it has any historical referentiality at all, and one of the arguments that lead to such doubt is the notion that the editors of Genesis 1–11 put it together out of bits that have separate origins and inconsistent ideas. Nevertheless, the overall flow of Genesis 1–11 matches that of important Mesopotamian stories covering similar events, so it makes sense to read the whole eleven chapters together. I will not take space here to show the linguistic and literary unifying features of Genesis 1–11 as we now have it,[11] but once we recognize how Genesis 1–11 is integrated into the flow of the book of Genesis and how these chapters parallel basic worldview-shaping materials from Mesopotamia, it presents no surprise to find that whoever put these chapters together did so in such a way that they display their unity at the literary and linguistic level.

9. From his 1497 letter to Radulphus; text in Frederic Seebohm, *The Oxford Reformers* (London: Longmans, Green, 1869), 51 (emphasis original). Colet was in a long line of scholars who made this kind of observation: Aristobulus (Jewish philosopher, mid-second century BC) tells us that Moses wrote with words that relate to "outward appearances" (Fragment 2, §3); Eusebius (church father, early fourth century AD) insists that the account in Genesis is popular, not philosophical (*Preparation for the Gospel* 11.7 [522d]); similarly Augustine, *On Genesis by the Letter* 2.6.13; 2.9.20; Aquinas, *Summa Theologica*, I.70.1, ad. 3; I.68.3.

10. The notion that Genesis is to be set over against other ancient origin stories is as old as the Jewish writer Josephus (first century AD) and the Christian apologists (notably Eusebius, in his *Preparation of the Gospel*, early fourth century).

11. I have argued this in my "Reading Genesis 1–2 with the Grain: Analogical Days," in *Reading Genesis 1–2: An Evangelical Conversation*, ed. J. Daryl Charles (Peabody, MA: Hendrickson, 2013), 73–92; "Historical Adam (Old Earth)," in *Four Views on the Historical Adam*, ed. Matthew Barrett and Ardel B. Caneday (Grand Rapids: Zondervan, 2013), 143–75; "Adam and Eve in the Old Testament," in *Adam, the Fall, and Original Sin*, ed. Michael Reeves and Hans Madueme (Grand Rapids: Baker Academic, 2014), 3–32.

The first readers of Genesis would have known about how animals and plants reproduce "according to their kinds"; Genesis tells them that this is because God wanted it that way. Mind you, this doesn't say anything about evolution, for or against; if a process resulted in something that God wanted, then God "made" it.

These early readers would also be led to reflect on how humans alone are in God's image and after his likeness, and they would be able to see how in Genesis 1–2 God displays features of his character: he shows intelligence in designing the world as a place for humans to live; he uses language when he says things; he appreciates what is "good" (morally and aesthetically); and he works and rests. He is also relational in the way he establishes a connection with humans that is governed by love and commitment (2:15–17). In all of this God is a pattern for humans. The Ten Commandments, for example, base the human Sabbath on God's Sabbath (cf. Gen. 2:2–3 with Exod. 20:11). So the "image and likeness" distinguishes us from the other animals; its purpose is to enable humans to establish communities and to exercise wise and benevolent dominion.

We do not need the author of Genesis to tell us to distrust the serpent in chapter 3; that serpent calls God a liar, insinuates that God has something he wants to keep from the humans (vv. 4–5), and incites them to disobey an explicit command. And for the serpent to suggest that the God who had already loaded these humans down with all manner of overflowing generosity in the garden (see, e.g., Gen. 2:9) was somehow stingy or sneaky is unimaginably disgusting. We also know that snakes do not talk—not even in the Bible! So if the snake is talking, it is because some Power is using it. After reading Genesis 3:1–7, we are sure that Power is evil. We do not need the author to tell us that when Eve ate and then gave some to Adam, it was a "disobedience" or "sin"; we can see that from what the narrative shows.

We also don't need the author to tell us that this was some kind of "fall"; again, we can see that easily enough. The humans were part of what was "very good" at first (Gen. 1:31); when we read of the "curses" that follow their disobedience (3:16–19), see that the humans are driven from the garden so that neither they nor their descendants can return (3:22–24), then see how one of their children lies to and then murders another (4:8), and then see how he produces descendants who decline so far from the ideal that they boast of excessive vengeance (4:23–24), we wonder where all that evil came from. We can easily infer that "*pain*ful toil" is an intruder from which people need relief (5:29 NIV); it was introduced in 3:16–17 ("pain"). Then a little later we read that "every intention of the thoughts of [humankind's] heart was only evil continually" (6:5 ESV) and that the great flood did not change that (8:21); surely this is not what the Maker intended. It cannot be part of the "very good" condition, so our author must want us to infer that it came from the disobedience. No biblical author calls the event a "fall," but that is a good descriptor. The term appears in the writings of the Greek-speaking church fathers by the early fourth century.[12]

But there is something else to say about this disobedience: God gave his command to Adam (in Gen. 2:16–17, "you" is masculine singular), and Eve appropriated it for her own (3:2, "we"; in 3:3, "you" is plural). The consequences of the disobedience affect not only Adam and Eve but also their descendants. So there must be some sense in which Adam represents humankind. As early as Irenaeus (*Against Heresies* 3.9.8) a Christian calls the arrangement with Adam a covenant, which would explain how Adam serves to represent humankind.[13]

Finally, the text of Genesis never tells us a lot of things we should like to know, such as what God had in mind for these two special trees (Gen. 2:9). And while we are to take the humans as "good" (1:31), that does not imply that they were what we might call morally fully matured. I find the explanation given by the Greek fathers Theophilus of Antioch and Irenaeus (and the modern Semiticists Franz Delitzsch and Terence Mitchell of the British Museum) quite persuasive: the first humans were morally good but not yet confirmed or matured in their goodness. In prohibiting the fruit of the one tree, God intended to give them a chance to exercise their moral muscles and so to advance to maturity.[14] Thus "the tree of the knowledge of good and evil" was "the tree by which they would come to know good and evil," preferably knowledge from above, like God (Gen. 3:22), who knows good and evil and always chooses the good—but possibly from below, as those mastered by evil (which is what happened).

All of this supports what Pope Pius XII said in his 1950 encyclical, *Humani Generis*: "The first eleven chapters of Genesis, although properly speaking not conforming to the historical method used by the best Greek and Latin writers or by competent authors of our time, do nevertheless pertain to history in a true sense" (sec. 38). Or, as I might put it, we should affirm that how the Bible tells the story gives us the divinely approved way of *picturing* the events and

---

12. E.g., Eusebius, *Preparation for the Gospel* 7.8 [307d], and Athanasius, *Against the Pagans* §3.

13. Jewish author Ben Sira (Ecclesiasticus 14:17; Greek version, ca. 130 BC) had already done so, as had the prophet Hosea (Hos. 6:7, eighth century BC)—though the proper sense of the Hosea passage is controversial.

14. Irenaeus, *Against Heresies* 4.38.1, 3; Theophilus, *To Autolycus* 2.24, 25, 27; Franz Delitzsch, *A New Commentary on Genesis* (Edinburgh: T&T Clark, 1888), 1:138; Terence Mitchell, "Eden, Garden of," in *New Bible Dictionary*, ed. I. Howard Marshall et al. (Downers Grove, IL: InterVarsity, 1996), 289. See chap. 11 below by Andrew McCoy for a further discussion of Ireneaus's understanding of original sin.

that there are actual events that the pictures *refer to*. This treats fairly both the common tradition of Christian thinking and the kind of literary material we have in this part of Genesis. And this insight into the storytelling in Genesis will give us both flexibility and clear guidance in thinking about relating the story to the questions raised by the sciences.

As I have indicated, Genesis 1–11 is both unified in itself and unified with the rest of Genesis: it forms the indispensable universal backdrop to God's choice of a particular group, the family of Abram, to be the vehicle of his blessing for the rest of the world. But what does this require as a foundation, if it is to be true? It requires that all the other peoples need God's light because they are estranged from him, and it requires that there be something in those peoples that can be enlivened to respond to that light, just as in Israel. In other words, these other peoples have a common origin with Israel, a common set of human capacities, and a common need. Furthermore, this estrangement from God is unnatural; it is out of step with how things ought to be. Something has come into human experience that produced that estrangement, and that something is sin (see Eccles. 7:29).[15]

Jesus

We often hear that it was Paul who made the most of Adam.[16] But the most important passage comes not from Paul but from Jesus. In Matthew 19:3–9, some Pharisees want to test Jesus in order to ensnare him into taking sides on a debate between their competing schools of thought. So they ask him whether it is lawful for a man to divorce his wife "for any cause," and Jesus replies: "Have you not read that he who created them from the beginning *made them male and female*, and said, '*Therefore a man shall leave his father and his mother and hold fast to his wife, and the two shall become one flesh*'?" (Matt. 19:4–5 ESV). Jesus's answer ties together Genesis 1:27 and 2:24 (italics). Since man and woman are now one flesh, joined together by God, they should not be separated. The Pharisees then ask why Moses allowed divorce (Matt. 19:7, citing Deut. 24:1–4), and Jesus explains that it was a concession: "*from the beginning* it was not so" (Matt. 19:8).

In this conversation Jesus portrays the creation account of Genesis 1–2 as setting the ideal for a properly functioning marriage for all humans; that was how God intended things to be "from the beginning." The family legislation

---

15. To see how this is the implication of this text, see my *Did Adam and Eve Really Exist?*, 70.

16. E.g., Daniel Harlow, "After Adam: Reading Genesis in an Age of Evolutionary Science," *Perspectives on Science and Christian Faith* 62, no. 3 (2010): 189; James Barr, *The Garden of Eden and the Hope of Immortality* (Minneapolis: Fortress, 1992), 4.

of Deuteronomy, on the other hand, does not set the ethical norm but has another function—namely, that of preserving civility in Israel: a function that has become necessary by some change of circumstances since "the beginning."[17] The obvious candidate for making that change—indeed, the *only* candidate—is the sin of Adam and Eve, with its consequences for all humans.

Paul

Now we come to Paul, that "pestilent fellow" (Acts 24:5). Paul styled himself an apostle with a calling from outside the normal avenue of the Jerusalem apostles, those who had known Jesus during his earthly life and ministry. This claim met with intense resistance, as described elsewhere in the New Testament. Nevertheless, the Jerusalem leadership were won over (see Acts 15:12–21; 21:17–25), and Christians have always regarded Paul's letters as authoritative Scripture. To acknowledge Paul as an apostle is to accept him as a divinely authorized teller and interpreter of the Big Story; we are concerned not primarily with what he as a man believed about the world but with the story he tells.

In recent decades, specialists in the apostle Paul have realized how firmly he rooted his arguments in the overarching narrative of the Old Testament—just as Jesus did. Romans 1:2–6 shows that Paul read the Old Testament as the early chapters of the biblical story, telling how God chose Abraham's family to be his fresh start on humankind, to restore what was damaged by sin; these chapters anticipate a new era in which the gentiles (or "nations") receive the light. Paul defines his gospel as the announcement that through the death, resurrection, and ascension of Jesus this new era has now begun (Rom. 1:2–6; Gal. 3:8–9; cf. Mark 1:15; see also Matt. 28:18–20).[18] Paul describes Christian believers, both Jewish and gentile, as those in whom God is renewing his image for proper human functioning in their individual and community lives (e.g., 2 Cor. 3:18; Col. 3:9–10), where the fractured family is once again united.

When it comes to comparing Adam and Jesus (Rom. 5:12–19; 1 Cor. 15:20–23, 42–49), Paul's argument likewise depends on a narrative. That is, someone did something (one man trespassed, Rom. 5:15), and as a result something happened (sin, death, and condemnation came into the world of human experience), and then Jesus came to deal with the consequences of it

17. For discussion of how this law functioned and its relation to the Bible's ethical ideals, see Christopher Wright, *Old Testament Ethics for the People of God* (Downers Grove, IL: InterVarsity, 2004), 349–51; and my *Genesis 1–4: A Linguistic, Literary, and Theological Commentary* (Phillipsburg, NJ: P&R, 2006), 144–45. For more see Wenham, *Story as Torah*, chap. 5.

18. On this point, see my "Echoes of Aristotle in Romans 2:14–15: Or, Maybe Abimelech Was Not So Bad after All," *Journal of Markets and Morality* 13, no. 1 (2010): 137.

all (by his obedience to make the many righteous). The argument achieves its coherence from its sequence of events; it is drastically inadequate to say that Paul is merely making a comparison here.[19]

Further, consider the notion that people are "in Adam" or "in Christ" (1 Cor. 15:22): to be "in" someone is to be a member of that people for whom that someone is the representative. The members have what is called "solidarity" with one another and with their representative, which involves some kind of participatory union (natural in the case of Adam and supernatural in the case of Christ). The actions of one member affect the whole group, and the representative (or "head") can act on behalf of the whole body. We have a sense of how this works on the natural level: I was born into a family, and had my parents emigrated before I was born, I would have legitimately "inherited" their new citizenship. But if my older cousin had emigrated, that would not have entailed citizenship to me or my younger siblings; he is not a proper representative.

This need not imply a genetic model of sin's transmission. Indeed, there is no reason to believe that our genes define us; nor do we need a medically detectable mechanism for passing along sin. Humans in a "people" share mutual connections that we cannot see or even properly describe; hence Paul's use of the "body" idea—borrowed from Hellenistic political philosophy—expresses quite well the notion of corporate solidarity found in the Hebrew Bible. And finally, all the evidence we have indicates that only actual persons can function as representatives "in" whom the members are.

But need this actual person be the *first* human? Paul does not address that directly, but a number of factors show that his argument does indeed rely on something like that as an unstated premise. First, in Romans 5:12–19 Paul explains how sin and death "came into the world": it was though the disobedience of the one man (Adam, v. 14). That is, sin and death are not natural or inherent to humankind; they "came in" at some point. But we should make sure we know what Paul means by "sin" and "death." Sin is clear and is parallel with other words such as "transgression" (v. 14), "trespass" (v. 15), and "disobedience" (v. 19)—words that provide a reasonable summary of what happened in Genesis 3. That means that "death" is intended to echo Genesis as well, especially Genesis 2:17 ("you shall surely *die*," ESV). In Paul, when words such as "dead" and "death" refer to a moral condition, they are talking about alienation, particularly alienation from God (see Rom. 6:23; 7:9, 13; 8:6; Col. 2:13). That is indeed the death that Adam and Eve suffered in Gen. 3:8–10. It was not their natural condition.

19. Contra James D. G. Dunn, *Romans*, Word Biblical Commentary (Dallas: Word, 1988), 289–90.

So sin and death have spread to "all people" (Rom. 5:12 NIV), even to "those whose sinning was not like the transgression of Adam" (v. 14 ESV). The point is that Adam acted on behalf of all humankind; it was through his act that these horrors came to us. The popular idea that "each of us is our own Adam" is utterly foreign to the argument—and would undo it, as Adam is unique. Then, in 1 Corinthians 15:45, Paul quotes Genesis 2:7 but adds two words: "The *first* man, *Adam*, became a living being." He goes on to say that we are made of dust like Adam was—"we have borne the image of the man of dust" (1 Cor. 15:48–49 ESV)—which, in light of Genesis 5:3 (Adam fathered a son after his image) seems straightforwardly an assertion of our descent from Adam. Then we notice that Paul's wording echoes the wording in the book of Wisdom. Compare Romans 5:12 ("sin *came into the world* through one man") with Wisdom 2:24 ("through the devil's envy death *entered the world*"); sin and death are intruders into God's world. Then compare 1 Corinthians 15:45 ("the *first man*, Adam") with Wisdom 7:1 ("I also am mortal, like *everyone else*, a descendant of the *first-formed* child of earth"), which confirms our impression that Paul is portraying Adam as the first of humankind.

Mind you, this role of intruder that Paul attributes to sin and the status of Adam as the "first" through whom sin and death came in are bound up with the narrative he is telling: God's good creation, humankind, was marred by the disobedience of their representative, Adam, at their headwaters; and Jesus's work of dying and rising is the first installment of setting the world back on the right track, heading to the consummation.[20]

Revelation

The last book of the Bible tells us where the whole story is headed. Consider Revelation 22:1–5:

> Then the angel showed me the *river* of the water of life, bright as crystal, flowing from the throne of God and of the Lamb through the middle of the street of the city; also, on either side of the river, *the tree of life* with its twelve kinds of fruit, yielding its fruit each month. The leaves of the tree were for the healing of the nations. *No longer will there be anything accursed*, but the throne of God and of the Lamb will be in it, and his servants will worship him. They will see his face, and his name will be on their foreheads. And night will be no

---

20. I share many points in common with N. T. Wright's reading of Paul in *Surprised by Scripture*, chap. 2, although I find that he engages in unnecessarily stark antitheses between, say, human salvation and the renewal of the world. The key difference, as I see it, is that Wright does not attend to the place of Adam at the *beginning* of humankind in Paul's story.

more. They will need no light of lamp or sun, for the Lord God will be their light, and they will reign forever and ever. (ESV)

John's Revelation is filled with all manner of symbolism, and therefore I make no claim to know what the scene he describes will *actually* be like. But I can say this: John portrays it as Eden come to its full fruition; notice the tree of life and the river. The place is a sanctuary, which is how Genesis portrays the garden. Revelation thus continues the narrative focus we found elsewhere: it portrays the final victory of God's purposes, using Edenic and sanctuary imagery to describe perfected human life in a cleansed creation.

What Story Shall We Tell?

Here is how I can tie all this together. As we've seen, the biblical material leads us to a creation-fall-redemption-consummation story line (or its variants) as the Big Story of the world. That story then should function as the worldview story for all humankind and especially for the Christian faithful.

When we are talking about Adam and Eve, we are concerned with the beginning stages of the story; that's why it matters to be clear regarding both what we must affirm and what room we have for exploration. It seems fairly straightforward that, if we are to make any sense of the passages we considered in Genesis, Matthew, and Paul's writing, we should take them as implying that all humankind comes from the same family, with a unified origin: they share the same distinctive capacities, the same predicament, the same prospects of conversion. In the nineteenth century, and from time to time still, we encounter theories (scientific and pseudo-scientific) that have the different kinds of humans (such as Semitic, Caucasian, Black African, East Asian) rising from separate creative acts or evolutionary developments in different places. The name for such theories was polygenesis (multiple origins), and it does not fit with the biblical story at all. (In human evolutionary studies today, the word "polygenesis" has another meaning, which I will discuss in a moment.)

Further, these biblical materials portray sin as an intruder, something that defiles and disrupts human life and damages the functioning of human societies. It is not part of human nature as God created it, and it will be utterly removed from the consummated creation. If sin is inherent in being human, then it follows that the consummation will make us less than fully human—a conclusion that cannot be reconciled with any kind of traditional Christianity. Sin "came in" by way of an event, or complex of events, early on in human history.

Finally, in light of the human distinctives that we have discussed here, which work into the image of God—an image that has been damaged and in which

Christians are "being renewed"—we can say that whatever process God used to produce humans, it went beyond merely using the natural properties of the things involved. Something had to be added—at the very least to produce what we call "mind."[21]

Guides for Good Scientific Thinking

So now we have the tools to begin thinking about the questions that the sciences raise. But we still have to be careful in order to do *good* thinking. Good scientific thinking is not defined as simply "what scientists say it is"; it must follow good critical thinking. Among other things, this means recognizing its limits. A geneticist is an expert in the genome, for example, and a paleontologist in the fossil record. At the same time, when they want to integrate their findings into the larger story of what it means to be human, their reasoning is open to review by all kinds of people; their expertise does not mean that their integrations automatically trump every critique.

The biblical story does not involve a scientific theory as such; nevertheless Christians, who have traditionally regarded the sciences highly, have been at pains to show that good scientific theories are compatible with their origins story. And thus we are able to put our questions more pointedly: Do the sciences require us to change—or even to abandon—elements of the Christian story in a way that renders a different story altogether?

There are differing definitions of the term "biological evolution." It can refer simply to (1) the idea that animals change over time. Or it might go further and insist that (2) the animals we know today are descended from the creatures we dig up in the fossils and that changes have been introduced into the animals' genetic makeup in the process. Or it might go even further and contend that (3) all present-day animals descend from only a few ultimate ancestors—or even from just one (echoing Darwin's words).[22] In its strongest form, biological evolution asserts that (4) the whole process is a purely natural one with no "extra help" from God. Some who hold this fourth version at

21. C. S. Lewis argued this in many places; see my exploration in "A Peculiar Clarity: How C. S. Lewis Can Help Us Think about Faith and Science," in *The Magician's Twin: C. S. Lewis on Science, Scientism, and Society*, ed. John G. West (Seattle: Discovery Institute Press, 2012), 69–106. Lewis drew on Arthur James Balfour, *Theism and Humanism* (New York: Hodder & Stoughton, 1915). Important figures who agree with Lewis include Alvin Plantinga, *Warrant and Proper Function* (New York: Oxford University Press, 1993); Thomas Nagel, *Mind and Cosmos: Why the Materialist Neo-Darwinian Conception of Nature Is Almost Certainly False* (New York: Oxford University Press, 2012).

22. In concluding his classic, *The Origin of Species* (1872; New York: Collier, 1909), Darwin imagines life as "having been originally breathed by the Creator into a few forms, or only one" (506).

least try to characterize the process as a purposeful one, but I would prefer to say that, while the story we tell should include purpose, we ought also to recognize God's freedom to inject new things into the unfolding—which seems likely in the formation of humankind.

Most Christians (and traditional Jews as well) have imagined Adam and Eve as the actual ancestors of all humankind. They were formed directly from the loose soil, or "dust," with no animal intermediates between the dust and Adam. Their formation was supernatural since the dust couldn't form itself, and since distinctive human capacities go beyond natural developments in any other animal. They sinned at the headwaters of the human race—that is, at the early stages of humankind's existence—in such a way that all humankind was brought into their condition by way of their representation of us all.

Many still prefer this simpler scenario, but we should recognize that the view of human descent in which we have common ancestors with the apes long predates modern genetics research. Figures from the late nineteenth and early twentieth centuries as diverse as Pope Pius XII, the very conservative American Presbyterian Benjamin Warfield, and the sophisticated Anglican C. S. Lewis all had similar ways of dealing with it: they felt that it raises no theological problems so long as we recognize the common origin of all humans and special action from God in producing the first humans in the image of God, a condition in which he could enter into a relationship with them. Exegetically, one could argue that the verb "formed" in Genesis 2:7 allows for this since it is not intended as a scientific description of the formation. The word itself does not exclude a process with intermediate steps.[23] For such thinkers, the sin of Adam as representative of humankind still plays a role. Some call this allowance for an involved process of formation "evolutionary," though that is a form of evolution that is not limited to natural processes.

But we still have the difficulty of squaring the Bible's apparent account of an original human pair with the modern genetic theories of a sizable population (which is what the word "polygenesis" now means). While I prefer the simpler picture, I can find room for a kind of expanded mere-historical-Adam-and-Eve-ism, such as C. S. Lewis and Derek Kidner have each expounded. They offered scenarios in which the "initial human population" (actually a difficult term, requiring nuance) was larger than just the first couple; but the first couple, Adam and Eve, bear some relationship to the whole group (such

---

23. Compare Ps. 103:14 (ESV footnote): God "knows how we are *formed*; he remembers that we are *dust*." Each of us is ultimately "formed of dust," even if the dust has gone through a few intermediate (genetic) steps. For all humans as made from dust, see also Pss. 90:3; 104:29; Eccles. 3:20; 12:7; Job 10:8–9.

as king and queen) that allows the representation to be legitimate.[24] Since both wrote well before the contemporary theories in genetics, neither can be accused of some sneaky effort to harmonize science and the Bible. We should always appreciate that these are just scenarios and not harmonizations.

Under such a scenario, Adam and Eve can be seen as king and queen of the initial human population—or of whatever percentage of humanity are actual image bearers; everyone who can be called genuinely human descends from this group. In the Bible Adam and Eve could be the "father and mother" of their people, and they could act as representatives of the whole people. Their relationship of covenantal solidarity would go beyond the legal fictions that we are accustomed to in modern states.[25]

Let's imagine this scenario: suppose that God entered into a relationship with this population, or the image-bearing subset of it, and he did so by way of Adam and Eve as their representatives. This relationship involved them in obeying a command, according to their capacity and for the sake of their maturation. In some way temptation from a Dark Power seduced them into disobedience. This took place at the headwaters of humankind. (I use the potentially vague term "headwaters" in order to allow for some flexibility regarding how long after their formation Adam and Eve sinned. It needs to be early enough so that their representation for all humankind is still mean-ingful, and certainly prior to any dispersal of humans beyond the environs of their origin.) If the fall did not take place under such circumstances, it is exceedingly difficult to grasp how God could justly account its effects to a population that had no proper connection to Adam and Eve.[26]

Perhaps there are some scientific problems with this latter scenario. But (1) those scientific problems stem from the current way of thinking about the subject, and all scientific theories are subject to review and revision to meet critiques or new evidence;[27] and (2) it's just a scenario, an illustration of one way to imagine the events. Other ways may occur to those with

24. Derek Kidner's *Genesis*, Tyndale Old Testament Commentary (Leicester, UK: Inter-Varsity, 1967), proposes a scenario in which Adam and then Eve are supernaturally upgraded from hominids to bear God's image. After them the rest of the first population is also super-naturally upgraded—keeping Adam and Eve as the "first" human beings. I am partial to this idea if we are convinced of a larger initial population.

25. Lewis himself admitted that the notion of solidarity was the key and also that he did not understand it. Kidner, however, does seem to have grasped it well.

26. That is why a view that posits an Adam way downstream from the initial population, with whatever representation he exercises as being arbitrary, does not do the job.

27. Critiques have been offered by people with scientific qualifications: e.g., on the biology, Ann Gauger, Douglas Axe, and Casey Luskin, *Science and Human Origins* (Seattle: Discovery Institute Press, 2012); on the mathematics by which the calculations have been made (which is therefore not the special province of the geneticists), Vern Poythress (formerly a mathematician),

enough imagination; but in any case, I consider it important to protect three basic affirmations:

1. the human race is one family with a unified origin (regardless of the initial population size);
2. humans arose by a process that goes beyond the impersonal; and
3. sin is an alien intruder into God's good creation and entered into human experience at some point in the headwaters of human history.

I say, then, that we can preserve the Big Story so long as we maintain the solidarity of the human race in Adam—both his contemporaries and those who came after him. This story has the virtues of being *robust* in that it can make room for scientific exploration, *critical* in that it guards our good sense against erroneous views, and *sense giving* in that it actually addresses our condition and enables us to live faithfully.

"Adam versus Claims from Genetics," *Westminster Theological Journal* 75 (2013): 65–82. No doubt replies exist to these. I simply note the critiques; I do not pass judgment on them.

II

The Irenaean Approach to Original Sin through Christ's Redemption

Andrew M. McCoy

No School like the Old(er) School

As developments in evolutionary science have increasingly challenged traditional Christian beliefs about human origins, many Christian scholars have
responded by reclaiming—if selectively at times—very early Christian theology
and doctrine. Behind this reclamation lie two related concerns: first, the way
in which evolutionary theory appears to complicate Augustine's influential
understanding of original sin and, second, the desire to draw on other early
and orthodox resources in the Christian tradition that seem more compatible
with aspects of evolution. Arguably no patristic thinker has received more
recent attention in this latter regard than Irenaeus of Lyons, who rightly could
be called the church's earliest biblical theologian.

   This chapter begins with a brief look at facets of Irenaeus that make
him of particular interest to those rethinking original sin in the context of
evolution. Irenaeus conceives of creation as created for development and
growth, and he even speaks of creation as created "imperfect." This leads
many to portray Irenaean theology as a foil to Augustine's view of Adam
and Eve "falling" from created perfection. These same readers, though,
often leave to the side aspects of Irenaeus that affirm original sin as an event

of the fall and as a result of the disobedient actions of Adam and Eve. I argue that contemporary readers should not neglect how Irenaeus reflects on creation and sin through his emphasis on the incarnation and Christ's redeeming work of recapitulation. The Irenaean concept of recapitulation is key to understanding his view of original sin and crucial to making proper use of his theology as a resource for conversation and engagement with evolutionary science.

(Re)Originating Sin in Irenaeus

There are at least three reasons Irenaean thought is initially attractive to those rethinking original sin in light of evolution. The first is the dynamic approach he takes to creation. Irenaeus views creation as intended for development and growth and as God-designed to become more than creation was when it first began.[1] As a result, many contemporary readers perceive a contrast between Irenaeus and Augustine, who understands creation to originate in a kind of timeless state of perfection in God. Both Augustine and Irenaeus believe creation was brought into being out of nothing (*ex nihilo*), but some argue that the Augustinian view risks aligning time itself with the sinful effects of the fall.[2] On that account, Irenaeus provides a helpful alternative to Augustine because Irenaeus clearly articulates time and the need for growth as part of the goodness of creation from the beginning.[3] This decidedly positive theological view of time also puts Irenaeus in the unusual situation of simultaneously appealing to two very different sets of contemporary audiences: (1) those inclined to preserve some aspect of biblical literalism (who, unlike Augustine, take seriously the seven days of Genesis as days) and (2) those seeking to reconcile Genesis with evolution (which, of course, involves development over time).

1. Irenaeus, *Against Heresies* 4.38.3: "His wisdom [is shown] in His having made created things parts of one harmonious and consistent whole; and those things which, through His super-eminent kindness, receive growth and a long period of existence, do reflect the glory of the uncreated One, of that God who bestows what is good ungrudgingly." Trans. Dominic Unger, Ancient Christian Writers 55–57 (New York: Paulist Press, 1992), 541.

2. Examples of this view include Colin Gunton, *The Triune Creator* (Grand Rapids: Eerdmans, 1998), 91; James K. A. Smith, *The Fall of Interpretation: Philosophical Foundations for a Creational Hermeneutic* (Downers Grove, IL: InterVarsity, 2000), 144–48.

3. The contrast between Irenaeus and Augustine on this issue is certainly arguable, as recent Augustine scholarship has made clear. For discussion of Augustine's own articulation of the dynamic and developmental nature of creation, see chap. 15 below by Stan Rosenberg; and Alister McGrath, "Augustine's Origin of Species: How the Great Theologian Might Weigh In on the Darwin Debate," *Christianity Today*, May 8, 2009, 38–41.

Second, those in this latter group often pay particular attention to how Irenaeus describes God's creation of humanity as imperfect from the beginning: "Created things must be inferior to Him who created them, from the very fact of their later origin; for it was not possible for things recently created to have been uncreated. But inasmuch as they are not created, for this very reason do they come short of the perfect. Because, as these things are of later date, so they are infantile; so they are unaccustomed to, and unexercised in, perfect discipline."[4]

The Irenaean view of Adam and Eve as not created fully mature and destined for further development has led more than a few contemporary theologians to rethink traditional ways of understanding sin and the fall. John Hick's "Irenaean Type of Theodicy" famously puts Irenaeus and Augustine in sharp contrast: "Instead of the fall of Adam being presented, as in the Augustinian tradition, as an utterly malignant and catastrophic event, completely disrupting God's plan, Irenaeus pictures it as something that occurred in the childhood of the race, an understandable lapse due to weakness and immaturity rather than an adult crime full of malice and pregnant with perpetual guilt."[5] Philosopher Richard Swinburne's own influential Irenaean theodicy, while differing in significant ways from Hick, nonetheless begins with similar conclusions about Irenaeus and original sin: "Irenaeus wrote that 'man was a child, not yet having his understanding perfected. Wherefore he was easily led astray by the deceiver.' That is, Adam was created as a weak creature and so already significantly prone to sin. If (non-suppressed) sinfulness was part of Adam's created nature, it follows that (barring divine intervention) we would have inherited sinfulness whether or not Adam himself had sinned."[6] Both Hick and Swinburne, in their own respective ways, draw on Irenaean language about human imperfection to argue that sin originates less through a fall of humanity into sin and more through a realization of sinful tendencies already inherent in creation from the beginning. As we will see below, both further make connections between their reading of Irenaean theology and issues at hand in evolution.

A third reason Irenaean theology appeals to those with evolutionary concerns is his emphasis on the centrality of Christ in both creation and redemption. For Irenaeus, all creation begins and ends in the Triune God revealed through the incarnate Christ.[7] At the same time, Irenaeus appears

4. Irenaeus, *Against Heresies* 4.38.3, trans. Unger, 542.
5. John Hick, *Evil and the God of Love*, 3rd ed. (New York: Palgrave Macmillan, 2010), 214–15.
6. Richard Swinburne, *Providence and the Problem of Evil* (Oxford: Clarendon, 1998), 39.
7. Irenaeus, *Against Heresies* 4.20.

to suggest at points that humanity inevitably falls into sin so that Christ will have someone to save. Hick cites *Against Heresies* 3.20.2 as an example: "This, therefore, was the [object of the] long-suffering of God, that man . . . may always live in a state of gratitude to the Lord, having obtained from him the gift of incorruptibility, that he might love Him the more; for 'he to whom more is forgiven, loveth more' (Luke vii.43)."[8] In passages such as this, both Hick and Swinburne find support for the idea that sin is an inevitable or intended part of God's design for creation necessarily leading to Christ's redemption.[9] Others influenced by them also draw similar conclusions.[10]

To summarize, contemporary Christians—with modern evolutionary science in mind—often read Irenaeus as an alternative to Augustinian original sin along the following lines:

1. God creates creation for the purpose of development and growth;

2. humanity, as created by God, is imperfect and not fully developed, and sin is a natural result of this reality and should be understood as an inherent or genetic aspect of God's creation from the beginning;

3. human sin is either a divinely unavoidable or divinely intentional aspect of God's work of creation so that the greater good of salvation in Christ might be achieved and so that creation might become all that it is created to be.

This reading of Irenaeus, framed primarily in terms of theodicy, is hardly limited to Christian concerns about faith and evolution. A recent introductory work of philosophy, explicitly influenced by the theodicies of both Hick and Swinburne, draws the conclusion that Irenaeus has an "apparent indifference

8. As cited by Hick, *Evil and the God of Love*, 213.

9. Richard Swinburne writes, "By inheriting, genetically, his desires and his free will; and by inheriting, no doubt in part culturally, his moral awareness, we later humans inherited that sinfulness. But we would have inherited sinfulness anyway, whether or not Adam had sinned, but for divine intervention." *Providence and the Problem of Evil*, 115.

10. For related views of evolution that indicate God cannot avoid allowing sin in the world, see Daryl P. Domning, *Original Selfishness: Original Sin and Evil in the Light of Evolution* (Burlington, VT: Ashgate, 2006); George L. Murphy, "Roads to Paradise and Perdition: Christ, Evolution, and Original Sin," *Perspectives on Science and Christian Faith* 58, no. 2 (2006): 109–18. For a related view of evolution that indicates God intends for there to be sin in the world, see John R. Schneider, "Recent Genetic Science and Christian Theology on Human Origins: An 'Aesthetic Supralapsarianism,'" *Perspectives on Science and Christian Faith* 62 (2010): 196–212. For my critical response to Schneider, see Andrew M. McCoy, "Becoming Who We Are Supposed to Be: An Evaluation of Schneider's Use of Christian Theology in Conversation with Genetic Science," *Calvin Theological Journal* 49 (2014): 63–84.

to Original Sin or any theology of the Fall."[11] To see whether this is truly the case, we now turn to aspects of Irenaeus that often get downplayed or completely ignored when contemporary readers utilize his theology to rethink original sin.

Returning to Original Sin in Irenaeus by Returning to Incarnation and Recapitulation

While Irenaeus did not live in the time of modern evolutionary science, he did face significant theological controversies about the nature of creation and human origins during his lifetime. The title and purpose of his most important work, *Against Heresies*, focuses on the problem of gnosticism and its influence on the developing church. The gnostic opponents of Irenaeus viewed the materiality of creation as inherently sinful and preached a spiritual salvation *from* the material world. Irenaeus, on the other hand, began with Christ's incarnation to argue that all creation—*including* all of its physical and material aspects—was created good and apart from sin and evil.[12] Irenaeus thus describes the origin of humanity as "modeled after the image and likeness of the incarnate Son," a creative act that happens "by the hands of the Father, that is by the Son and the Holy Spirit."[13]

Humanity's origin in perfect relationship with God's two "hands" leads Irenaeus to perceive original sin in a way quite contrary to many contemporary portrayals of his theology. Irenaeus clearly understands the event of Adam and Eve's disobedience as a fall.[14] He also describes the actions of Adam and Eve in their biblical terms and, like much Christian tradition including Augustine, describes their disobedience as an event that disrupts creation and changes it for the worse: "For in Adam the hands of God had become accustomed to set in order, to rule, and to sustain His own workmanship, and to bring it and place it where they pleased. Where, then, was the first man placed?

11. Michael B. Wilkinson with Hugh N. Campbell, *Philosophy of Religion: An Introduction* (New York: Continuum, 2010), 178. See also the entirety of chap. 16, "The Problem of Evil II—Irenaean Theodicy and Swinburne."

12. Thomas Weinandy, "St. Irenaeus and the *Imago Dei*: The Importance of Being Human," *Logos* 6, no. 4 (2003): 16–17.

13. Irenaeus, *Against Heresies* 5.6.1, trans. Unger, 566.

14. See Gustaf Wingren, *Man and the Incarnation: A Study in the Biblical Theology of Irenaeus* (Edinburgh: Oliver & Boyd, 1959), 17: "The Gnostics likewise rejected the Law and the Old Testament which God the most high had given, and so Irenaeus was forced not only to try to demonstrate how both the Old and New Testaments were derived from God, and how both the Law and the Gospel were addressed to men by the same God, but also to make it clear to his own period that Adam was created by God to live, body and soul, in accordance with His will. For this very reason it is important to speak of Adam's sin as a *fall*" (emphasis original).

In paradise certainly, as the Scripture declares: 'And God planted a garden [*paradisum*] eastward in Eden, and there He placed the man whom He had formed.' And then afterwards, when [the man] proved disobedient, he was cast out thence into this world."[15]

Irenaeus further describes the consequences of sin as a falling away from creation's intended design for development by the divine "hands" of the Son and the Holy Spirit.[16] Yet, at least in his extant writings, Irenaeus does not provide a developed concept of original sin in the way Augustine does.[17] Instead, he tends to speak of sin only in the context of also speaking about the God revealed in Christ. His primary concern is to situate sin in theological relationship with Christ's involvement throughout the entire time of creation, from its beginning in relationship with God to its redemption in Christ's incarnate person and work.

Two important implications result from this approach, both of which are helpfully identified in Thomas Holsinger-Friesen's recent study of how Irenaeus reads Genesis. Holsinger-Friesen notes, first, that Irenaeus does not choose between reading Genesis in terms of chronological narrative and reading it in terms of Christology but instead holds together differentiated aspects of the Old and New Testaments "in order to demonstrate that together they articulate a single economy which may be termed a 'Christian' depiction of reality."[18] Contemporary Christian readings of Genesis are no different in this overall regard, though such contemporary readings are certainly now confronted with centuries of additional biblical scholarship; modern concerns with historical, anthropological, and sociological criticism; and challenging developments in evolutionary science. Even amid such complexities, contemporary readers who want to read Genesis from within the whole of Christian scripture continue to look to Genesis "for its ability to cast illumination on

15. Irenaeus, *Against Heresies* 5.5.1, trans. Unger, 564–65.

16. Irenaeus, *Against Heresies* 4.39.3: "If however, thou wilt not believe in Him, and wilt flee from His hands, the cause of imperfection shall be in thee who didst not obey, but not in Him who called [thee]" (trans. Unger, 523).

17. Thomas Holsinger-Friesen, *Irenaeus and Genesis: A Study of Competition in Early Christian Hermeneutics* (Winona Lake, IN: Eisenbrauns, 2009), 120: "One particularly notable feature in *Adversus Haereses* is that Irenaeus appears rather uninterested in talking about human fallenness as a subject of its own." Holsinger-Friesen in a footnote also cites Cyril O'Regan's observation that "outside of what it excludes, Irenaeus's position on sin is relatively underdeveloped." O'Regan points out that Irenaeus "does not attempt to correlate *disobedience* with all the biblical namings for sin," nor does he "probe in the way an Augustine does the motivational structure of sin, in which the categories of *self-love* and *pride* loom large." See Cyril O'Regan, *Gnostic Return in Modernity* (Albany, NY: SUNY Press, 2001), 165 (emphasis original).

18. Holsinger-Friesen, *Irenaeus and Genesis*, 223.

events from creation to the eschaton and to explain their interconnectedness *within* this one economy."[19]

Second, Holsinger-Friesen argues that the manner in which Irenaeus reads and interprets Genesis from within this christological economy has implications for how Christians think about scriptural interpretation and also interactions Scripture has with other narratives about the origins of creation. Irenaeus, on the one hand, criticizes the gnostic presumption that the Genesis narratives as written cannot satisfactorily portray God's relationship with humanity because the divine would never truly condescend to create the material. In this case, Scripture ceases to function as Scripture because the gnostic interpretation cannot explain how the narrative itself communicates God's creation as created good. On the other hand, Irenaeus prioritizes Christ as the means for upholding the Genesis narratives over against competing gnostic counternarratives about the creation of the world. Christ's incarnation provides divine confirmation that God, as portrayed in Genesis, truly created all creation as good from the beginning and not intrinsically evil, as gnostic arguments suggest.

In short, Irenaeus is more concerned with explaining all creation history as Christ's history than he is with classifying the type of history at work in the Genesis narratives. Discrete categorization of historical concerns is a much more modern pursuit. For those struggling with original sin in the light of evolution, such a concertedly theological account, rooted in Christology, would indeed seem to provide resources for developing meaningful conversations.[20] Yet an Irenaean approach to sin also does not entail simply giving up on the sinlessness of creation before the fall or giving up on the fall itself as an actual event of human disobedience. As Irenaeus writes,

> For we have shown that the Son of God did not begin to exist then, having been always with the Father; but when he became incarnate and was made man, He recapitulated in Himself the long unfolding of humankind . . . that in Christ Jesus we might receive what we had lost in Adam, namely to be according to the image and likeness of God. In fact, it was not possible for humankind, which had once been conquered and had been dashed to pieces by its disobedience, to refashion itself and obtain the prize of victory. Again, it was not possible for the human race, which had fallen under sin, to receive salvation. And so the Son, Word of God that He is, accomplished both, by coming down from the

19. Holsinger-Friesen, *Irenaeus and Genesis*, 223 (emphasis original).
20. Holsinger-Friesen, *Irenaeus and Genesis*, 223–24. "If what is sought in a christological reading of Genesis is theological perspective and orientation . . . rather than fixed, self-sufficient knowledge about beginnings then drawing on the Genesis narrative to engage extra-textual lines of enquiry (such as modern science) can be a productive enterprise."

Father and becoming incarnate, and descending even to death, and bringing the economy of our salvation to completion.[21]

Portrayals of Irenaean theology in the context of evolutionary concerns often ignore his references to Adam and Eve's disobedience and suggest that, in a more contemporary age, when biblical texts are often no longer read "literally," such disobedience can be understood as merely a sign of the need for development in humanity that Irenaeus articulates elsewhere. This kind of reading ignores the fact that Irenaeus first and foremost reads all history in terms of Christ, and so the incarnation undergirds his reading of Scripture and his interpretation of sin as a loss that invades God's good creation and destroys the potential for humanity to grow as God intends in God's image and likeness over time. Precisely for this reason, Irenaeus speaks of the work of Christ's incarnate person to transform humanity—that "long unfolding of humankind" through a salvation of recapitulation.

Hick rightly picks up on growth "towards perfection" as an aspect of creation and redemption in Irenaeus, but he understands creation's redemption only in terms of an elevated future. He views sin as "natural" and as an immanent aspect of evolution over time, but this conclusion would be far more at home with the gnostic opponents of Irenaeus than with Irenaeus himself.[22] Hick misses how Irenaean recapitulation confirms the goodness of creation from the beginning as Christ's incarnate redemption restores creation's past. Over against the kind of view Hick endorses, Irenaeus states, "He had Himself, therefore, flesh and blood, recapitulating in Himself not a certain other, but that original handiwork of the Father, seeking out that thing which had perished."[23] Irenaean recapitulation complicates any reading of God's economy of salvation simply in terms of evolutionary development. Evolution, as a process in the time of creation, only impacts creation as it moves toward the future. Through recapitulation, however, Irenaeus affirms that Christ's redemption ever and always makes the past new even as it elevates creation toward perfection in Christ.

Recapitulation is a central—but often misunderstood—aspect of Irenaean thought that ultimately bears significantly on how one understands Irenaeus on original sin. Recapitulation refers to Christ's action throughout history

21. Irenaeus, *Against Heresies* 3.18.1–2, trans. Unger, 87–88.
22. See Michael Reeves and Hans Madueme, "Threads in a Seamless Garment: Original Sin in Systematic Theology," in *Adam, the Fall, and Original Sin: Theological, Biblical, and Scientific Perspectives*, ed. Hans Madueme and Michael Reeves (Grand Rapids: Baker Academic, 2014), 211–14.
23. Irenaeus, *Against Heresies* 5.14.2, trans. Unger, 591.

to save creation by transforming the past, present, and future of humanity. For Irenaeus, this means Christ elevates human development toward perfection in God by restoring humanity to that which God originally intended for creation before the fall of Adam and Eve into sin. Contemporary theology, however, often portrays this tandem of elevation and restoration in Irenaean recapitulation as a tension.[24] The result—especially amid an intellectual climate of evolutionary concerns—has been emphasis on the elevation theme within Irenaean thought apart from adequate attention to recapitulation as restoration. Hick, for example, writes, "I have accordingly called this the Irenaean type of theodicy. Instead of seeing humanity as having been created in innocent perfection and then falling, it sees us as having been created—as we now know, through the long process of evolution—as immature beings capable of growing through the experience of life in a challenging world. We are to grow gradually, in this life and beyond it, towards our perfection, which lies in the future, not in the past."[25] No issue is more central to readings of Irenaeus that seek to address evolutionary concerns by using his theology as an alternative to Augustine on original sin than the fact that Irenaeus speaks of humanity as created "imperfect." As Swinburne argues, "Adam could not have sinned without already having some bad desires to which he yielded—and bad desires are themselves a natural evil."[26] This raises the question of how the perfection of the incarnate Christ can in any sense restore a creation and humanity that was never perfect from the beginning.

None of the surviving texts of Irenaeus indicate creation or humanity emerged from God fully realized. Yet neither should his description of humanity as created "imperfect" or "childlike" be understood to suggest that humanity was created sinful or that Irenaeus believes evil is a natural aspect of creation.[27] Again, to hold this view is to endorse a key aspect of the gnostic views of material creation that Irenaeus sought to refute. On the contrary, the imperfection of humanity at creation refers to its trajectory for development

---

24. Robert F. Brown, "On the Necessary Imperfection of Creation: Irenaeus' *Adversus Haereses* iv, 38," *Scottish Journal of Theology* 28 (1975): 17: "Interpreters of [Irenaeus's] Recapitulation (*anakephalaiosis*) doctrine routinely note that Christ's work brings two different benefits to the human race. First, humanity is restored to its status before the fall of Adam, thereby abolishing sin and its effects. Second, it is elevated or perfected to a higher form of being than that of the originally created human nature." I discuss the perceived tension between these two themes (and the need to affirm them as mutually compatible in Irenaean thought) further in McCoy, "Becoming Who We Are Supposed to Be," 68–74.

25. Hick, "Preface to the 2010 reissue," in *Evil and the God of Love*, xii–xiii.

26. Swinburne, *Providence and the Problem of Evil*, 109.

27. Matthew C. Steenberg, *Irenaeus on Creation: The Cosmic Christ and the Saga of Redemption*, Vigiliae Christianae Supplements (Leiden: Brill, 2008), 176: "The human person is weak, but he is not naturally evil."

within perfect relationship with the Triune God. Perfection of creation is not absolute for Irenaeus; it is relational. He proposes that human potential for growth and maturity is part of the goodness of creation but is potential that can only be realized through unbroken relationship with God's two hands, the Son and the Holy Spirit. Douglas Farrow writes, "The 'imperfection' is this: The love for God which is the life of man cannot emerge *ex nihilo* in full bloom; it requires to grow with experience. But that in turn is what makes the fall, however unsurprising, such a devastating affair. In the fall, man is 'turned backwards.' He does not grow up in love of God as he is intended to. The course of his time, his so-called progress, is set in the wrong direction."[28] For this reason, Irenaeus believes the greatest limit on human potential—death—enters human experience as a result of the fall.[29] All human aspects of life and development are affected by sin—again, not because progress no longer happens in creation but because creation's progress no longer happens in and through perfect relationship with God.

Irenaeus's theology of recapitulation ultimately results from bringing together his reading of Genesis with his emphasis on the revelation of God in Christ. As Matthew Steenberg writes, "Irenaeus does not turn to these [Genesis] texts so much to learn the nature of sin, but to read them Christologically, and by means of the revelation of sin and redemption found in Christ to demonstrate the consistent recapitulative work of God for the human creature."[30] Original sin for Irenaeus is not simply something he abstracts from redemption, but, crucially, neither is sin something that he finds to be natural to creation. Christ's recapitulation acts redemptively to restore the trajectory along which humanity was originally intended to grow, and in so doing, Christ returns the ever-developing time and space of creation back into perfect relationship with God and toward its intended destiny.

Irenaean Recapitulation as Resource for Conversations about Original Sin and Evolution

Amid questionable readings of his theology and the significant challenges posed by evolution, a careful reading of Irenaeus on the issue of Christ's

28. Douglas Farrow, "St. Irenaeus of Lyons: The Church and the World," *Pro Ecclesia* 4 (1995): 348.

29. On Irenaeus and death, see Steenberg (*Irenaeus on Creation*, 190–92), who explains that Irenaeus presents death as a punishment for sinful disobedience but that he is also "the first author" to present death as God's postfall limitation on unrestricted sin (by limiting human life). That said, Steenberg observes further inconsistencies in the overall Irenaean presentation of death as a result of sin.

30. Steenberg, *Irenaeus on Creation*, 154.

recapitulation provides substantial doctrinal support for continuing to uphold the concept of original sin as the result of human action against God in time. Irenaeus affirms sin as *un*natural by showing how creation must be intrinsically related to the incarnate Christ and not intrinsically related to sin. This does not mean there is no room for discussion about the interpretation of Genesis, about *how* Adam and Eve should be understood to exist in history, or of varying theories about *how* their fall into sin occurred or what sin now means. Yet Irenaeus provides strong support for affirming that the fall happened in some way as an event in history, that sin is invasive, and that sin is neither a natural aspect of creation nor a result reducible to genetics. Christ's recapitulation of our humanity necessarily means redemption of creation as originally created from the beginning all the way through Christ's life, death on the cross, resurrection, and ascension. Otherwise, the incarnation is something other than what creation was before or something that Christ sheds and discards once he overcomes sin on the cross and rises from the dead and ascends. Irenaeus argues that if Christ, in his perfection, "took flesh" of anything besides the original humanity that God made for relationship with himself, then Christ's redeeming recapitulation does not redeem, and Christ is not truly incarnate.[31] At the same time, Irenaeus does not deny that the resurrected and ascended Christ, in his humanity, is more than what humanity was when first created. Irenaeus provides the means to speak of creation as always intended by God to grow and develop, a divine intention restored in Christ's redemption. The glorified heavenly body of the Lord Jesus, though certainly more than creation now, cannot be understood as anything less than what we were originally created to be. Otherwise, the doctrine of the incarnation becomes skewed and falters as a doctrine.[32]

The way in which Irenaeus grounds this understanding of original sin in the context of Christ's redemption also does not make either the doctrine of the incarnation or recapitulation contingent on sin itself. Rather, the inverse; it is to ensure that our doctrine of sin doesn't become that which defines our understanding of God or creation. In this way Irenaeus presents both helpful

---

31. Irenaeus, *Against Heresies* 5.14.2, trans. Unger, 590: "But if the Lord became incarnate for any other order of things, and took flesh of any other substance, He has not then summed up human nature in His own person, nor in that case can He be termed flesh." See also Douglas Farrow, *Ascension and Ecclesia: On the Significance of the Doctrine of the Ascension for Ecclesiology and Christian Cosmology* (Grand Rapids: Eerdmans, 1999), 55: "When the existence of evil is put down to the fact of creation rather than to the actions of sinning creatures, creaturely existence is that which must be overcome, not sin and its consequences."

32. Gunton, *Triune Creator*, 223: "Any suggestion that [Christ's] body is not formed of the matter of this fallen world breaks the links between creation and redemption and renders the saviour irrelevant to this world."

opportunities and meaningful boundaries for Christian doctrinal reflection in conversation with evolutionary science.

The issue of death in creation provides a good example. Though Irenaeus (like so many in the early church) views death as a result of the fall, those making present use of his theology could potentially make room for evolutionary theories of death, suffering, and predation, provided that aspects of death, suffering, and predation are qualified in some way as experiences of human finitude and development and not sin. John Walton articulates this kind of view in his recent *Lost World of Adam and Eve*. With a nod toward Irenaean theology, Walton ascribes death and specific aspects of suffering to "non-order" in the developing creation and not the "disorder" that enters the world through the fall and sin.[33] Whatever one thinks of Walton's proposal (or even of how he applies his understanding of Irenaean theology), the manner in which he differentiates creation and its development from the invasiveness of sin at the moment of the fall could be understood, at the very least, as an Irenaean impulse.

Walton's proposal also moves moral evil in humanity apart from what has traditionally been called natural evil and is not unrelated to the approach to Augustine taken by Stanley Rosenberg in chapter 15 below. Rosenberg does not discuss Irenaeus, but he argues clearly that Augustine locates evil in "corruption within souls" and within "spiritual, reasoning creatures" but *not* within all the aspects of creation that manifest death, disease, and decay and those that are results of the process of evolution. Phenomena within nature after the fall should thus not be thought of as fallen or part of sin, because experiences of death, disease, and decay are simply "acknowledgment that the creation is fundamentally contingent, limited, and different from God." Undoubtedly, many will find such a view attractive exactly because it helps to maintain an account of the fall that—like that of both Irenaeus and Augustine—describes original sin as the result of human disobedience of God in time, while also allowing room for evolutionary processes to be understood as part of creation's inherent contingency rather than the by-product of sin.

Conclusion

Ultimately, an Irenaean view of original sin must be shaped by how Irenaeus understands creation to begin and end in Christ. Irenaeus affirms that God intends the dynamic and changing aspects of creation that are aspects of the

33. John H. Walton, *The Lost World of Adam and Eve: Genesis 2–3 and the Human Origins Debate* (Downers Grove, IL: IVP Academic, 2015), esp. 153–60.

world variously observed by natural and physical sciences. But over against how he is sometimes read, Irenaeus does not affirm that sin originates in God's purposes for the development of creation, nor that sin and evil can be understood simply as immanent aspects of the evolutionary process. The Irenaean doctrine of recapitulation makes this distinction crucial and also demonstrates why—even if creation emerges through processes of decay and destruction—Christian faith must continue to proclaim that humanity fell into sin through willful action against God in time.

12

Original Sin and the Coevolution of Nature and Culture

BENNO VAN DEN TOREN

> Certainly, nothing jolts us more rudely than this doctrine, and yet, but for this mystery, the most incomprehensible of all, we remain incomprehensible to ourselves. The knot of our condition was twisted and turned in that abyss, so that it is harder to conceive of man without this mystery than for man to conceive of it himself.
>
> Pascal, *Pensées* #131

One does not need to agree with Pascal's entire understanding of the doctrine of original sin to affirm the deep insight of his sharp observation: this doctrine is at the same time a stumbling block for Christians and non-Christians alike and yet brings an enormous depth to the understanding of our human condition. It realistically explains why humankind seems to be universally bound to the disastrous effects of personal and communal self-destructive attitudes and behavior. It also explains why humans cannot simply accept this mire of their

For a more technical treatment of the issues discussed in this chapter, see Benno van den Toren, "Human Evolution and a Cultural Understanding of Original Sin," *Perspectives on Science and Christian Faith* 68, no. 1 (March 2016): 12–21, http://www.asa3.org/ASA/PSCF/2016/PSCF3-16Toren.pdf. I thank Emily Burdett and my fellow editors to this volume for their knowledgeable and insightful comments on earlier versions of this chapter.

existence as the unavoidable reality of being human but must keep believing that life was meant to be better and more meaningful. In Pascal's own words, the doctrine explains the *grandeur* and the *misère*, the greatness and misery, of the human condition and why the two exist side by side in such a way that they do not diminish each other but rather intensify each other. Our misery is all the more outstanding because we long for such *grandeur* and carry the traces, memories, and hopes of a much better and grander existence in our inmost beings.

Yet the doctrine remains a mystery that stretches our minds and imagination. For Pascal, the mystery centered on the close connection between unavoidable corruption and universal culpability. In the history of theology, it has also raised many questions related to theodicy: How can a good God allow the existence of evil? Or, more particularly: Why would a good God create a world in which the sin of parents unavoidably corrupts their entire offspring? In the context of the dialogue of the Christian faith with modern evolutionary thinking, other elements are added to the mystery: How can humanity be culpable of its evil nature when that nature seems simply the consequence of an evolutionary development in which we have inherited various forms of egocentricity, aggression, and ill-directed desires from our prehuman ancestors? And how can we believe in original sin when it seems increasingly difficult to conceive of a first couple in a state of righteousness somewhere on the line of human evolutionary development?

This combination of the clarity and mystery attached to this doctrine provides us with a healthy caution about the *relative importance* of our explorations. In this essay, I intend to show that in the light of recent insights into human evolution the cultural model of original sin acquires new depth and relevance. Pascal's insight points to the *importance* of this exercise. Given the centrality of this doctrine to the Christian understanding of the human condition and to the Christian understanding of the grand story of salvation history, these questions have significant intellectual and apologetic importance.

The questions are important because many non-Christians have difficulty believing the doctrine of original sin in the context of evolutionary science. These are not the only issues with the doctrine—many people feel a deep existential resistance to the idea that humans are radically corrupt, and this may be more significant than the issues raised by evolutionary science. Such existential resistance must be dealt with in its own way, partially by explaining that this does not devalue the human but rather presents a hopeful picture of a world that is meant to be—and can be—different. Yet, whatever the effect of such existential resistance to the doctrine of original sin, the intellectual issues placed on the table by evolutionary scientists carry real weight for a number of people. Such questions also have intellectual importance for Christians who want to deepen the understanding of their faith, as expressed in Anselm's adage *fides quaerens intellectum*, "faith seeking understanding." Christians believe that the world that is explored by the sciences is the same world with which the Scriptures and Christian theology are concerned. Therefore, seeking resonance is entirely warranted and desirable.

Pascal's insight points not only to the importance, however, but also to the *relative* importance of this exercise of relating the doctrine of original sin to evolutionary science. Our faith does not depend on our ability to come up with an instant satisfactory answer to these conundrums. We believe in original sin because this is how we discover ourselves to be in our encounter with Jesus Christ and in our reading of the Christian scriptures. We believe in original sin because of its explanatory power: it makes ultimate sense of the grandeur and misery of the human condition. This by itself gives us reason to believe in the doctrine even if for the time being we have not yet worked out how this relates to current understandings of evolutionary science. This may be because evolutionary science is in a number of areas still patchy and in flux, or it may be because we do not yet understand how the two relate. This by itself does not undermine the validity of our belief in the doctrine—and reality—of original sin.

Consider two parallels. In the light of evolutionary science it may be hard to understand how we can trust that our senses and reasoning give us some access to knowledge and truth beyond the immediate pragmatic needs of our survival. Yet our experience of the world is such that we still have good reason to believe that our reasoning is not just about the evolutionary survival of our genes but also about understanding reality for its own sake. That is the paradox of Richard Dawkins making truth claims about blind evolutionary processes aimed at the survival of genes: his evolutionary argument seems to undermine the trustworthiness of the very processes of reasoning that he uses to argue his case. Yet he is not willing to concede that the way we use reason and many other aspects of human existence suggests that there may be more to human existence than what current evolutionary science is able to understand—or possibly what evolutionary science may be able to understand in principle.[1]

Similarly, in the light of evolutionary science, I may find it hard to understand how my feelings of love for my wife can be anything more than an epiphenomenon of sexual attraction aimed at producing as many and as potent offspring

---

1. Cf. Richard Dawkins, *The Blind Watchmaker* (London: Penguin, 1986); Dawkins, *The Selfish Gene* (London: Granada, 1978; repr., New York: Oxford University Press, 1989). For an argument against naturalistic explanations on the basis of an analysis of how human knowledge is warranted, see Alvin Plantinga, *Warrant and Proper Function* (New York: Oxford University Press, 1993), 194–238; cf. Plantinga, *Where the Conflict Really Lies: Science, Religion, and Naturalism* (New York: Oxford University Press, 2011), 307–50.

as possible. My direct experience of this relationship tells me, however, that there is more to love than this. This experience may be so robust and confirmed by a range of other experiences that I can reasonably believe it shows that love can be much more than sexual attraction even if for the moment I do not understand how this relates to the current evolutionary picture.

The doctrine of original sin is not a single doctrine but rather a network of doctrines. One element of the doctrine is "originating original sin" (*peccatum originale originans*), which refers to *the first sin* of the first human couple that is the origin of all later sins and sinfulness. In this essay, I instead focus on what is called "originated original sin" (*peccatum originale originatum*), which refers to the reality that every human in the world as we currently know it is born into sin: though the species was created good, every individual human is born with a sinful disposition, a tendency to sin and an inability not to sin. The sinfulness of humankind means not only that humans do sinful actions but also that every human born in this world is bound to or enslaved by sin. In this essay, I argue that current evolutionary theory rather unexpectedly provides a new theoretical framework that helps us deepen our doctrinal understanding that human sinfulness is not part of human nature yet is unavoidably inherited from our parents and from the communities in which we are raised.

To make my argument, I first introduce how evolutionary biology has increasingly undermined the modern nature-culture divide. I then explore how our radical dependence on the cultural socialization in our communities coheres with, confirms, and fleshes out the doctrine of original sin. In conclusion, I return to the wider doctrinal web, showing that a cultural understanding of the inheritance of original sin enriched by recent insights from evolutionary anthropology helps us avoid the opposite dangers of (semi-)Manichaeism, on the one hand, and (semi-)Pelagianism, on the other. I also conclude that recent evolutionary insights contribute significantly to a major theodicy question raised by the doctrine of original sin: Why would a good God create a world in which the sin of remote ancestors disposes their entire offspring to destructive sinful behavior? New understandings of the deeply cultural nature of human existence suggest that this is the natural counterpart of the greatness of humans being created in the image of God, as God's created co-creators.

Blurring of the Nature-Culture Dichotomy in Recent Evolutionary Theory

One of the consequences of recent developments in evolution is the blurring of the boundary between nature and culture. Traditional understandings of human nature worked with a fundamental distinction between human nature and the various cultures humankind develops on the basis of natural potential. Human nature is basically given and the *prerequisite* for the development of various cultures. Recent developments in evolutionary theory show the evolution of human nature and of cultures can no longer be separated because the two coevolved and mutually depend on each another.[2]

Biological human nature can no longer be discussed apart from culture because it is cultural through and through. Culture is not an accessory to the species' nature or a second layer added to a nature that exists independent of culture. Human nature as it currently presents itself never existed without culture. It cannot survive, let alone thrive, without its cultural form and embedding. The development of culture is the fruit of the unique evolution of human nature. These two aspects of its evolution are, in its current form, inextricably linked. As Jonathan Marks observes, "Nature and culture act as a synergy. If the human is like cake, culture is like the eggs, not like the icing—it is an inseparable part, not a superficial glaze."[3] Let me unpack some of the relevant evolutionary research.

First, recent evolutionary evidence suggests that the development of the human brain in its current form coevolved with our super sociality and ability for cooperation, with our ability for so-called joint attention and theory of mind. The growth of the human brain is furthermore closely linked with the development of language.[4] Given that the ability to use symbolic language is one of the main tools for both the transmission and the development of culture, the human brain is not only what made culture possible; the brain itself evolved parallel to the development of language, sociality, and culture and cannot be understood apart from it.

Second, the principle of so-called niche construction states that biological evolution cannot be explained simply by the adaptation of organisms through genetic evolution to different ecological environments. Species do not only adapt to different environments, but they also adapt environments to themselves.[5] Trees patiently grow their roots in tiny cracks in mountain

2. William H. Durham, *Coevolution: Genes, Culture, and Human Diversity* (Stanford, CA: Stanford University Press, 1991); Ralph Wendell Burhoe, "The Source of Civilization in the Natural Selection of Coadapted Information in Genes and Culture," *Zygon* 11, no. 3 (1976): 263–302; Philip J. Hefner, "Culture Is Where It Happens," *Zygon* 40, no. 3 (September 2005): 523–27.

3. Jonathan Marks, *What It Means to Be 98% Chimpanzee: Apes, People, and Their Genes* (Berkeley: University of California Press, 2003), 177.

4. Cf. Terrence William Deacon, *The Symbolic Species: The Co-evolution of Language and the Human Brain* (New York: Norton, 1997).

5. F. John Odling-Smee, Kevin N. Laland, and Marcus W. Feldman, *Niche Construction: The Neglected Process in Evolution* (Princeton: Princeton University Press, 2003).

rocks and create shade from sun and wind in which dust may collect, smaller organisms may live, and new seeds can germinate. Thus, they create their own environment in places that were before uninhabitable. Earthworms improve the soil so that other nutritious organisms may prosper and in turn improve the environment for the earthworms themselves.

Humans also construct their own environments in places that are very hostile: they build igloos in the arctic, irrigation channels in the desert, pale dwellings in swamps, and high-rises in densely populated areas. Human niche construction is, however, much more flexible and versatile than the niche construction of other species. Humans' capacity to adapt their environment is not just engraved in their genetic memory; it is transmitted and inherited by culture. This means that the genetic variation between humans living in a great variety of environments is slim and even negligible—the most visible difference in pigmentation, for example, can be compensated by cultural means such as sun hats or vitamin supplements. This also means that humans can adapt much faster to new environments because cultural change can happen so much quicker than genetic change.[6] In all these different environments, the physical survival and procreation of humans radically depends on their cultural inheritance. They simply cannot do without it.

A third aspect of human evolution that shows how the genetic evolution and cultural evolution of the human species are intertwined relates to the relationship between humans and their offspring. Already in 1940, German philosopher and anthropologist Arnold Gehlen pointed out that the human is a *Mängelwesen*, or "needy being."[7] Unlike other animals, humans cannot survive with their biological equipment and instinctively inherited capabilities. Human infants need a long period of socialization (or cultural formation) by their parents. Only after such enculturation is the child able to survive. This cultural character of human existence again reflects itself in the child's physical form: human children develop much more slowly than other animals of the same size, and human females are able to care for their offspring by living much longer beyond their fertile age.

Humans are unique in the animal kingdom because of the human capacity to develop culture. The fact that we share 98.6 percent of our DNA with chimpanzees doesn't mean that we are no different from apes, any more than

6. K. N. Laland, J. Odling-Smee, and M. W. Feldman, "Cultural Niche Construction and Human Evolution," *Journal of Evolutionary Biology* 14, no. 1 (January 8, 2001): 22–33.

7. Arnold Gehlen, *Der Mensch: Seine Natur und seine Stellung in der Welt* (Wiesbaden: Akademische Verlagsgesellschaft Athenaion, 1978), 12:12; translated by Clare McMillan and Karl Pillemer as *Man, His Nature and Place in the World* (New York: Columbia University Press, 1988).

the fact that computer chips are made of silicon means that they are no different from desert sand. We may share much of our biological nature with apes, but our unique identity is formed by being advanced cultural beings. In the words of Jonathan Marks: "You are not an ape; you are an *ex*-ape."[8]

Theologically, this deeply enculturated nature of human existence can be related to our creation in the image of God. The notion of the image is multifaceted.[9] It encompasses being created for a covenant relationship with God and for relations within the human community, but it also includes being created for a special role in the rest of creation. We are God's "created co-creators."[10] Because human existence isn't fixed by genes and instincts, humans have, in the words of Gehlen, an "openness to the world"—a certain freedom that allows them to develop their environment, to develop culture, and to relate to the world around them in different ways. This is their greatness. But it also means that humans are radically dependent on their parents and community for their socialization. This dependence on their cultural upbringing for good or for evil is a necessary corollary to this openness to the world and this creativity that characterizes human existence. This dependence of the human on cultural socialization by their community resonates with the doctrine of original sin and is the focus of the next section.

Human Socialization, Cultural Transmission, and Original Sin

One can find phenomena among other species that resemble human culture. The humpback whale's song has certain features of human language, and the chimpanzee's use of sticks to extract ants from ant holes represents a rudimentary use of tools. However, when one looks to a Neolithic settlement or a modern city, it is clear that human culture has developed on a completely different scale. The difference is not just quantitative but qualitative. Apart from chimpanzees that have had extensive training by humans, animal languages have never become symbolic languages, thereby allowing for the creation of a "symbolic universe," a universe in which different ideas have meaning because of how they relate to other ideas that together create a web

8. Jonathan Marks, "You Are Not an Ape," guest editorial, TEDxEast, August 23, 2012, http://global.oup.com/us/companion.websites/fdscontent/uscompanion/us/static/companion.websites/9780190210847/pdf/17.pdf.

9. See, e.g., Charles Sherlock, *The Doctrine of Humanity* (Downers Grove, IL: InterVarsity, 1996); Benno van den Toren, *Christian Apologetics as Cross-Cultural Dialogue* (London: T&T Clark, 2011), chap. 4.

10. Philip J. Hefner, *The Human Factor: Evolution, Culture, and Religion* (Minneapolis: Fortress, 1993), chaps. 2, 15.

of meaning.[11] Similarly, tools in other species remain rudimentary and never attain functionality beyond what is immediately apparent.

The unique development and complexity of human culture and human artifacts is due to what Michael Tomasello has called the "ratchet effect."[12] A ratchet is a tool that allows pulling in a cable that stands under high tension bit by bit, as the cable length gained is secured every time it moves forward. In the same way, human culture develops over many generations. Cultural discoveries made in one generation can be transmitted to later generations that can build on these earlier discoveries. Thus, a modern digital library is the result of a long, cumulative process beginning with oral communication via early forms of writing and book printing to the development of libraries and search tools, while interacting with the development of social structures and management systems. It is this ratchet effect that allows human openness to the world and adaptation to many different environmental niches.

This ratchet effect is made possible by the unique way human children and adults learn in comparison to their closest relatives, such as chimpanzees and bonobos. This difference has been highlighted by a variety of studies by cognitive scientists and has often been labeled as a difference between "imitation learning" and "emulation learning."[13] Animals, particularly chimpanzees, capuchin monkeys, and crows, are indeed able to learn using specific tools by looking at other members of the group or to humans. This can be perceived in natural environments where certain uses of tools spread through communities and are maintained over generations. It can equally be seen in laboratory situations. This is, however, always or mainly *emulation* learning. Emulation learning means that the animal sees how a certain tool (such as a rake) can be effectively used for a certain procedure (such as pulling food near so that it can be eaten) and starts doing it for itself. It focuses on the results of actions rather than on the details of the behavior.[14] Imitation learning is unique—or significantly more developed—in human children.[15] Human children learn

11. Deacon, *Symbolic Species*, 79–92.

12. Michael Tomasello, "The Human Adaptation for Culture," *Annual Review of Anthropology* 28 (1999): 512.

13. Tomasello, "Human Adaptation"; Michael Tomasello, Sue Savage-Rumbaugh, and Ann Cale Kruger, "Imitative Learning of Actions on Objects by Children, Chimpanzees, and Enculturated Chimpanzees," *Child Development* 64, no. 6 (1993): 1688–1705.

14. Victoria Horner and Andrew Whiten, "Causal Knowledge and Imitation/Emulation Switching in Chimpanzees (*Pan troglodytes*) and Children (*Homo sapiens*)," *Animal Cognition* 8, no. 3 (2005): 164–81.

15. See Andrew Whiten et al., "Emulation, Imitation, Over-Imitation and the Scope of Culture for Child and Chimpanzee," *Philosophical Transactions of the Royal Society B: Biological Sciences* 364, no. 1528 (2009): 2417–28, which nuances Tomasello's conclusions while confirming his main thrust.

by imitating practices of educators even if they do not directly understand the meaning of these practices. Human children will, for example, imitate an adult who turns the light on by pushing a light switch with the head, even if using a hand would be easier or more efficient.[16] This is not confined to laboratory situations but can be perceived in many real-life situations, such as the simple habit of continuing to cut meat in the same way as one's mother without understanding the underlying reason.[17]

Such imitation learning allows for the learning of practices and languages that are opaque in the sense that their usefulness is not immediately clear to the one learning them.[18] Children are hardwired to imitate their parents and educators, particularly if these educators approach them in a teaching mode—that is, when it is clear that educators are not acting randomly but intend to teach something of value.[19] This aptitude or ability allows children to learn simple and even complex symbolic languages and allows the use of complex tools and complex series of actions that can be used in further experimentation and in exploration far beyond what is immediately obvious.

This highly developed ability for cultural learning in humans constitutes not only a strength but also a weakness. It means that humans are predisposed to imitate their parents and caregivers both for good and for evil. They are able to imitate complex practices that will prove ultimately useful, even if their initial use is far from clear, such as putting garbage in a bin and repeating the letters of the alphabet before they can read. But it also predisposes children to imitate futile or harmful practices, such as the tendency to fear for sorcery when you spot an owl in a tree (as was common in central Africa, where my family lived for a number of years) or to believe that harsh military action is the appropriate response to terrorist attacks. In the grander picture, our dependence on cultural socialization by our parents and caregivers is the necessary counterpart of our openness to the world. We are by nature highly enculturated. Our natural survival depends on a high degree of culture, and we can only survive if we are socialized in the particular cultural mold of our community.

Cultural socialization may be one of the mechanisms—possibly the main mechanism—for understanding the working of the inheritance of sin from the

16. Andrew N. Meltzoff, "Infant Imitation after a 1-Week Delay: Long-Term Memory for Novel Acts and Multiple Stimuli," *Developmental Psychology* 24, no. 4 (1988): 470.

17. G. Gergely and G. Csibra, "Sylvia's Recipe: The Role of Imitation and Pedagogy in the Transmission of Cultural Knowledge," in *Roots of Human Sociality: Culture, Cognition and Interaction*, ed. N. J. Enfield and Stephen C. Levinson (New York: Berg, 2006), 229–55.

18. Gergely and Csibra, "Sylvia's Recipe."

19. Gergely and Csibra, "Sylvia's Recipe." Cf. Giacomo Rizzolatti, "Imitation: Mechanisms and Importance for Human Culture," *Rendiconti Lincei: Scienze Fisiche E Naturali* 25, no. 3 (2014): 285–89.

generations before us: we can only grow up as humans if we are socialized and enculturated within a specific family and community from which we inherit a culture both for good and for evil.[20] Because of their limited physical equipment, humans wouldn't even be able to survive unless their environment was extremely favorable and unless cared for by other animals, such as the stories of children raised by wolves suggest. I can only become a *fully* developed human by imbibing the culture of my parents. I appropriate their ways of behavior, I inherit their tools and living environment, I am socialized in the social structures in which they function, and I inherit the symbolic universe with which they structure and give meaning to the world. In this way, I inherit both good and evil values, both resourceful and wasteful practices, both truthful and distorting aspects of their symbolic universe, both the blessing and the curse of their understanding of life inscribed in their practices and language. It is only after I have been enculturated in what has been given to me that I can add my own small critical addition to this cultural framework that has been shaped over many millennia and uncountable generations.

Concluding Reflections

When drawing our considerations on the possibilities of a cultural understanding of original sin together, we must point out both the positive results and the limitations of these explorations.

The doctrine of original sin cannot be isolated from the wider Christian doctrinal network. It is crucial in avoiding both (semi-)Pelagianism and (semi-)Manichaeism in theological anthropology.[21] In the first place, it undergirds the need for redemption, not just as forgiveness of sins but also as redemption from the slavery of sin. The understanding of original sin in the context of evolutionary science pictured here suggests that we are indeed bound to the sinful practices we inherit from our parents, educators, and community. From our parents we copy what to desire most and how to strive for it, how to handle competition, and how to value—or abuse—the people we meet and the earth that sustains us. We are biologically hardwired to imitate their practices, for good or for evil, before we can even begin to look critically at the

---

20. There are indeed some stories of children abandoned as little babies and raised by wolves or other animals, but they were unable to develop the characteristics that make us human, such as the use of language, tools, and so many other aspects of complex human cultures.

21. In considering the importance of the doctrine of original sin for avoiding Pelagianism and Manichaeism, I have been inspired by James K. A. Smith, "What Stands on the Fall? A Philosophical Exploration," in *Evolution and the Fall*, ed. William T. Cavanaugh and James K. A. Smith (Grand Rapids: Eerdmans, 2017), 48–64.

relative usefulness and goodness of those practices. This was the crucial issue in the debate between Augustine and Pelagius on original sin in the early fifth century and in the continuing debates in the church concerning later forms of Pelagianism and semi-Pelagianism. Here we are not asking the question of whether humans have a genuine two-way freedom to either accept or reject the offer of the gospel. The understanding of original sin sketched here can well be combined with a notion that the Holy Spirit makes such freedom possible when overcoming the power of sin. The issue is rather that, as the church has repeatedly declared, humans are sinful "by propagation, not just by imitation."[22] Sinful acts are not just isolated acts that confer guilt on us but that we could as well have refrained from committing. Sinful acts are an expression of our sinful nature, which is driven by ill-directed desires. We are therefore in need not only of forgiveness of our debts but also of redemption from our slavery to or imprisonment in sin. This understanding of human sinfulness is a strong tenet in the wider biblical narrative, in which sin is an issue not just of debt that needs to be forgiven but of a force that binds us. It is also confirmed by a wide range of empirical data that shows humans cannot simply decide to live differently and do so on the basis of their inherent powers but, instead, are bound by who they have become through the pressures of the society around them, through their personal history, and through the history of the generations before them.[23]

The doctrine of original sin not only has a role in guarding against forms of (semi-)Pelagianism but, second, is equally crucial in avoiding the opposite danger of Manichaeism. If Pelagianism represents too optimistic a view of the human condition, Manichaeism is too pessimistic. Manichaeism—to which Augustine himself adhered for some time before his conversion to the Christian faith—has a dualist worldview that maintains that good and evil are two equally fundamental realities in eternal opposition. It presents the view that the entire physical reality, including human bodily existence, is inherently evil. A number of Christian heresies in the early church courted the Manichaean worldview and believed that human historical and corporal existence was intrinsically evil. This has major consequences for salvation: if bodily existence is inherently evil, salvation cannot mean the salvation of the body but only of the soul from its imprisonment in bodily existence.

It is hard to avoid the opposite dangers of Pelagianism and Manichaeism simultaneously. The moment one wants to stress the anti-Pelagian line that "sin

---

22. *Catechism of the Catholic Church* (New York: Doubleday, 1995), §404.
23. Henri Blocher, *Original Sin: Illuminating the Riddle* (Grand Rapids: Eerdmans, 1999), 93–99.

is not only inherited by imitation, but by propagation," there is the risk that one may fall into the Manichaean trap of making sin part of created human nature. If, to the contrary, one wants to stress that our sinfulness is not part of our created nature, there is the risk that it may become so accidental to who we are that one may fall into the opposite trap of Pelagianism.

A strength of the model of cultural inheritance presented above and suggested by recent evolutionary theory is that it avoids both traps. Earlier cultural understandings of the inheritance of original sin in the liberal Protestant tradition could easily be accused of semi-Pelagianism. Modernity worked with a sharp nature-culture distinction that allowed human nature to exist independently of its cultural form, which was supposedly added to it. On this account, human nature could be transmitted intact, untouched by sin. But, if nature and culture are as deeply intertwined as recent evolutionary theory suggests, we cannot inherit our nature from the community that births and raises us without inheriting its culture, including its sinful biases. We do have a certain freedom to contribute to the shaping of the cultures we inherit, but we can only begin doing so after we have been deeply shaped by this culture both for good and for evil.

This understanding of the enculturated nature of human existence and of the inheritance of sin can also avoid the opposite danger of Manichaeism. A number of theologians working on the interface between science and theology have proposed that original sin is a theological term for the destructive biases inherited from our prehuman evolution, such as our bent to aggression, egoism, and destructive lust.[24] This is highly problematic because it makes sinfulness part of who we are fundamentally (of our created beings) rather than what we have become. It seems more helpful to see these desires as neutral and as having become sinful only in the ways we use them and by the ways they have been sinfully shaped by the cultures of which we are part. For example, sexual desire only becomes sinful lust when it is ill directed rather than channeled in ways that contribute to meaningful relationships. Or our inborn need to protect what is essential to the survival of ourselves and our nearest and dearest only becomes sinful when that energy is directed destructively. Both egotistic and altruistic tendencies seem to be part of our biological makeup, and this cocktail only becomes sinful if we do not learn to balance our genuine proper needs with appropriate concern for others.[25] These drives are strong and deeply

24. So, e.g., Patricia A. Williams, "Sociobiology and Original Sin," *Zygon* 35, no. 4 (2000): 783–812; Philip J. Hefner, "Biological Perspectives on Fall and Original Sin," *Zygon* 28, no. 1 (1993): 77–101.

25. Denis Edwards, *The God of Evolution: A Trinitarian Theology* (New York: Paulist Press, 1999), 65–66; Karl Rahner, "The Theological Concept of Concupiscentia," in *Theological Investigations* (London: Darton, Longman and Todd, 1974), 1:347–82.

rooted but can be distinguished from the sinful shape they take in particular cultural constellations. The power of these drives means, however, that once ill directed, they are very difficult to tame and steer in constructive directions.

In these explorations I have concentrated on originat*ed* original sin—that is, on the transmission of sin through the generations—and have not considered the other aspect of originat*ing* original sin, or the way the first sin entered the world. On the one hand this means that these considerations do not help to answer the complex questions recent evolutionary theory raises for that aspect of the doctrine of original sin. On the other hand, it means that the cultural understanding of the transmission of sin through the generations can be combined with a variety of scenarios concerning the origin of sin in the human race.[26] While I personally prefer an understanding of one historic fall along the lines presented by Gijsbert van den Brink,[27] this understanding of the transmission of original sin can also be combined with a gradual fall, parallel falls, or an ahistoric fall.[28] One added advantage of linking this understanding of the transmission of original sin to a historic fall is that doing so allows for the transmission of sin not only down the generations but also sideways through communities. Unlike certain Augustinian understandings of the transmission of original sin that require that all sinners are biological descendants of Adam, a cultural understanding of sin allows for sin to be transmitted horizontally to others in a given group or to other groups as well, through what we might call "contamination."

As a final concluding reflection, I would like to point to the important contribution of this cultural understanding of the doctrine of the transmission of original sin for the Christian question of theodicy. Certain influential theoretical explanations of the unity of the human race in sin raise baffling questions for our understanding of the goodness of God: Why would a good God establish a covenant that would make all humanity guilty of the sin of its federal head (as in the federal theory)? Why would a good God create a world in which all Adam's descendants were in him and fell in him (as in "realist" understandings of the unity of the human race)? The cultural understanding of the inheritance of the sinfulness of our parents in the light of the breakdown of the nature-culture divide in recent evolutionary theory suggests an answer to this specific question of theodicy. It suggests that inheritance of the sinfulness of our parents and caregivers is a natural corollary or counterpart of our creation in God's image. A theological interpretation of the process

26. For a variety of scenarios, see Denis R. Alexander, *Creation or Evolution: Do We Have to Choose?*, 2nd ed. (Oxford: Monarch, 2014), 288–94, 316–19.

27. See chap. 8 above.

28. As exemplified in chap. 13 below by Christopher Hays.

of human evolution suggests that God used this process to create us as his "created co-creators." He gave us relative independence over against the world so that we were not bound by our genes and instincts but could creatively contribute to the becoming of this world by engaging in culture formation. This openness does imply that we are *Mängelwesen*, needy beings, who can only survive after a long process of socialization by our parents. Yet it inevitably means that we inherit both the strength and the weakness, both the good and the evil, of the cultural practices and symbolic universe of our parents. The doctrine of original sin is therefore a natural counterpart of our creation in the image of God. As Pascal showed, the *grandeur* and *misère* of the human condition are closely related, and both cry for the Redeemer.

13

A Nonhistorical Approach

The Universality of Sin without the Originating Sin

CHRISTOPHER M. HAYS

No Adam, no fall. No fall, no sin. No sin, no cross. No cross, no resurrection. One often witnesses this narrative in Christian debates about evolution. The implication is this: as Adam goes, so goes the gospel. But is the syllogism sound? Can humanity's need for redemption really only be explained by Adam's fall? The thesis of this chapter is that one can indeed affirm the Christian doctrine of sin without believing in the historicity of Adam and Eve.[1] I begin by arguing that it is erroneous to interpret Genesis 2–3 as a record of events that happened in time and space. That decision has consequences for our doctrinal theory: it precludes the ideas of a single originating sin and thus original guilt. Consequently, the essay turns to explain that the ideas of originating sin and original guilt can be set aside without violating the integrity of the New Testament witness (with special attention given to Romans 5, a *locus classicus* for the doctrine of sin). Nonetheless, to confirm that the doctrine of sin can still be affirmed without a historical fall, the chapter concludes by showing that the universality of sin can be amply explained by a confluence of evolutionary, cultural, spiritual, and supernatural factors.

1. Note that this view does not imply a rejection of the doctrine of atonement, since this chapter strongly affirms the universality of sin, which requires the redemptive action of God.

Reasons Not to Read Genesis 2–3 as Historical

Before I explain why I do not affirm the historicity of the events in Genesis 2–3, it is important to clarify that I do not thereby deny the inspiration or truthfulness of Genesis 2–3. Rather, I would argue that the sorts of truths God communicates through Genesis 2–3 are neither historical nor scientific. It is, admittedly, a common error of modernism to confuse "truth" with "history" and to assume that a narrative must be historical to be true.[2] Yet even a quick reflection on, for example, biblical parables reminds us that stories can speak divine truths even though the events in stories did not actually transpire in time and space. So the first question we have to ask is this: What sort of literature is Genesis 2–3?

Genre-Related Considerations

We probably need to admit at the outset that Genesis does not fit neatly within any known ancient genre; in many ways it is *sui generis*. That does not mean, however, that we cannot note similarities Genesis bears to other ancient texts and thus calibrate our expectations about the sorts of literature Genesis might include. For example, it is well known that Genesis 2–3 has significant similarities to ancient Near Eastern texts that are not historical (e.g., the Atrahasis Epic, the Enuma Elish, the Epic of Gilgamesh, and the Memphite Theology), both in terms of the topics treated (the nature of the gods and the elements of creation, the purpose for which humans were created, etc.) and the stock literary features included.[3] With these texts, Genesis shares motifs such as foods that confer immortality,[4] a snake that impedes the reception of immortality, the acquisition of godlike knowledge (associated with the initiation of sexual intercourse), and the creation of humans from a mixture of

2. See further Christopher M. Hays, "Towards a Faithful Criticism," in *Evangelical Faith and the Challenge of Historical Criticism*, ed. Christopher M. Hays and Christopher B. Ansberry (Grand Rapids: Baker Academic, 2013), 14–17; Christopher M. Hays and Stephen Lane Herring, "Adam and the Fall," in Hays and Ansberry, *Evangelical Faith and the Challenge of Historical Criticism*, 28–31; Hans Frei, "The 'Literal Reading' of Biblical Narrative in Christian Tradition: Does It Stretch or Will It Break?," in *The Bible and Narrative Tradition*, ed. Frank McConnell (Oxford: Oxford University Press, 1986), 36–77.

3. See, e.g., Peter Enns, *The Evolution of Adam: What the Bible Does and Doesn't Say about Human Origins* (Grand Rapids: Brazos, 2012), 35–59; Christopher B. Hays, *Hidden Riches: A Sourcebook for Comparative Study of the Hebrew Bible and Ancient Near East* (Louisville: Westminster John Knox, 2014), 41–73.

4. Cf. the Adapa myth, in which the protagonist forfeits immortality because he is tricked into not eating the food and waters of life. See William W. Hallo and K. Lawson Younger, eds., *The Context of Scripture*, vol. 1, *Canonical Compositions from the Biblical World* (Leiden: Brill, 2003), 129, lines 75–84.

clay and a divine substance. These similarities indicate that Genesis is probably in the same generic ballpark as, for example, the Enuma Elish. Since the Enuma Elish and the Atrahasis Epic are not considered historically reliable, that legitimately raises the question of whether Genesis 2–3 is historical.

The presence of etiologies in Genesis also militates against the probability of its historicity.[5] Etiologies appear (on the surface!) to be explanations of why things are the way they are; a modern generic equivalent might be Rudyard Kipling's "Just So Stories" about how the elephant got its trunk and how the leopard got its spots. Genesis 2–3 includes etiologies for the Sabbath (2:1–3), marriage (2:24), and why snakes wriggle on their bellies (3:14). Some of these etiologies are historically problematic. For example, insofar as the fossil record provides compelling evidence that snakes were slithering long before hominids emerged, one might question the historicity of that snake etiology in Genesis (i.e., I do not think snakes lost their legs because of tempting humanity). By extension, the nonhistoricity of the etiology in Genesis 3:14 increases the probability that the surrounding text may also be nonhistorical.

This does not mean that the etiologies in the Bible are *wrong*. Quite the contrary. The real purpose of an etiology is not to explain how a given phenomenon arose. Rather, etiologies tell origin stories (sometimes fantastically) as a way of making moral or theological points. The reason Kipling narrates how the camel got his hump is not to explain the lump on the backs of dromedaries but to warn against sloth. Likewise, the purpose of the story of the snake losing its legs is not to explain the historical origin of slithering but to warn against the dangers of tempting others to sin. So etiologies are often true without being historical.

In brief, there are significant genre-related reasons to think that Genesis 2–3 might not be best read as a historical text. But the evidence is not confined to extrabiblical literature.

Internal Considerations

The text of Genesis itself gives indications that the creation and fall narratives should not be read as historical. For example, Genesis 1 and 2 contain conflicting accounts of the sequences of creation. Genesis 1:11–13 claims that plants were created on the third day, prior to humans, who were created on the sixth day (1:26–31); by contrast, Genesis 2:4–7 says that humans were created before there were any plants. Likewise, Genesis 2:19 asserts that the

---

5. Steven L. McKenzie, *How to Read the Bible: History, Prophecy, Literature—Why Modern Readers Need to Know the Difference and What It Means for Faith Today* (Oxford: Oxford University Press, 2005), 29–36; Bill T. Arnold, *Genesis*, New Cambridge Bible Commentary (Cambridge: Cambridge University Press, 2008), 10–11.

birds and land animals were created after humans, whereas Genesis 1:20–25 locates their creation prior to humans. Similarly, Genesis 1:3–5 indicates the separation of day and night on the first day, followed by the creation of the sun, moon, and stars on the fourth day (1:14–19); yet, from an astronomical point of view, celestial bodies are commonly prerequisite for visible light in the universe. These problematic sequences detract from the probability that Genesis 1–3 should be considered historical.

Similarly, the name of the protagonist in Genesis 2–3 suggests that the text has a symbolic character. The first human is called *adam* (meaning "human"; cf. Gen. 9:5–6; 16:12) because he is made from *adamah* (meaning "dirt" or "earth"; Gen. 2:6–7). In other words, his name is more or less "Earth-human," on the grounds that he is made from dirt. It seems reasonable to suggest that a story about a person named Earth-human, who was made from earth, is probably a different sort of text from one beginning "Winston Churchill was born on November 30, 1874, to the Lord Randolph Churchill and the Lady Jenny Jerome."

Scientific Considerations

Scientific evidence is also pertinent in our evaluation of the historicity of Genesis 2–3. The depiction of Adam's creation, from dust and divine breath, obviously does not align with creation through evolutionary mechanisms. Likewise, the Bible seems to indicate that—even if evil existed in the world prior to Adam and Eve's sin (as the presence of the malicious snake character clearly indicates)—Adam and Eve did not have a propensity toward that evil. In contrast, evolutionary science suggests that instincts toward violence, sexual promiscuity, and selfishness are part of our evolutionary inheritance. Hominids survived, and their genetic legacy advanced in part because of these impulses that are *sinful* for morally conscious beings. So the idea that humans did not have a sinful impulse prior to their fall runs contrary to evolutionary theory (see further below).

A commonly encountered literal reading of Genesis 3:20 indicates (in contradistinction to Gen. 4:14–17) that Adam and Eve were the sole progenitors of all humanity, whereas the current scientific account of human origins indicates that humans emerged in a population of around ten thousand hominids. Likewise, paleogenetics reveals that the genomes of modern European humans are 1–4 percent Neanderthal DNA and that around 5 percent of the genomes of modern Melanesians are derived from another *Homo* species, known as Denisovans.[6] This complicates a narrative about all humans descending from

6. For a helpful introduction to this topic, see Dennis Venema, "Neanderthals, Denisovans and Human Speciation," *Letters to the Duchess* (blog), Biologos Forum, September 23, 2011, http://biologos.org/blog/understanding-evolution-neanderthals-denisovans-and-human-speciation.

a single pair of the first *Homo sapiens*. Finally, the popular reading of Genesis according to which death is the result of the fall is incompatible with evolutionary theory, according to which death is an integral part of the process of generation and mutation by which humans evolved.[7]

Finally, the presence of a talking snake and *two* types of magical fruit (one that grants immortality and another that grants godlike knowledge), and the assertion that woman was created from the rib of a man, all suggest that Genesis 2–3 does not convey scientifically accurate data.

I hasten to add, nonetheless, that these scientific inaccuracies in Genesis do not somehow falsify the messages of the creation narratives. Genesis's prescientific account of human origins reflects how ancient Near Eastern people understood humans to have come to exist ("anthropogeny"). The Atrahasis Epic, for example, says humans were made from clay and divine saliva. Thus, Genesis's depiction of humanity's creation from dirt and God's breath fits with ancient suppositions: humans are a mix of earth and divinity.[8]

This raises the question of whether it is theologically acceptable for the biblical texts to include statements that are contradicted by well-substantiated scientific theory. Happily, theologians have long recognized that God communicates in ways that are comprehensible within the parameters of his audience's historical moment, knowing that humans cannot be expected to possess knowledge that would only be accrued after additional millennia of investigation. This idea is called *accommodation*, and it has a long Christian pedigree. (For example, John Calvin applied the doctrine of accommodation to the heliocentric controversy, and Origen and Gregory of Nyssa appealed to it in their explanations of Old Testament anthropomorphism.)[9]

Divine accommodation helps explain why the biblical texts often seem to run afoul of what we now know from science.[10] Biblical authors appear to have surmised that the sun circled the earth (Ps. 19:6; Eccles. 1:5); we know that the earth circles the sun, which in turn spins within the vortex of our

---

7. It bears mentioning in this context that Gen. 2:9 and 3:22 indicate that death was the natural state of affairs and that Adam and Eve were only preserved from it by the tree of life.

8. See Tremper Longman III, "What Genesis 1–2 Teaches (and What It Doesn't)," in *Reading Genesis 1–2: An Evangelical Conversation*, ed. J. Daryl Charles (Peabody, MA: Hendrickson, 2013), 106–7.

9. On the doctrine of accommodation, including a helpful historical survey, see Kenton L. Sparks, *God's Word in Human Words: An Evangelical Appropriation of Critical Biblical Scholarship* (Grand Rapids: Baker Academic, 2008), chap. 7.

10. This paragraph depends on the helpful treatments of John H. Walton, *Ancient Near Eastern Thought and the Old Testament: Introducing the Conceptual World of the Hebrew Bible* (Grand Rapids: Baker Academic, 2006), 165–78; Denis Lamoureux, "No Historical Adam: Evolutionary Creation View," in *Four Views on the Historical Adam*, ed. Matthew Barrett and Ardel B. Caneday (Grand Rapids: Zondervan, 2013), 37–65.

galaxy. Biblical authors speak of the sky as a solid "firmament" holding back a primal sea and into which the stars were laid (Gen. 1:6–8; Job 37:18); we know today that the sky is atmospheric gas and that the stars, which are exponentially larger than our planet, lie billions of light years away. Biblical authors spoke of the mustard seed as the smallest of all seeds (Mark 4:31); we recognize that many other seeds are smaller than mustard.

In principle, then, we can feel comfortable with the logical possibility that a biblical text might reflect the suppositions of its prescientific authors and still communicate truly about God and his relationship with humanity. But, if we are comfortable with saying that God's goal in inspiration was not to teach the ancient astronomy, geography, or botany that appear in the Scriptures, we should not feel obliged to affirm the ancient explanation of humans' biological origins present in the Bible either.

Against Cherry-Picking: A Word of Hermeneutical Caution

Before wrapping up this section, a word of hermeneutical caution is in order. Scholars trying to reconcile Genesis with modern science often engage in a process of exegetical cherry-picking. In recognition that Genesis 1–3 is not a scientific text, interpreters frequently categorize various mythological-sounding bits as symbolic (e.g., the tree of knowledge of good and evil), while selecting other bits as historically reliable (e.g., taking the description of Adam's farming as evidence that the fall must have happened after the Neolithic era, when rudimentary farming developed). This picking and choosing is often practiced by excellent scholars; my concern, however, is that the process is methodologically arbitrary. It may be true that Genesis 2–3 includes historical and nonhistorical elements, but how do we distinguish the former from the latter? On what basis do we decide that one element is historical (e.g., an originating couple) while another is nonhistorical (e.g., a talking, intelligent, quadrupedal snake)? I think that, in general, the implicit filter is that the former sort of elements seems plausible whereas the latter sort seems quite implausible.

The problem is that the generic and hermeneutical decisions one makes in order to justify categorizing some bits of Genesis 2–3 as nonhistorical *imperil the hermeneutical legitimacy of seeing other bits as historical*.[11] If I set aside the composition of humanity from dust because that is a stock element of ancient Near Eastern creation narratives, then how do I justify holding on to other features of Genesis 2–3 as historical? To pick another genre of biblical literature that possesses historical verisimilitude, consider the parables. If I

---

11. Note that I use the word "imperil" and not "falsify."

am right in thinking that the parable of the prodigal son (Luke 15:11–32) does not refer to a real historical man who took his inheritance early and squandered it in another country, then on what basis could I claim that the prodigal son's self-righteous brother was in fact a historical figure? Since I believe that "parable" is a nonhistorical genre, I am not justified in selectively claiming that certain events or characters are historically referential. I would suggest that we should be similarly circumspect about our treatment of the historicity of Genesis 2–3.

This is not to say that it is impossible that the text could blend the historical and nonhistorical; for example, many critical scholars would affirm that the prophet Jonah did exist and prophesy against Nineveh, but these same scholars would doubt the historicity of his sojourn in the fish's belly. But if one argues that such a mixture exists, it would be methodologically important to provide criteria by which to discern between the elements that are and are not historically accurate.

Hamartiological Ramifications of a Nonhistorical Reading of Genesis 2–3

If the fall narrative in Genesis is not historical, then what happens to our doctrine of sin?[12] (The technical term is *hamartiology*, from the Greek word for sin, *hamartia*.) To get a handle on that question, let's examine five constituent elements of the traditional Protestant doctrinal theory of sin:[13]

1. *Culpability*: Sin makes us guilty and thus worthy of punishment (Rom. 6:23).
2. *Universality*: Sin is a universal phenomenon. Given time, everyone will sin (Rom. 3:23).
3. *Concupiscence* (or more colloquially, *corruption*): Everyone will sin because human wills are corrupt and, to a degree, averse to God (the famous Latin phrase is *aversio ad Deo*; Rom. 7:7–24).[14]
4. *Originating sin* (*peccatum originale originans*): All human sins find their origin, or source, in the first sins of Adam and Eve.[15]

---

12. It is logically possible that there was a historical fall that is described only symbolically in the Genesis narrative—a topic that will be addressed in the next section of this chapter.

13. For the difference between doctrine and theological *theory*, see chap. 2 above.

14. This is to say that human desires are often distorted in a way that hinders our relationship with God but not that every human desire is wrong.

15. But not all evil is so originated; Satan's fall is always considered to be anterior to Adam and Eve's fall.

5. *Original guilt*: All humans are *culpable* of the sins of Adam and Eve and thus worthy of punishment, even if they have not yet personally committed sins (as in the case of children who die in infancy).[16]

The pertinent question for this essay is this: What happens to hamartiological doctrinal theory if Genesis 3 is not a historical text? If Adam and Eve are not historical figures, then clearly their fall did not happen historically and cannot be considered the originating sin. So, element 4 gets scratched off the list. But, if there was never an originating sin, then, logically, one cannot be guilty of the originating sin (for one cannot be guilty of something that never happened). Thus, element 5, original guilt, gets removed too.

The nonhistoricity of Genesis 3 does not, however, have any bearing on element 1, culpability; sin merely has to exist as sin for it to be punishable, irrespective of how sin came into being. Likewise, element 2, universality, is not abrogated by a nonhistorical reading of Genesis 3; as long as one believes in the existence of concupiscence (element 3), one has a sufficient explanation for the universality of sin.

This leaves us with three big questions, to which we dedicate most of the rest of the chapter:

1. Even if the fall narrative in Genesis is not historical, there must have been a first sin at some point. Should we identify that first sin as the originating sin?
2. Even if Genesis does not require belief in originating sin or original guilt, does the New Testament (especially Paul) affirm them?
3. Can we affirm concupiscence (i.e., moral corruption) without believing in the historicity of the fall?

Why Not to Identify the First Sin with the Originating Sin

In the last section, the attentive reader may have objected that, even if Genesis 2–3 does not describe events that literally happened in history, logically there must have been *a* first sin (perhaps described symbolically by the Adam and Eve narrative). Assuming that nonhuman animals cannot be described as sinning in the same way that humans do (insofar as they are not conventionally

16. It is worth emphasizing that original guilt is part of the traditional Protestant and Catholic hamartiologies, but it is *not* part of the Eastern Orthodox doctrinal theory. See the masterful survey by David Weaver, "The Exegesis of Romans 5:12 among the Greek Fathers and Its Implication for the Doctrine of Original Sin: The 5th–12th Centuries," *St. Vladimir's Theological Quarterly* 27, no. 4 (1983): 133–59; and 28, no. 1 (1984): 231–57.

considered morally conscious figures, by dint of not possessing the capacity for rational or moral deliberation), there must have been *a* first morally conscious hominid. At some point, even making all the necessary caveats about gradualism and speciation and the emergence of humans in a larger population, some hominid must have been the first to have the neurological hardware and the experiences necessary (1) to realize that some actions were evil and (2) to choose to commit an evil action. So we can ask the question: Why not identify that first sin with the originating sin?

The problem with identifying the first sin (whenever it happened) with the originating sin is that the evolutionary account of the first sin in the last paragraph would not have made that first sin the source, the singular *origin*, of all subsequent sins. That person would not have been the progenitor of all subsequent sins (1) because they would not have been the progenitor of all subsequent humans and (2) because they were not the first being to commit the sinful action. Rather, the sinful action committed (be it violent, gluttonous, sexual, etc.) would have been the sort of action that the rest of the species or community had long since been committing; our first sinner would simply have been the first to be morally aware that his or her action was wrong. The fact that thereafter other humans would come to realize that their actions were sinful (perhaps even as a result of communication with the first sinner) would not mean that their sinful actions had been brought about by the first sinner's sin. For these reasons, as well as because of my concern about historical cherry-picking, I do not think that we should confuse the logically necessary first sin with the Christian notion of a single originating sin.[17]

Paul and the Fall

We turn now to the second big question posed above: Does the New Testament (especially Paul) require that we affirm a historical reading of Genesis 2–3?[18] After all, Paul speaks of Adam as if he were a historical figure, and Protestants have traditionally thought that Paul affirmed original guilt. These

17. This does not deny that ancient sins contribute to the multiplication of subsequent sins. As will be argued below, cultural and sociological forces certainly cause sins in one generation to foster evil in the next, in a way that is analogous to the traditional notion of the transmission of original sin. The point being resisted here is that all sins can be traced back to a single originating sin made by the first human individual or couple.

18. It may seem like a leap to go straight from Genesis to the New Testament, but after Gen. 1–5, the fall account is never again mentioned in the Old Testament, and Adam is explicitly named only in the genealogy of 1 Chron. 1:1. For a more detailed account of the argument in this section, see Hays and Herring, "Adam and the Fall," 34–50.

are disconcerting objections, but on closer examination one sees that they need not cause concern.

Did the Apostle Teach the Notion of Original Guilt?

The crucial text in this debate is Romans 5:12–21, to which Western Christians have traditionally pointed in defending original guilt. It is an especially important passage because there is no evidence that anyone before Paul adhered to the idea of original guilt; previous Jewish writers who did affirm the historicity of the fall believed that sin and death spread as a result of *concupiscence* since people had their wills corrupted as a result of the originating sin.[19] So by traditional Western Christian reckonings, Paul is considered the originator of the idea. But I do not think we have understood Paul aright on this point.

Scholars agree that in Romans 5:12–21 Paul is celebrating the greatness of Christ's sacrifice, which brings about new life (physical and spiritual; see 5:21), by contrasting it with Adam's fall, which brought about death (physical and spiritual). The crucial question is this: *How* does Paul claim that Adam's sin brought about death for humanity? Was it through original guilt or through concupiscence? Does Paul say that humans die because Adam's guilt is imputed to them such that they are punished for that guilt? Or does he say that Adam brought sin into the world such that other humans sin and are punished for their own sins?

The answer to the question is perfectly clear from the outset of Paul's discourse: "Sin came into the world through one man, and death came through sin, and *so death spread to all because all have sinned*" (Rom. 5:12). Paul sees death as the result of Adam's sin and explains that, by extension, all humans die because all humans sin. In just half a sentence, Paul summarizes elements 1 and 2 of the doctrinal theory described above: culpability and universality. Furthermore, in verse 20, when Paul says that "the law came in order that [*hina*] transgression might abound" (translation mine), he reveals his belief that humans have a sinful aversion to God's will (concupiscence), sinning more as they encounter the revelation of the law (see further Rom. 7:7–24). So in Romans 5:12–21 Paul affirms elements 1 through 3 of the doctrine of sin described above.

But nowhere in this text does Paul explicitly affirm original guilt (element 5). The verses often adduced as affirmations of original guilt are Romans 5:15–18:

> If the many died through the one man's trespass, much more surely have the grace
> of God and the free gift in the grace of the one man, Jesus Christ, abounded

19. Sirach 25.24; Apocalypse of Moses 32.2; Testament of Adam 3.5; 4 Ezra 7:118–20.

for the many. And the free gift is not like the effect of the one man's sin. For the judgment following one trespass *brought* condemnation, but the free gift following many trespasses *brings* justification. . . . Therefore just as one man's trespass *led* to condemnation for all, so one man's act of righteousness *leads* to justification and life for all.

The key question is *how* Adam's trespass brought about judgment for many. Many have argued, on the basis of Romans 5:16 and 18, that the judgment is issued because people are guilty of Adam's sin. But verses 16 and 18 do *not* say that. Quite the contrary, they are totally silent about the mechanism relating the judgment to the trespass; even the verbs "brought" and "brings" in verse 16 and "led" and "leads" in verse 18 (italicized above) are supplied by the translators because Paul included no verbs in those clauses. Paul just wrote the Greek equivalent of the following: "one man's trespass → unto condemnation for all" (v. 18) and "the judgment of one [trespass] → unto condemnation" (v. 16). He never says that all are condemned *because* they are guilty of what Adam did. Rather, he expects his readers to supply the mechanism by which to relate the transgression to the judgment.

Paul expects his readers to know how to relate the transgression of Adam to their own experience of judgment and death because he explained that relationship at the outset of his discussion: "Sin came into the world through one man, and death through sin, and so death spread to all *because all have sinned*" (Rom. 5:12). Paul never says humans are punished for Adam's sins; he says explicitly that they are punished because of their own sins.[20]

Indeed, the analogy to Christ's salvific death confirms this relationship. Paul does not believe that all people automatically have Christ's righteousness imputed to them; they receive it as a result of an act of faith (see, e.g., Rom. 4:5, 22–24). In the same way, Paul does not believe that people automatically have Adam's guilt imputed to them; they are made guilty and worthy of punishment, like Adam, as a result of their own acts of sin. In short, Paul believes that humans have corrupted wills as a result of which they sin and

---

20. Western Christians came to interpret this passage as teaching original guilt because of a mistranslation by Augustine. Not being an excellent Greek philologist, Augustine translated the phrase "*because [eph' hō]* all sinned" in 5:12 as "*in whom [in quo]* all sinned," thus rendering the text as follows: "Sin came into the world through one man—and death came through sin, and thus death spread to all men—*in whom [in quo]* all sinned." Augustine of Hippo, "A Treatise on the Merits and Forgiveness of Sins" 1.11, in *Saint Augustine: Anti-Pelagian Writings*, ed. Philip Schaff, trans. Peter Holmes, *The Nicene and Post-Nicene Fathers of the Christian Church*, series 1, vol. 5 (New York: Christian Literature, 1887), 19. In this way, Augustine came to think that Paul believed that all people sinned "in Adam" when he sinned. Today, however, Augustine's translation of *eph' hō* has been roundly rejected.

merit death and judgment. One sees the same hamartiology in James 1:13–15 and in many of Paul's Jewish predecessors.

So the fact that a nonhistorical reading of Genesis 2–3 precludes the idea of original guilt does *not* create problems from a New Testament perspective, insofar as the idea of original guilt is not found in the New Testament either.

Paul's Supposition of the Historicity of Genesis 2–3

Even though Paul does not teach the idea of original guilt, there is still the more basic fact that Paul does seem to have believed that Adam was a historical figure. This raises the question: Can we read Genesis 2–3 as nonhistorical if Paul assumed it was historical?

In the first place, we need not affirm every supposition that a biblical author carries over from their culture. As we already discussed, biblical authors often reflect the scientific and historical suppositions of their broader culture. Psalm 19 says the sun orbits the earth, and Jesus spoke about the mustard seed as the smallest of all seeds. But insofar as we do not believe that the psalmist was writing a treatise on astronomy or that Jesus was preaching botany, these continuities between the suppositions of the biblical authors and the (inaccurate) knowledge of their contemporaries should not bother us. The same goes for Paul's assumption about the historicity of Adam and the fall. Insofar as Paul's Jewish contemporaries took for granted that Adam was a historical figure, it is only reasonable that Paul would have assumed the same. So, unless we think that Paul's goal in Romans 5 was to defend the historicity of Adam's fall, we do not have a hermeneutical quandary.

There is a second matter to address: even allowing that Paul did not aim to convince his audience of the historicity of the fall, if the cohesion of Paul's argument depends on the historicity of an event that did not occur, that could theoretically imperil the veracity of what he aimed to affirm. Happily, this does not seem to be the case in Romans 5. In that text, Paul's goal is to expound how people are justified by faith unto eternal life through the grace of Jesus. Paul invokes the fall narrative as a way of contrasting the former state of humanity with the fortunes of those in Christ, thus rhetorically magnifying the greatness of Christ's action. But the truthfulness of Paul's argument about Christ's work does not hang on the historical veracity of the rhetorical foil he uses to celebrate redemption in Christ. It is not problematic to believe that salvation comes to humans through Christ's action without believing that Adam's fall is the source of all human death. Similarly, it was perfectly reasonable for the scribe in Luke 10:25–37 to accept Jesus's commandment that he should become a neighbor to anyone in need, even though the scribe would have believed in the historicity of neither the rhetorical foils Jesus created (the priest and the Levite who passed by the man brutalized by bandits) nor the good Samaritan. Without being historical, a story can be a perfectly valid point of analogy or contrast.

Finally, the nonhistoricity of Adam's fall in no way undermines the necessity of Christ's death and resurrection. Sometimes one hears it asserted that if Adam had not fallen, then Jesus would not have had to die. But this is not terribly sound logic. Christ's redemptive death does not become frivolous if human sins did not originate in Adam's fall. On the contrary, as long as humans sin and require forgiveness, Christ's death is supremely necessary. In other words, it is not elements 3 to 5 of Christian hamartiology (above) that necessitate Jesus's sacrifice; rather, elements 1 (the culpability of sin) and 2 (the universality of sin) make Christ's death crucial. Even if Adam and Eve never fell, the historical reality of my sin, your sin, and the sins of all humanity makes Christ's crucifixion both necessary and profoundly important.

In short, there is nothing about Paul's argument in Romans 5 that makes it problematic to deny the historicity of Genesis 2–3 because

- Paul's case does not rest logically on the historicity of the fall;
- it is not hermeneutically unique to say that Paul shares some of his contemporaries' erroneous suppositions about history or science;
- Paul does not argue for the existence of original guilt;
- Jesus's death is not rendered superfluous if Adam was not a historical figure.

Paul believes in the culpability and universality of sin, and he believes in concupiscence. He does not believe in original guilt. We only part company with respect to whether Adam's fall was the source of all sin—that is, whether there was a single originating sin.

An Integral Hamartiology

One big question remains: If the fall is not the reason for universal sin, then what is? No one would deny the universality of sin; if there is any Christian belief that can be empirically confirmed, the universality of sin is it! The question instead is this: *Why* is sin universal if it is not a result of what Adam and Eve did? Appealing to concupiscence (the corruption of human desires) only begs the question: *Why* are we concupiscent?

There is no reason to identify a single hamartiological culprit, to think that there is only one factor at play in concupiscence. I would suggest that concupiscence is a product of the confluence of *biological, sociological, cultural-evolutionary, spiritual,* and even *supernatural* factors, which I discuss below in turn.[21]

First, evolutionary biology provides a useful starting point for this conversation,[22] as it helps correct an inaccurate interpretation of Genesis according to which the creation was perfect prior to human rebellion.[23] For all the beauty of creation and the altruistic impulses fostered by evolution notwithstanding, natural selection favors behaviors such as violence, sexual promiscuity, and selfishness. Chimps kill members of their own species; spider monkeys perpetrate infanticide against the male offspring of their rivals;[24] mother tamarin monkeys will even take the lives of their own babies if their troop lacks a sufficient proportion of adult males.[25] These behaviors make sense at an evolutionary level: animals that practice violence against one another or against problematic offspring have a better chance of passing on their genes and seeing their offspring to reproductive maturity. In other words, there are significant ways in which natural selection favors the propagation of selfish behavior that runs contrary to Christian ideals of charity, self-sacrifice, monogamy, and so on.

Insofar as humans emerged through the process of natural selection, these same impulses (violence, selfishness, sexual concupiscence) ostensibly contributed to our emergence and remain present in our genetic composition. This suggests that we are, to a degree, spring-loaded toward behaviors that, among morally conscious beings, are properly categorized as sinful. (Even if, e.g., sexual promiscuity is not morally opprobrious for a terrier in heat, insofar as terriers are not morally conscious beings.) This should not be understood in terms of genetic determinism, as if we were held captive by the whims of our evolutionary inheritance.[26] Rather, evolutionary biology

---

21. Stephen J. Duffy, "Our Hearts of Darkness: Original Sin Revisited," *Theological Studies* 49 (1988): 597–622; Jerry D. Korsmeyer, *Evolution and Eden: Balancing Original Sin and Contemporary Science* (New York: Paulist Press, 1998), 125.

22. See the extended discussions of Patricia A. Williams, *Doing without Adam and Eve: Sociobiology and Original Sin* (Minneapolis: Fortress, 2001); Daryl P. Domning, *Original Selfishness: Original Sin and Evil in the Light of Evolution* (Burlington, VT: Ashgate, 2006).

23. Genesis never suggests that the creation was morally perfect. God says that it is very good (Gen. 1:31), but never that it is pristine. Indeed, the presence of the serpent (Gen. 3) and a tree of knowledge of good and evil (Gen. 2:9) indicate that, even if the biblical authors could not explain the origin of evil, they were aware of its primal antiquity.

24. Sara Alvarez et al., "Male-Directed Infanticide in Spider Monkeys (*Ateles* supp.)," *Primates* 56 (2015): 173–81.

25. Jeffrey Kluger, "Scientists Rush to Understand the Murderous Mamas of the Monkey World," *Time,* June 15, 2011, http://content.time.com/time/health/article/0,8599,2076786,00.html.

26. Biological conditions can incline us toward certain behaviors, but they do not oblige us to enact them. Genes do not steamroll free will.

helps explain why we have strong inclinations to behaviors that we would reject as contrary to God's will for humanity. In brief, evolutionary biology contributes to concupiscence; our physicality as humans helps explain our *aversio ad Deo* ("aversion to God").

Nonetheless, our being is not exhausted in our biology. So, second, sociology reveals that our engagement with reality is shaped by our interactions with other humans. As infants, we develop an apparatus of understanding in cooperation with those around us; our communities and culture shape what we believe, how we know, and therefore who we are.[27] There will inevitably be a high degree of transmission of values from one generation in a community to another, both for good and for ill. The same social mechanisms that imbue love for family can equally imbue xenophobia, and while these values and suppositions are not immovable, they are durable. We may not be puppets on strings pulled by our culture, but we are at very least like fish in a current. We have a strong inclination to persist in and therefore to perpetuate the sins of the community in which we were born. Morality has inertia. In short, sociology explains how our communities contribute to the reality of concupiscence. Not only do we follow bad examples; bad examples contribute to our moral constitution.

These evolutionary and cultural accounts of concupiscence need not be seen as alternatives. Quite the contrary, both factors contribute to our formation as concupiscent entities. Indeed, the previous chapter pointed out just how intimately the biological and cultural are intertwined.[28] So, third, cultural evolution explains that human flourishing owes in significant part to our tendency to *imitate* uncritically rather than to *emulate* behaviors we understand. Logically this would accelerate the intergenerational tendency toward sinful patterns of behavior, insofar as one generation uncritically imitated the vicious practices of its predecessors. Biology in no small part enables and facilitates cultural transmission, in favor of both altruistic tendencies and concupiscence.

Affirming that evolutionary and sociological elements contribute to the universality of sin need not exclude attention to the domains that have historically been the focus of hamartiological discussion. So, fourth, human spirituality certainly plays a major role in the dynamics of concupiscence. Our most profound existential deficiency and poverty, as spiritual entities, is that of not being fully with God.[29] A sense of distance from God increases the likelihood of sin, which in turn amplifies the sense of distance from God and

27. Peter Hünermann, "Experience of 'Original Sin'?," *Concilium* 1 (2004): 110.
28. See chap. 12 above by Benno van den Toren.
29. Cf. Korsmeyer, *Evolution and Eden*, 62–63.

thereby heightens the probability of even further sin. Sin is self-propagating, and that contributes to the dynamics of our moral corruption (concupiscence).

Finally, I am inclined to think that there are malevolent supernatural forces that tempt humans. Being attentive to natural sciences, under the conviction that all truth is God's truth, does not mean that one need become a philosophical naturalist; believing that science describes the natural world well does not mean that science excludes the existence of the supernatural, whether in reference to God or to lesser supernatural beings. I see little reason to abjure belief in a devil or demons *tout court*, and I find Michael Lloyd's discussion of an angelic fall to be compelling.[30] If evil angels exist, as Christian tradition has always maintained, then they too should be considered contributing agents in the momentum of concupiscence, in our rebellion against God.

To summarize, one can elaborate a compelling account of concupiscence (and thus the universality of sin) without appealing to an Adamic fall. Evolutionary biology, sociocultural dynamics, spiritual privation, and supernatural antagonism all combine to create a situation of profound temptation. As a result of these dynamics, humans are so strongly enticed toward sin that, even though we can in any given moment choose not to sin, we remain, in the long haul, certain to sin. The Christian doctrine of sin does not fall without Adam.

30. See chap. 17 below by Michael Lloyd.

CONCLUSION TO PART 2

Benno van den Toren

The Project: Creating Space

A main intention of the instigators of the research project Configuring Adam and Eve, which resulted in this volume, was to create space at the interface of theological anthropology and evolutionary science. We hypothesized that we could create more space (or less reverentially, more "wiggle room") between traditional Christian doctrine and the science with which it was supposed to clash if we could mine different theological theories that have been developed to understand these doctrines. Each of the theological theories might relate differently to the relevant aspects of current evolutionary theory, experience tensions in different places, allow for consonance at others, and simply address different issues where again other aspects of the doctrine are concerned.

This desire to create space is not motivated by a wish to make Christian doctrine immune to scientific insights and vice versa. If the truth is one, and if the Father of Jesus Christ is also the Creator of the universe, we do expect both discourses to refer to the same reality and to invite us to discover truth about the one world in which we live as creatures and objects of God's love in Christ. The doctrine of original sin speaks about the same human studied in evolutionary science. Yet we want to give careful attention to the question of whether there might be a variety of ways in which doctrines, through the mediation of different theological theories, relate to the findings of evolutionary science, looking for the real tensions but also for compatibility or possibly even consonance in places where it may not yet have been detected. In the whole process we have become increasingly aware that we do not only need to reckon with the proper nature of doctrinal discourse and scientific discourse. We have to be even more precise and distinguish between roles and functions of the different genres of the scriptural text, Christian doctrine, and theological theory on the one hand and scientific findings, different levels of theory building, and philosophical extrapolations of these theories on the other.

Throughout the chapters in part 2, it has become clear that the doctrine of original sin has two main aspects: original sin as the first sin in history (*peccatum originale originans*) and original sin as the sinfulness we inherit at birth, as hereditary sinfulness (*peccatum originale originatum*). The dialogue with evolutionary science raises different issues for both elements of the doctrine—in the latter case focused on the question of the unity of the human race and in the former on the question of whether one can (and should) find space for a historic first sin in the current scientific pictures of the evolutionary development of *Homo sapiens*. With regard to both aspects of the doctrine of original sin, our hypothesis has been confirmed as our discussion has provided us with a number of theological theories and concepts that create space and allow for creative dialogue and interaction with the relevant science.

The Results: Mapping the Space

With regard to the first sin, Christopher Hays presents a number of hermeneutical reasons why he believes that the doctrine of original sin is exclusively about the sinfulness we inherit rather than about how sin came into the world. Other authors in this section disagree for hermeneutical or theological reasons, but they nevertheless do not find the current findings and theories presented in evolutionary science incompatible with a historically first sin.

Gijsbert van den Brink makes the logical point that there necessarily must have been a first moment that one of our ancestors crossed the threshold to full humanity and responsibility before God. Only after this event (which would be linked with our species existing for the first time "in the image of God") could the first sin have happened. This insight might well be in line with Andrew McCoy's insights drawn from the church father Irenaeus of Lyons. Many people think of the original state of the first Adam and Eve as a state of perfection, yet the notion of perfection can have two different meanings. It can mean that something or someone is without default, but it can also mean that someone is perfected, having reached the highest state that can be attained. According to Irenaeus, Adam was not perfect in the latter sense, for he could only reach that through a historical relationship with God through union with Christ. Yet he was created not sinful but perfect in the first sense, in the way we can call a child "perfect," even though there is much growth that we still hope for.[1]

Andrew Pinsent adds another layer to the question of Adam's perfection by drawing on the Augustinian and Thomistic insight that what happened at the fall should be thought of as the loss of special grace. This grace was originally given to humanity as the *imago Dei* and allowed the first Adam to control his natural drives that would otherwise lead to his destruction. These drives are not wrong in themselves but need this special grace to properly guide them in a direction that promotes human flourishing. In this understanding, the consequences of the first, or original, sin can in principle not be detected in evolutionary history because they constitute the loss of a special divine gift that may only have been present for a relatively short period.

With regard to the unity of the human race in sin, different theological theories allow for different ways to understand this unity. Pinsent argues that this unity should be thought of as a unity of common descent but reads the modern genetic notion of a "mitochondrial Eve" and "Y-chromosomal Adam" as an argument against a polygenetic origin of the modern human population and possibly as an indication of an original human pair from whom we all descend—even though this does not necessarily mean that this couple would have been the only human couple at the time. John Collins argues on the basis of his federal approach that the unity of the human race is of a covenantal nature, and Adam and Eve can therefore well have been representatives of a wider community, conceivably as their king and queen. Benno van den Toren elaborates the strong cultural unity of human communities through the generations, allowing for a notion of inheritance of sinful cultural traits that is far stronger than mere imitation. These different models allow for different ways in which a first sin may have influenced the entirety of humanity, through the generations and—in the case of the federal and cultural models—also sideways within the same community.

Each of these models may have issues in relation to current developments in evolutionary theory that need further reflection. How, for example, does one conceive of the unity of the human race (federal, cultural, or otherwise) in the light of current theories that estimate that the population at the

---

1. Note that I use the perfection of a child here as a metaphor, not as a theological statement about original sin.

bottleneck at the origin of the human species consisted possibly of around ten thousand individuals,[2] consisting presumably of small communities of hunter-gatherers who spread out over the different continents in early stages? Furthermore, if one stresses the immaturity of the first humans rather than their perfection—and moreover the imperfect world in which they lived— does the difference between the human existence before and after the fall not become so small that one might need to reevaluate the weight it can carry as an explanation for the existence of evil? The last question by itself shows that the issues raised in this part cannot be treated independently from the issues related to the image of God and the origin of evil discussed in the other parts of this volume. Given the rapid developments in the field of human evolutionary biology, it may be wise not to foreclose conclusions by opting for one of these theological theories. It seems better to underline that the analysis of the theories in this part reveals that there are promising resources for further reflection while the debate over the doctrine of original sin and human evolution progresses. Insights from different theories might well be combined for a new theological synthesis to arise out of this fermentation process.

Further Reading

Alexander, Denis R. *Creation or Evolution: Do We Have to Choose?* 2nd ed. Oxford: Monarch, 2014.

Barrett, Matthew, and Ardel B. Caneday, eds. *Four Views on the Historical Adam.* Grand Rapids: Zondervan, 2013.

Blocher, Henri. *Original Sin: Illuminating the Riddle.* Grand Rapids: Eerdmans, 1999.

Collins, C. John. *Did Adam and Eve Really Exist? Who They Were and Why You Should Care.* Wheaton: Crossway, 2011.

Domning, Daryl P. *Original Selfishness: Original Sin and Evil in the Light of Evolution.* Burlington, VT: Ashgate, 2006.

Hefner, Philip J. *The Human Factor: Evolution, Culture, and Religion.* Minneapolis: Fortress, 1993.

McFarland, Ian A. *In Adam's Fall: A Meditation on the Christian Doctrine of Original Sin.* Oxford: Wiley-Blackwell, 2010.

Reeves, Michael, and Hans Madueme, eds. *Adam, the Fall, and Original Sin: Theological, Biblical, and Scientific Perspectives.* Grand Rapids: Baker Academic, 2014.

2. See Dennis R. Venema, "Genesis and the Genome: Genomics Evidence for Human-Ape Common Ancestry and Ancestral Hominid Population Sizes," *Perspectives on Science and Christian Faith* 62, no. 3 (2010): 173–74.

Schwager, Raymond. *Banished from Eden: Original Sin and Evolutionary Theory in the Drama of Salvation*. Leominster, UK: Gracewing, 2006.

Steenberg, Matthew C. *Irenaeus on Creation: The Cosmic Christ and the Saga of Redemption*. Vigiliae Christianae Supplements. Leiden: Brill, 2008.

Walton, John H. *The Lost World of Adam and Eve: Genesis 2–3 and the Human Origins Debate*. Downers Grove, IL: IVP Academic, 2015.

Wiley, Tatha. *Original Sin: Origins, Developments, Contemporary Meanings*. Mahwah, NJ: Paulist Press, 2002.

Williams, Patricia A. *Doing without Adam and Eve: Sociobiology and Original Sin*. Minneapolis: Fortress, 2001.

PART 3

Evil and Evolution

Michael Lloyd, EDITOR

The engagement of the church with new scientific discoveries has not always been a model of good public relations—think Galileo, think Darwin. Whatever the truth of the matter, the widespread belief is that the church insisted on a geocentric universe for centuries after the evidence went decisively against the Ptolemaic system.[1] And the enduring image of bishops getting trounced in debates with Darwinians, however distorted a perception, is certainly still dominant in the corporate memory of contemporary Western society.[2]

In part 3, we shall be considering the implications of modern evolutionary science and genetics for the problem of evil. Here it is the former, in particular, that raises questions with which we need to engage, for to accept with geological and biological science that pain, predation, disease, and death predate the emergence of humans would seem to rule out the previously widespread theodical maneuver of attributing natural disasters and natural evil of all

---

1. See Allan Chapman, *Stargazers: Copernicus, Galileo, the Telescope and the Church* (Oxford: Lion Hudson, 2014).
2. See Allan Chapman, *Slaying the Dragons: Destroying Myths in the History of Science and Faith* (Oxford: Lion Hudson, 2013).

kinds to the dislocation of the created order brought about by the human fall.[3] If such suffering predates the emergence of the only known creatures of sufficient moral awareness to be held morally accountable, then God would seem to be the only agent to whom responsibility for such suffering could be attributed. The problem with evolution for Christian belief has never been scientific as such; it has always been moral. God could have used evolution as his means of creating the world and its competing life forms, but why would a good God have chosen such a violent way of achieving that goal? That is the challenge posed by evolutionary science to any belief in a loving God and therefore to Christian belief in particular.

The nature of that challenge is outlined in chapter 14 by Ben Mitchell. He highlights the (often neglected) hermeneutical challenges that theistic evolutionists face. There are biblical texts that were historically read as presenting a narrative of creation that would be at odds with an evolutionary narrative, and according to Mitchell, "theistic evolutionists are going to have to offer persuasive alternative readings of these texts that neither undermine the authority of the biblical text nor reshape the basic contours of the narrative." He further (rightly) insists that such readings must not diminish or in any way compromise the gospel as gospel, and he suggests that only a full-bloodedly christological and trinitarian narrative is likely to be substantial enough to meet these challenges.

These challenges are then taken up by the other contributors. In chapter 15, Stanley Rosenberg presents an Augustinian approach in the light of evolutionary and genetic science, focusing on Augustine's belief that, as all things come from nonbeing, they have a tendency to return to nonbeing (if not held in being by the miraculous intervention of God). Rosenberg presents Augustine as seeing disease, decay, and death as characteristics not so much of *fallenness* as of *finitude*—and thus as necessary features of a finite world, at least until it is radically redeemed at the eschaton. He therefore suggests that Augustine is far more able to cope with the findings and challenges of evolutionary biology than is often assumed.

In chapter 16, Michael Lloyd argues that theodicies that do not incorporate a doctrine of the fall are subject to serious challenges. That raises the issue of evolution acutely, as evolution makes it highly problematic to attribute all suffering to the disobedience of the human race. He argues that evolution does not actually rule out a historic human fall, but he admits that such a

---

3. I say "seem" here because attempts have been made to articulate the human fall in such a way as to ascribe to it the animal suffering that preceded it. See, e.g., William A. Dembski, *The End of Christianity: Finding a Good God in an Evil World* (Nashville: B&H Academic, 2009).

fall cannot bear the weight of accounting for prehuman suffering and death. In chapter 17, he therefore looks at alternative doctrines of the fall that can account for prehuman natural evil. He believes that taking seriously the fall-of-the-angels tradition enables one to see suffering as inimical to the purposes of God—which he sees as being theologically, christologically, and pastorally vital.

In chapter 18, Richard Swinburne offers what he calls an Irenaean approach to the problem of evil in the light of evolutionary theory and modern genetics. This carefully argued chapter examines the requirements of a satisfactory theodicy and then proceeds to offer a theodicy that, he argues, meets those requirements. Swinburne suggests that there are some moral virtues that depend on the occurrence of suffering and pain and that are so beneficial to human significance that they warrant God's permission of the suffering. He then considers how this greater or higher good argument might apply to animals who may not be capable of such moral virtue and who may not be compensated in a future life for the suffering they have endured.

In chapter 19, Christopher Southgate explores free process and only way arguments. The former build on the freewill defense, in which the good of human freedom is used to outweigh the evils that it makes possible, and argue that it is not just individual human freedom that is valuable but also the freedom of the whole nexus of creaturely interactions—and that that freedom can be seen as outweighing the suffering, waste, and frustration of the natural order. He then outlines and defends an only way argument, in which he argues that it is plausible to assume that God could not have created a physical world containing the goods and values of the world as it is, without it also containing the pains and disvalues from which our world suffers.

In chapter 20, Vince Vitale offers his unique non-identity theodicy, which argues that our existence—as the particular individuals that we are—depends in significant part on the history that preceded our births, both the pleasurable aspects of that history and the painful ones. If, therefore, God values the creation of you and me and every other individual human in particular, then that gives him some reason for allowing our universe to include its vulnerabilities to suffering. To complain that God should have so governed cosmic history to prevent all creaturely suffering is implicitly to demand that we and our loved ones should never have been created. Vitale then applies the same argument to animal suffering.

The contributors to part 3 have two hopes in particular. First, they hope that the diversity of their contributions will demonstrate the enormous space that theodicy still enjoys. Here are five ways of continuing to believe in the goodness of God, while fully taking into account the consensus of modern science. And this selection is not comprehensive—there are plenty of other positions we could have included (if we had been permitted another hundred pages or so!). It is not the case that evolutionary science has significantly shrunk the space in which theodicy can operate. And, second, Ben Mitchell calls on all contributors to this debate to "focus on cultivating Christian virtues and spiritual practices that may make the conversation less hostile and volatile." All the contributors to this volume hope that they have modeled a form of engagement with one another that will make for such a conversation. They believe that light tends to be generated in inverse proportion to heat, and they have tried to express themselves accordingly.

14

Questions, Challenges, and Concerns for the Problem of Evil

C. Ben Mitchell

Jews and Christians have affirmed down the ages that God is good and that the good God made the world good. So declares the first book of the Hebrew Bible: "God saw everything that he had made, and indeed, it was very good" (Gen. 1:31). At the same time, however, the experience of the world with its struggle, travail, suffering, and death has posed a perennial problem—namely, the problem of evil, or what eighteenth-century metaphysician Gottfried Leibniz coined as "theodicy" (a justification of God's actions).[1] Stated simply, the problem is this: If an omnipotent, omniscient, and omnibenevolent deity made a good world, what accounts for the obvious and palpable evil in that world? Or to put the clutch of questions as Scottish philosopher David Hume famously expressed them, "Is [God] willing to prevent evil, but not able? Then he is impotent. Is he able, but not willing? Then he is malevolent. Is he both able and willing? Whence then cometh evil?"[2]

Most Enlightenment philosophers mounted the argument from the problem of evil not as a means of questioning the truthfulness of the claim that God is

1. Gottfried Leibniz, *Theodicy: Essays on the Goodness of God, the Freedom of Man, and the Origin of Evil*, trans. E. M. Huggard (1709; repr., Hartford, CT: Yale University Press, 1952).
2. David Hume, *Dialogues concerning Natural Religion*, 2nd ed. (1779; repr., Indianapolis: Hackett, 1998), 186.

good but rather of the claim that God *is*.[3] That is to say, the problem of evil has been traditionally used as an argument against theism. Bertrand Russell, for example, made much of the problem of evil in a 1927 essay still being read by nearly every first-year philosophy student, "Why I Am Not a Christian."[4] More recently, the so-called four horsemen of atheism—Richard Dawkins, Daniel Dennett, Sam Harris, and the late Christopher Hitchens—have each employed the problem of evil to one extent or another to argue against the existence of God.

Christian Philosophy and the Problem of Evil

Hebrew and Christian scriptures, especially the poetic books and Wisdom literature, grapple with the perplexity of the problem of evil. For instance, Psalms and the book of Job speak to the problem in poignant ways. Likewise, philosophers and theologians in the Christian tradition have engaged the problem on several levels, including analytical, theological, and pastoral responses.[5] Two prominent approaches to the problem of evil include the freewill defense and the greater good defense.

Freewill Defense

One of the ablest contemporary defenders of Christian theism is Alvin Plantinga, John A. O'Brien Professor of Philosophy Emeritus at the University of Notre Dame and the inaugural holder of the Jellema Chair in Philosophy at Calvin College. In his volume *God, Freedom, and Evil*, Plantinga summarizes the freewill defense in the following way:

> A world containing creatures who are significantly free (and freely perform more good than evil actions) is more valuable, all else being equal, than a world

3. Joseph F. Kelly, *The Problem of Evil in the Western Tradition: From the Book of Job to Modern Genetics* (Collegeville, MN: Liturgical Press, 2002); Marilyn McCord Adams and Robert Merrihew Adams, eds., *The Problem of Evil* (Oxford: Oxford University Press, 1990); John Hick, *Evil and the God of Love*, 3rd ed. (New York: Palgrave Macmillan, 2010; first published 1966); Kenneth Surin, *Theology and the Problem of Evil* (Oxford: Basil Blackwell, 1986).

4. Bertrand Russell, *Why I Am Not a Christian, and Other Essays on Religion and Other Subjects* (New York: Simon & Schuster, 1957).

5. Alvin Plantinga, *God, Freedom, and Evil* (Grand Rapids: Eerdmans, 2002; first published 1974); Norman L. Geisler, *The Roots of Evil* (Grand Rapids: Zondervan, 1978); James Walsh and P. G. Walsh, eds., *Divine Providence and Human Suffering*, Message of the Fathers of the Church (Wilmington, DE: Glazier, 1985); Peter Kreeft, *Making Sense out of Suffering* (Ann Arbor, MI: Servant, 1986); Richard Swinburne, *Providence and the Problem of Evil* (Oxford: Clarendon, 1998); John S. Feinberg, *Where Is God? A Personal Story of Finding God in Grief and Suffering* (Nashville: Broadman & Holman, 2004).

containing no free creatures at all. Now God can create free creatures, but He can't cause or determine them to do only what is right. For if He does so, then they aren't significantly free after all; they do not do what is right freely. To create creatures capable of moral good, therefore, He must create creatures capable of moral evil; and He can't give these creatures the freedom to perform evil and at the same time prevent them from doing so. As it turned out, sadly enough, some of the free creatures God created went wrong in the exercise of their freedom; this is the source of moral evil. The fact that free creatures sometimes go wrong, however, counts neither against God's omnipotence nor against His goodness; for He could have forestalled the occurrence of moral evil only by removing the possibility of moral good.[6]

In other words, one of the consequences of God creating free human creatures is that, in their freedom, they may use their wills in ways that are inconsistent with God's own goodness or the goodness of God's created order. Thus, evil is a result of free human agency.

Greater Good Defense

Another account of the problem of evil is the one often attributed to second-century philosopher and theologian Irenaeus, bishop of Lugdunum in Gaul (modern-day Lyons, France). According to this view, although humans were created in the image of God, they remain imperfect and are gradually being perfected into the likeness of God. Evil and suffering are offered as the best way to refine human nature or to develop the soul. Without the struggle against evil and suffering, humans could not perfect their own natures. Later, Origen used two metaphors for the soul-making character of the fallen world. First, the world is a school where humans learn and mature, and a school's primary purpose is to educate, not to entertain. Similarly, God's purposes for us are more pedagogical than hedonistic. As one of the leading proponents of (a version of) the greater good defense, John Hick puts it this way:

> I think it is clear that a parent who loves his children, and wants them to be-come the best human beings that they are capable of becoming, does not treat pleasure as the sole and supreme value. . . . If, then, there is any true analogy between God's purpose for his human creatures, and the purpose of loving and wise parents for their children, we have to recognize that the presence of pleasure and the absence of pain cannot be the supreme and overriding end for which the world exists. Rather, this world must be a place of soul-making.[7]

6. Plantinga, *God, Freedom, and Evil*, 30.
7. Hick, *Evil and the God of Love*, 258–59.

The second of Origen's metaphors is that the world is a hospital where the human soul is being healed. The point here is that in a hospital the medicine may be unpleasant and the surgery may be painful—or even, in some ways, destructive—but both are justifiable if they bring about the healing of the patient. Thus, the evil and suffering one experiences serve the greater good of making one a better human.

John Hick is not alone in advocating an Irenaean view of the problem of evil. Richard Swinburne and other recent philosophers have also viewed evil as an opportunity for the greater human good.[8] That is, evil is a necessary condition for a world in which humans overcome obstacles and struggles in order to develop certain virtues, and many higher-order goods (e.g., altruism, self-sacrifice, courage, perseverance, compassion) are simply not possible if there is no evil to be overcome. Presumably, without the struggle, human existence would be flat, textureless, and unimprovable.

The Problem of Natural Evil

To this point I have emphasized how the freewill and greater good defenses account for moral evil—that is, the suffering that results from human moral choices. But what about natural evil? What about earthquakes, tsunamis, and blizzards? What about animal predation, aging, and death? How does one account for "Nature, red in tooth and claw," as Alfred Lord Tennyson put it?

This problem was most certainly part of Charles Darwin's concern as he sought to work through the implications of his own theory of evolution. In a now-famous exchange with his friend Asa Gray, the American naturalist, Darwin exclaimed, "I own that I cannot see as plainly as others do, and as I should wish to do, evidence of design and beneficence on all sides of us. There seems to me too much misery in the world. I cannot persuade myself that a beneficent and omnipotent God would have designedly created the Ichneu-monidae with the express intention of their feeding within the living bodies of caterpillars, or that a cat should play with mice."[9] The Ichneumonidae is a family of parasitic wasps that plant their eggs within the bodies of spiders, caterpillars, and other hosts. As the pupa develops, it effectively eats its host from the inside out. And everyone will be familiar with the apparent delight a cat takes in torturing its prey. These examples of animal cruelty were too much for Darwin to fathom. How could God be the author of such a grisly

8. For a statement of Richard Swinburne's position, see chap. 18 below.
9. Charles Darwin to Asa Gray, "Letter no. 2814," May 22, 1860, Darwin Correspondence Project, http://www.darwinproject.ac.uk/DCP-LETT-2814.

world? "What a book a devil's chaplain might write on the clumsy, wasteful, blundering, low, and horribly cruel works of nature."[10]

Likewise, contemporary scientists Karl Giberson and Francis Collins lament the intractability of the problem of evil. It "poses the most ancient and persistent objection to God's existence," they write, and "has no simple answer; alas, it also has no complex answer. In fact it has no satisfactory answer whatsoever."[11] They go on to echo Darwin's concern about the problem of natural evil: "The God of the Bible would not play a cruel joke on mice by designing cats to torture them. (What did the mice ever do to deserve that?) Nor would this God give the bacterium that causes bubonic plague its remarkably well-designed power to kill some two hundred million people—many of them innocent children—over the past two millennia."[12]

The Evolutionary Defense

As we have seen, for many evolutionists, the problem of evil has been a decisive factor in coming to atheistic conclusions. Natural evil is indisputably real and cannot be explained as a consequence of the moral failure of humans; therefore a good God cannot exist, or so the argument goes. However, according to some theists, the problems of both natural evil and moral evil find some resolution in the theory of evolution. As it has itself evolved, theistic evolution in effect provides its own theodicy. Theistic evolution—and what has come to be known in some circles as evolutionary creationism[13]—extricates God from the problem of natural evil (for, on the assumptions of this position, moral evil is a natural, evolutionary by-product of natural evil).

To relieve the felt pressure, evolutionary creationists maintain that natural suffering and death must be the results of natural processes. God created through the big bang, using evolution as the means.[14] Again, as Giberson and

10. Charles Darwin, "A Low & Lewd Nature," *Darwin*, ed. Adrian Desmond and James Moore (New York: Norton, 1991), 449.

11. Karl Giberson and Francis Collins, *The Language of Science and Faith: Straight Answers to Genuine Questions* (Downers Grove, IL: InterVarsity, 2011), 127, 128.

12. Giberson and Collins, *Language of Science and Faith*, 133.

13. For more on this language, see materials from the organization BioLogos at http://biologos.org.

14. Some account still needs to be given of *why* God has created by these means, especially given the competitive and violent nature of the evolutionary process. In the present volume, Christopher Southgate (chap. 19) argues that the way that God has created our world is the only way in which a physical world containing free and creative beings could have been created, and Michael Lloyd (chap. 17) argues that evolution has only taken a competitive and violent form because of the dislocation engendered by the angelic fall.

Collins have said, "Here, evolution actually makes a valuable contribution to Christian theology. In contrast to the challenges that evolution has posed to traditional belief—and we do not mean to minimize those—we now find that evolution has a most useful positive and constructive insight to offer."[15]

What Is at Stake?

Both Jews and Christians have affirmed that it is God "who made heaven and earth, the sea, and all that is in them" (Ps. 146:6). Indeed, the very first verse of the Bible declares, "In the beginning God created the heavens and the earth" (Gen. 1:1 NIV). Moreover, the Nicene Creed (AD 325), the ancient liturgical confession of the Christian church, commences with the declaration, "I believe in one God, the Father almighty, maker of heaven and earth, of all things visible and invisible."

Many biblical commentators and theologians in the Christian tradition have maintained that God made the world *ex nihilo* (from nothing) and that, in the beginning at least, God made the world to be good. The first chapter of Genesis chronicles God's creation of the various elements: light, the waters, the dry land, and so on, over a six-day period. At the conclusion of each day of creation, "God saw that it was good" (Gen. 1:12). Grounded in the biblical text and the theology of the fathers of the church, it is not too strong to say that this—that when God made the world it was good—has been the dominant view among orthodox Christians (although there have been divergent views on the length of time designated by a "day").

Further, based on a straightforward reading of the biblical text, most orthodox Christians have believed that God created the first pair of humans, Adam and Eve, and placed them in a garden paradise: "Then God said, 'Let us make humankind in our image, according to our likeness; and let them have dominion over the fish of the sea, and over the birds of the air, and over the cattle, and over all the wild animals of the earth, and over every creeping thing that creeps upon the earth'" (Gen. 1:26).

Adam and Eve lived in the presence of God as they cared for and tended the garden paradise. The Genesis text goes on to say, "Out of the ground the LORD God made to grow every tree that is pleasant to the sight and good for food, the tree of life also in the midst of the garden, and the tree of the knowledge of good and evil" (Gen. 2:9). A few verses later, we find that "the LORD God took the man and put him in the garden of Eden to till it and keep

---

15. Giberson and Collins, *Language of Science and Faith*, 133.

fall from the architecture of the faith, what will the repercussions be?
ng mild, like tossing a pebble into a pond with the ripples absorbed
 the system? Or something more serious, like the great fall of Humpty
 where all the king's exegetes and all the king's theologians couldn't put
back together again? Christians need reliable answers to such questions.[16]

dly, this problem is nothing new in the faith-and-science dialogue.
bout reading the Book of God and the so-called Book of Nature
rt of the conversation for a very long time.[17] Nevertheless, that the
rsist so robustly in the debate is evidence of their importance to
olved. BioLogos, an organization that advocates for the compat-
istic evolution and the Christian faith, for instance, devotes a large
 website to common questions around biblical interpretation.[18]
BioLogos acknowledges how important the biblical witness is
nding origins.

ersation is by no means merely academic. Obviously at stake are
nterpretations of the Bible and the evidence of science. But, crudely
 are also at stake. Madueme and Reeves trace some of the recent
titutions firing professors for taking one view or another on these
d the chapter on "Adam and Modern Science" in their book was
 a pseudonym, presumably to preserve the author's reputation
job. The Galileo affair was not just a historical event, so to speak.
 it doubly important that Christians especially attend not only
ns but also to the virtues necessary to participate in the con-
east one organization, the Colossian Forum, has emerged not
sues at the center of the debate(s) but to focus on cultivating
ues and spiritual practices that may make the conversation less
atile.[19] Whether the project will succeed is an open question.

ieme and Michael Reeves, eds., *Adam, the Fall, and Original Sin: Theological,
tific Perspectives* (Grand Rapids: Baker Academic, 2014), ix–x. Several con-
lations of the doctrine of original sin and the fall include John E. Towes, *The
Sin* (Eugene, OR: Wipf & Stock, 2013); Tatha Wiley, *Original Sin: Origins,
ntemporary Meanings* (Mahwah, NJ: Paulist Press, 2002); Ian A. McFarland,
leditation on the Doctrine of Original Sin (Oxford: Wiley-Blackwell, 2010).
dley Brooke, *Science and Religion: Some Historical Perspectives* (Cambridge:
sity Press, 2014); David C. Lindberg and Ronald L. Numbers, eds., *God
ical Essays on the Encounter between Christianity and Science* (Berkeley:
rnia Press, 1986); Peter Harrison, *The Bible, Protestantism, and the Rise of
ambridge: Cambridge University Press, 2001); Harrison, *The Fall of Man
 of Science* (Cambridge: Cambridge University Press, 2009); Harrison, *The
e and Religion* (Chicago: University of Chicago Press, 2015).
logos.org/common-questions/biblical-interpretation.
rmation on the Colossian Forum, see http://colossianforum.org/.

it. And the LORD God commanded the man, 'You may freely eat of every tree of the garden; but of the tree of the knowledge of good and evil you shall not eat, for in the day that you eat of it you shall die'" (vv. 15–17).

Alas, as the narrative progresses, we find that Adam and Eve did indeed disobey God, eat the forbidden fruit, and suffer the consequences of their rebellion—on both them and the entire created order. In the following verses, God indicts the serpent who tempted the first couple and pronounces the curses that will be brought about because of their disobedience:

The LORD God said to the serpent,

> "Because you have done this,
>   cursed are you among all animals
>   and among all wild creatures;
> upon your belly you shall go,
>   and dust you shall eat
>   all the days of your life.
> I will put enmity between you and the woman,
>   and between your offspring and hers;
> he will strike your head,
>   and you will strike his heel."

To the woman he said,

> "I will greatly increase your pangs in childbearing;
>   in pain you shall bring forth children,
> yet your desire shall be for your husband,
>   and he shall rule over you."

And to the man he said,

> "Because you have listened to the voice of your wife,
>   and have eaten of the tree
> about which I commanded you,
>   'You shall not eat of it,'
> cursed is the ground because of you;
>   in toil you shall eat of it all the days of your life;
> thorns and thistles it shall bring forth for you;
>   and you shall eat the plants of the field.
> By the sweat of your face
>   you shall eat bread
> until you return to the ground,
>   for out of it you were taken;

you are dust,
and to dust you shall return."

(Gen. 3:14–19)

On the basis of these ancient stories, Christians traditionally have drawn a number of important conclusions. First, the world was created by divine fiat out of no preexisting matter, *ex nihilo*. Second, the world was created good, but through human disobedience it became cursed. On this view, the sin of a single pair of specially created humans, Adam and Eve, is the cause of the evil that is in the world. In other words, since the created order was originally paradisal, moral evil is the source of natural evil. This is called the doctrine of the fall, which was the result of that original sin.

Much later, the apostle Paul would develop these doctrines soteriologically. In Romans 5, for instance, Paul locates the origin of death in the first act of human disobedience: "Sin came into the world through one man, and death came through sin, and so death spread to all because all have sinned" (Rom. 5:12). Or, as he exults in his letter to the Corinthian believers, "But in fact Christ has been raised from the dead, the first fruits of those who have died. For since death came through a human being, the resurrection of the dead has also come through a human being; for as all die in Adam, so all will be made alive in Christ" (1 Cor. 15:20–22). The sin and death that result from the first Adam's disobedience have been victoriously overcome through the second, or last, Adam's obedience, death, and resurrection. Because all humans since Adam (except Jesus) have sinned (thereby revealing that they are "in Adam"), they die. All who are "in Christ"—that is, are united with him by faith—will be made alive.

Finally, Paul himself acknowledges the cosmic effects of that first sin and points to an eschatological hope that the curse will one day be removed through the redemptive work of God in Christ. In the meantime, Paul says, creation groans:

I consider that the sufferings of this present time are not worth comparing with the glory about to be revealed to us. For the creation waits with eager longing for the revealing of the children of God; for the creation was subjected to futility, not of its own will but by the will of the one who subjected it, in hope that the creation itself will be set free from its bondage to decay and will obtain the freedom of the glory of the children of God. We know that the whole creation has been groaning in labor pains until now; and not only the creation, but we ourselves, who have the first fruits of the Spirit, groan inwardly while we wait for adoption, the redemption of our bodies. (Rom. 8:18–23)

One day, as this reading of the text goes,

He [God] will dwell with them;
they will be his peoples,
and God himself will be with them;
he will wipe every tear from their eyes
Death will be no more;
mourning and crying and pain will b
for the first things have passed away.

"'The wolf and the lamb will graze toget
the ox; and dust will be the serpent's foo
all My holy mountain,' says the LORD"
the horrendous effects of the fall will be r
of Jesus the Messiah.

There are a few reasons for rehearsin
ground. The first is to be reminded of t
ing biblical texts. It is relatively easy to
these texts to offer a certain account o
plays a prominent role in the biblical
of humanity's original parents appears
the origin of evil in the world.

Second, Christians who take this st
ously worry that theistic evolutionist
reliability of the Bible and ultimately c
ness of the God who inspired the aut

Finally, because the outline just pr
rative arc of the Scriptures of the Ol
gospel (the good news) of Jesus Chr
way worry that theistic evolution u
young-earth creationists, some old-e
views are informed by a plain read
going to have to offer persuasive alte
undermine the authority of the bil
of the narrative, if they are to be t

As evangelical theologians Han
the introduction to their book, A

Adam and the fall do not float free
dent ideas. They are central node
meshed in a much broader, orga

16. Hans Mad
Biblical, and Scien
temporary reform
Story of Original
Developments, Co
In Adam's Fall: A
17. See John H
Cambridge Unive
and Nature: Histo
University of Calif
Natural Science (C
and the Foundation
Territories of Scien
18. See http://bi
19. For more in

---

and the
Somethi
back int
Dumpty,
the faith

Admitte
Questions
have been p
questions p
everyone in
ibility of the
section of it
In doing so,
for understa

This conv
trustworthy i
perhaps, jobs
history of ins
questions. Ar
written unde
and, perhaps,

This make
to the questic
versation. At
to solve the is
Christian virt
hostile and vo

it. And the LORD God commanded the man, 'You may freely eat of every tree of the garden; but of the tree of the knowledge of good and evil you shall not eat, for in the day that you eat of it you shall die'" (vv. 15–17).

Alas, as the narrative progresses, we find that Adam and Eve did indeed disobey God, eat the forbidden fruit, and suffer the consequences of their rebellion—on both them and the entire created order. In the following verses, God indicts the serpent who tempted the first couple and pronounces the curses that will be brought about because of their disobedience:

The LORD God said to the serpent,

> "Because you have done this,
>> cursed are you among all animals
>> and among all wild creatures;
> upon your belly you shall go,
>> and dust you shall eat
>> all the days of your life.
> I will put enmity between you and the woman,
>> and between your offspring and hers;
> he will strike your head,
>> and you will strike his heel."

To the woman he said,

> "I will greatly increase your pangs in childbearing;
>> in pain you shall bring forth children,
> yet your desire shall be for your husband,
>> and he shall rule over you."

And to the man he said,

> "Because you have listened to the voice of your wife,
>> and have eaten of the tree
> about which I commanded you,
>> 'You shall not eat of it,'
> cursed is the ground because of you;
>> in toil you shall eat of it all the days of your life;
> thorns and thistles it shall bring forth for you;
>> and you shall eat the plants of the field.
> By the sweat of your face
>> you shall eat bread
> until you return to the ground,
>> for out of it you were taken;

> you are dust,
>   and to dust you shall return."
>
> (Gen. 3:14–19)

On the basis of these ancient stories, Christians traditionally have drawn a number of important conclusions. First, the world was created by divine fiat out of no preexisting matter, *ex nihilo*. Second, the world was created good, but through human disobedience it became cursed. On this view, the sin of a single pair of specially created humans, Adam and Eve, is the cause of the evil that is in the world. In other words, since the created order was originally paradisal, moral evil is the source of natural evil. This is called the doctrine of the fall, which was the result of that original sin.

Much later, the apostle Paul would develop these doctrines soteriologically. In Romans 5, for instance, Paul locates the origin of death in the first act of human disobedience: "Sin came into the world through one man, and death came through sin, and so death spread to all because all have sinned" (Rom. 5:12). Or, as he exults in his letter to the Corinthian believers, "But in fact Christ has been raised from the dead, the first fruits of those who have died. For since death came through a human being, the resurrection of the dead has also come through a human being; for as all die in Adam, so all will be made alive in Christ" (1 Cor. 15:20–22). The sin and death that result from the first Adam's disobedience have been victoriously overcome through the second, or last, Adam's obedience, death, and resurrection. Because all humans since Adam (except Jesus) have sinned (thereby revealing that they are "in Adam"), they die. All who are "in Christ"—that is, are united with him by faith—will be made alive.

Finally, Paul himself acknowledges the cosmic effects of that first sin and points to an eschatological hope that the curse will one day be removed through the redemptive work of God in Christ. In the meantime, Paul says, creation groans:

> I consider that the sufferings of this present time are not worth comparing with the glory about to be revealed to us. For the creation waits with eager longing for the revealing of the children of God; for the creation was subjected to futility, not of its own will but by the will of the one who subjected it, in hope that the creation itself will be set free from its bondage to decay and will obtain the freedom of the glory of the children of God. We know that the whole creation has been groaning in labor pains until now; and not only the creation, but we ourselves, who have the first fruits of the Spirit, groan inwardly while we wait for adoption, the redemption of our bodies. (Rom. 8:18–23)

One day, as this reading of the text goes, in a new paradise,

> He [God] will dwell with them;
> they will be his peoples,
> and God himself will be with them;
> he will wipe every tear from their eyes.
> Death will be no more;
> mourning and crying and pain will be no more,
> for the first things have passed away. (Rev. 21:3–4)

"'The wolf and the lamb will graze together, and the lion will eat straw like the ox; and dust will be the serpent's food. They will do no evil or harm in all My holy mountain,' says the LORD" (Isa. 65:25 NASB). In other words, the horrendous effects of the fall will be reversed through the victorious work of Jesus the Messiah.

There are a few reasons for rehearsing this biblical and theological background. The first is to be reminded of the hermeneutical challenges of reading biblical texts. It is relatively easy to see how Christians have understood these texts to offer a certain account of origins. The creative work of God plays a prominent role in the biblical narrative. Likewise, the disobedience of humanity's original parents appears to play a profound role in explaining the origin of evil in the world.

Second, Christians who take this straightforward reading of the text seriously worry that theistic evolutionist accounts undermine the authority and reliability of the Bible and ultimately challenge the authority and trustworthiness of the God who inspired the authors of the biblical text.

Finally, because the outline just provided, brief as it is, represents the narrative arc of the Scriptures of the Old and New Testaments and thus of the gospel (the good news) of Jesus Christ, Christians who read the text in this way worry that theistic evolution undermines that gospel. Because six-day young-earth creationists, some old-earth creationists, and others believe their views are informed by a plain reading of the text, theistic evolutionists are going to have to offer persuasive alternative readings of these texts that neither undermine the authority of the biblical text nor reshape the basic contours of the narrative, if they are to be taken seriously.

As evangelical theologians Hans Madueme and Michael Reeves remark in the introduction to their book, *Adam, the Fall, and Original Sin*,

> Adam and the fall do not float free in Scripture like rootless, atomistic, independent ideas. They are central nodes that hold together and are completely enmeshed in a much broader, organic, theological matrix. If we remove Adam

and the fall from the architecture of the faith, what will the repercussions be? Something mild, like tossing a pebble into a pond with the ripples absorbed back into the system? Or something more serious, like the great fall of Humpty Dumpty, where all the king's exegetes and all the king's theologians couldn't put the faith back together again? Christians need reliable answers to such questions.[16]

Admittedly, this problem is nothing new in the faith-and-science dialogue. Questions about reading the Book of God and the so-called Book of Nature have been part of the conversation for a very long time.[17] Nevertheless, that the questions persist so robustly in the debate is evidence of their importance to everyone involved. BioLogos, an organization that advocates for the compatibility of theistic evolution and the Christian faith, for instance, devotes a large section of its website to common questions around biblical interpretation.[18] In doing so, BioLogos acknowledges how important the biblical witness is for understanding origins.

This conversation is by no means merely academic. Obviously at stake are trustworthy interpretations of the Bible and the evidence of science. But, crudely perhaps, jobs are also at stake. Madueme and Reeves trace some of the recent history of institutions firing professors for taking one view or another on these questions. And the chapter on "Adam and Modern Science" in their book was written under a pseudonym, presumably to preserve the author's reputation and, perhaps, job. The Galileo affair was not just a historical event, so to speak.

This makes it doubly important that Christians especially attend not only to the questions but also to the virtues necessary to participate in the conversation. At least one organization, the Colossian Forum, has emerged not to solve the issues at the center of the debate(s) but to focus on cultivating Christian virtues and spiritual practices that may make the conversation less hostile and volatile.[19] Whether the project will succeed is an open question.

16. Hans Madueme and Michael Reeves, eds., *Adam, the Fall, and Original Sin: Theological, Biblical, and Scientific Perspectives* (Grand Rapids: Baker Academic, 2014), ix–x. Several contemporary reformulations of the doctrine of original sin and the fall include John E. Towes, *The Story of Original Sin* (Eugene, OR: Wipf & Stock, 2013); Tatha Wiley, *Original Sin: Origins, Developments, Contemporary Meanings* (Mahwah, NJ: Paulist Press, 2002); Ian A. McFarland, *In Adam's Fall: A Meditation on the Doctrine of Original Sin* (Oxford: Wiley-Blackwell, 2010).

17. See John Hedley Brooke, *Science and Religion: Some Historical Perspectives* (Cambridge: Cambridge University Press, 2014); David C. Lindberg and Ronald L. Numbers, eds., *God and Nature: Historical Essays on the Encounter between Christianity and Science* (Berkeley: University of California Press, 1986); Peter Harrison, *The Bible, Protestantism, and the Rise of Natural Science* (Cambridge: Cambridge University Press, 2001); Harrison, *The Fall of Man and the Foundations of Science* (Cambridge: Cambridge University Press, 2009); Harrison, *The Territories of Science and Religion* (Chicago: University of Chicago Press, 2015).

18. See http://biologos.org/common-questions/biblical-interpretation.

19. For more information on the Colossian Forum, see http://colossianforum.org/.